Christina Jordan, Imke Polland (eds.)
Realms of Royalty

Culture & Theory | Volume 52

Christina Jordan, Imke Polland (eds.)
Realms of Royalty
New Directions in Researching Contemporary European Monarchies

[transcript]

The publication of this volume was supported by the International Graduate Centre for the Study of Culture (GCSC) at Justus Liebig University Giessen and the Dr.-Herbert-Stolzenberg Foundation.

Bibliographic information published by the Deutsche Nationalbibliothek
The Deutsche Nationalbibliothek lists this publication in the Deutsche Nationalbibliografie; detailed bibliographic data are available in the Internet at http://dnb.d-nb.de

© 2020 transcript Verlag, Bielefeld

All rights reserved. No part of this book may be reprinted or reproduced or utilized in any form or by any electronic, mechanical, or other means, now known or hereafter invented, including photocopying and recording, or in any information storage or retrieval system, without permission in writing from the publisher.

Cover layout: Maria Arndt, Bielefeld
Cover illustration: Jeff Coons, Christina Jordan, Imke Polland

Print-ISBN 978-3-8376-4583-5
PDF-ISBN 978-3-8394-4583-9
https://doi.org/10.14361/9783839445839

Contents

Preface and Acknowledgements | 7

Introduction: Mapping New Realms in the Study
of Contemporary European Monarchies
Christina Jordan and Imke Polland | 9

ROYAL PUBLIC INTERACTIONS AND TRANS/NATIONAL RELATIONS (19TH-21ST CENTURY)

"We'll Never be Royals" – or Will We?
Exploring Meghan Markle's Impact
on the British Royal Family Brand
Pauline Maclaran and Cele C. Otnes | 29

Your Media Majesty:
Three Kings and Radio in the Inter-War Years
Deirdre Gilfedder | 47

European Royals and their Colonial Realms:
Honors and Decorations
Robert Aldrich and Cindy McCreery | 63

Between Politics and Dynastic Survival:
19th-Century Monarchy in Post-Revolutionary Europe (1815-1918)
Torsten Riotte | 89

MONARCHY ON PAGE, STAGE, AND SCREEN

Who's Queen? Elizabeth I in Contemporary Culture
Susanne Scholz | 107

"Empires of all kinds collapse, but the fake tsars,
they last forever." Modern and Contemporary Memories
of Tsar Šćepan Mali (1767-1773)
Stefan Trajković Filipović | 129

Long May He (Not) Reign?
Literary Depictions of a 'Meddling' Future Monarch
Prince Charles in Mike Bartlett's Play *King Charles III* (2014) and
in Catherine Mayer's Biography *Charles: The Heart of a King* (2015)
Marie-Theres Stickel | 149

Gendered Strategies of Power:
Queen Elizabeth II as a Politician in the Plays
The Audience **(2015 [2013]) and** *Handbagged* **(2013)**
Eva Kirbach | 169

ROYAL REPRESENTATIONS IN CONTEMPORARY POPULAR CULTURAL CONTEXTS

The (In)Significance of Queen Victoria in Neo-Victorian Comics
Natalie Veith | 193

Monarchy and the Alien:
Three Queens as Sites of Memory in *Doctor Who*
Marie Menzel | 211

'Party at the Palace': Popular Cultural Celebrations
in the Context of Queen Elizabeth II's Golden and Diamond Jubilee
Christina Jordan | 233

AFTERWORD

Afterword: The British Monarchy and Brexit
Imke Polland | 253

Authors | 265

Preface and Acknowledgements

> "But I see the world has changed. And one must modernise."
> *[The Queen 2006: 01:36:40]*

The quote from the film *The Queen* holds true for contemporary European monarchies; it also pertains to research on monarchies. These age-old institutions offer many starting points for exploring aspects that are of crucial interest to contemporary research in the fields of cultural, media, and literary studies, historic enquiry, and many more.

In order to approach, explain, evaluate, and make sense of the cultural phenomena that contemporary monarchies confront us with, this volume sets out to explore the various realms of influence, functions, and ramifications of contemporary European monarchies. Its chapters offer explorations of the nexus between monarchies, their cultural representations, and contemporary societies from various theoretical perspectives, pertaining to a broad range of historical contexts and encompassing a variety of genres (from plays and biography to cinema). The three sections range from the historical to the contemporary (19th-century to 21st-century contexts), and from the socio-political (honors, exile, speeches) to the popcultural (comics, film, and television).

This volume emerged from a conference held at the International Graduate Centre for the Study of Culture (GCSC) at Justus Liebig University, Giessen, Germany in April 2017. At this conference, PhD students, postdocs, and university professors from various disciplinary backgrounds, e.g. History, the Study of British Literature and Culture, or Marketing and Consumer Research, gathered to discuss facets of researching contemporary European monarchies and thus paved the way for this book.

Publishing the results of these discussions would not have been possible without substantial support. We thank the GCSC for financially and logistically supporting the conference and for contributing a substantial amount to the printing costs of this volume. We would also like to express our sincere thanks to the Dr.-Herbert-Stolzenberg-Foundation for awarding the prize for excellence in higher education teaching 2017 to us and our seminar *Two Elizabethan Eras: Literary and Intermedial Portraits of Elizabeth I and Elizabeth II*, taught at the English department at Justus Liebig University Giessen. We are delighted to dedicate the prize money to the realization of this book project.

We give our heartfelt thanks to our doctoral supervisor Prof. Dr. Dr. h.c. Ansgar Nünning, whose academic and personal support and encouragement we greatly value. More thanks go to a wonderful team, without whose dedication this book would not exist – especially Rose Lawson, who assisted us with proofreading and her valuable comments. We thank the student assistants at JLU's English department, Nele Grosch, Laura Howe, and Janna Thonius, who supported us in repeatedly and attentively checking the articles and bibliographies. Thank you to Franziska Eick for her assistance with the formatting and compilation of the manuscript and to Simon Ottersbach for many helpful suggestions on how to make the project run smoothly. We would like to thank Jeff Coons who took the photograph for the book cover. We would also like to thank Annika Linnemann at transcript for her support during the preparation of the manuscript. Finally, we would like to extend our thanks to the contributors to this volume, whose thorough work addresses many questions on conceptualizing, theorizing, exemplifying, and analyzing the "Realms of Royalty" and point out avenues for future research.

Giessen, November 2019
Christina Jordan & Imke Polland

Introduction:
Mapping New Realms in the Study
of Contemporary European Monarchies

Christina Jordan and Imke Polland

CONTEMPORARY EUROPEAN MONARCHIES
AS AN OBJECT OF RESEARCH

For centuries, monarchies have dominated European politics and power relations and they still permeate European cultures, even if sometimes in a post-political form. Having carved out new spheres of influence for themselves and having exchanged hard- against soft-power instruments (cf. Müller/Mehrkens 2016), the royal families of Europe are currently encountering a wave of popularity, especially as regards the celebration of royal events and the commercialization and ongoing production of fiction about royal history. The latest remediations for stage and screen focus particularly on the British monarchy, e.g. the popular Netflix series *The Crown* (2016–) or ITV's *Victoria* (2016-2017), theatre plays such as Mike Bartlett's *King Charles III* (2014) or Peter Morgan's *The Audience* (2015 [2013]) as well as films such as *The King's Speech* (2010) and *Mary Queen of Scots* (2018).

In an age of increasing royal celebrity – a trend that began in the 19th century (cf. Plunkett 2003) and was repeatedly diagnosed by several scholars (e.g. Couldry 2001; Blain/O'Donnell 2003; Nairn 2011 [1988]; Minier/Pennacchia 2014) – the notions of what monarchy is and should be about in contemporary Europe are shaped by and renegotiated in response to the logics of these cultural developments. More than ten years ago, Blain and O'Donnell have stated that notions and forms of celebrity are constantly changing, "in its current phase having also been increasingly associated with ordinariness" (2003: 163), basing their observation on the increase in reality TV shows and the altering effects these had on celebrity culture. Reacting to these recent developments and to a great extent fashioned by them, a notion of "royal ordinariness" (Widholm/Becker 2015: 10) has indeed developed. This is exemplified by the recent royal weddings to 'commoners' in Denmark (2004), Great Britain (2011 and 2018), and Sweden (2015) or by the new middle-class appearance of the royal heirs' family lives, which is frequently thematized in the media (e.g. amongst others, Prince William and Catherine or Prince Harry and Meghan in the UK as well as Crown Princess Victoria and Daniel in Sweden).

The current state of Europe's royal houses, their having-become, and their importance for the contemporary cultural sphere are the areas of interest that lie at the heart of this volume. These topics inspire some of its central questions: Why do royals still seem to play such an important role for contemporary European societies? What renders them culturally important? In how far do the concept of monarchy and its representations change in the face of constant media developments and ever-changing media consumption practices, societal needs and demands? And, consequently, how does research on monarchies have to react to its ever-changing objects of interest?

The present volume addresses these questions and thus fills a gap in current academic debates about European monarchies. Despite the ubiquitous media presence of European royals and the sheer number of royal events since 2000, the topic of 21st-century royalty has received an astonishingly modest amount of academic attention, especially by scholars of literature, media, narrative, and culture. Ruth Adams rightfully diagnoses a "widespread neglect of topics relating to the British monarchy by academia, an inattention that is perhaps 'perplexing,' given its prominence in British culture and society, and the strong emotional attachment demonstrated by a significant proportion of the population." (2016: 265) Notwithstanding a number of interesting recent publications (cf. especially the recent volumes of the Palgrave Series 'Studies in Modern Monarchy' [Glencross/Rowbotham/Kandiah 2016; Müller/Mehrkens 2016; Banerjee/Backerra/Sarti 2017], but also Merck 2016, Laing/Frost 2017, Woodacre et al. 2019), the topic of contemporary European monarchies begs for more attention in the study of culture. A first approximation in this direction is proposed by Pankratz and Viol's collected volume entitled *(Un)Making the Monarchy*, which approaches the monarchy from a constructivist perspective "trying to come to grips with texts and discourses, making and (un)making specific versions of the British monarchy" (2017: 17). The present volume further responds to this demand, offering a range of contributions that explore the nexus between monarchy and contemporary European cultures, which encompasses a variety of fictional and non-fictional media and genres, from newspaper articles, live radio and television broadcasts to plays and TV series to cinema and comics. Beginning with tracing developments by addressing trans/national perspectives on royal families as well as their public interactions from the 19th century until today, proceeding with fictional imaginations of monarchies, and ending with a section on negotiations of 21st-century representations of royalty in popular cultural contexts, this collection of essays by young and established scholars in the fields of history, marketing, literary and cultural studies provides perspectives on European monarchies in diverse cultural contexts. Moving from the historical to the contemporary, through the socio-political and the fictional, the volume's goal is to capture the complex and myriad ways in which contemporary European monarchies permeate cultural spheres.

In addition, responding to royalty's cultural ubiquity, the study of monarchies is particularly interesting for literary and cultural studies, because it offers a wide range of fictional and non-fictional materials and foci of research. It allows to scrutinize categories such as identity, gender, heritage as well as dichotomies such as tradition/modernity, public/private, or national/transnational. Due to its numerous cultural facets, contemporary royalty also challenges established approaches by demanding interdisciplinarity and combining the expertise of fields of research, which are aptly equipped to do justice to this complex object of research.

Furthermore, studying the variety of cultural negotiations of contemporary monarchies serves to shed light on developments regarding societies' norms and values, its concerns and its dominant forms of expression, preferred media and genres. Neil Blain and Hugh O'Donnell's observations and analysis of monarchies' economic, psychological, and cultural importance is still valid for present-day royalty:

"It may be true that the phenomenon of monarchy in the media is primarily economic and secondarily political – as well as cultural and psychological. However, we might say that the phenomenon manifests itself in a circuit of production and reception in which eventually it seems to have acquired economic and political importance *because* it is originally of cultural and psychological importance. That is to say, even if royal media production is driven most strongly by economic benefit to the media industry, and political (or psychological) gratification to its proprietors or custodians, it is also true that exposure to royal events and personalities finally manifests itself as an imagined psychological need, conditioned by cultural reality: or indeed as a cultural reality, conditioned by psychological need, depending on one's philosophical inclination. Either way, it becomes immensely hard to deny the reality of a public and private need for royal narratives and imagined participation in royal lives." (2003: 60)

Explorations of the role of the institution of monarchy within contemporary European societies and cultures can go in many directions. To provide some conceptual and theoretical orientation points for navigating this varied topic of research, the following sections of this introduction offer perspectives that we find helpful for coming to terms with the cultural phenomena that monarchies and contemporary notions about them confront us with. Part two of this introduction discusses contemporary monarchies as cultural phenomena, because they are constructs which "we can only approach [...] via texts, material practices, and discourses" (Pankratz/Viol 2017: 17). Against the background of discussing transformations of monarchies as well as of the research *on* monarchies itself, in part three, we provide a brief historical contextualization. We argue that especially interdisciplinary approaches are needed to be able to adequately address contemporary royalty as an object of research. Proceeding from this assumption, the final part of this introduction then maps out the structure of the volume and gives an overview of its contributions, illustrating how the different articles approach the multifaceted research topic of European monarchies. We conclude by outlining some trajectories for further research.

MONARCHIES AS CULTURAL PHENOMENA: COMING TO TERMS WITH CONTEMPORARY NOTIONS OF ROYALTY

Having forfeited most of their political power, European royals have nevertheless maintained or even increased their cultural significance.[1] As historically grown complexes of institutional power, symbolic value, and 'treasure chests' of historic and fictional narratives, monarchies may be regarded as cultural phenomena. They do not merely exist for the sake of their own continuity, but because people value the institutions and choose to support them. Charged with meanings, as these institutions thus are, they do important cultural 'work.'

A prime example is the ITV documentary *Diana, Our Mother: Her Life and Legacy* (2017) produced on the occasion of the 20th anniversary of Diana's death. This 90-minute program not only attracted an estimated number of about seven

---

1   Müller/Mehrkens (2016) have already spelled out the increasing uses of soft power by royal heirs in the cultural sphere for the 19th century. Jürgen Kramer delineates "the reinvention of the role of the monarchy as a symbolic force in the 19th century" (2017: 21).

million viewers, but it also joined other forms of cultural remembrance taking place at that time. In the documentary, Princes William and Harry flip through family photo albums and talk about their individual memories of their mother Diana. Thus, they make their personal psychological and emotional work available to the public, who can reprocess their own emotional involvement. It can be said that – in light of remembering an occasion, which has often been called a collective national trauma – the princes mourn on behalf of the nation.

An occasion on which the monarchy, in this case the Spanish King Felipe VI, recently added a cultural layer to a political discussion, is the Catalan push for independence. In October 2017, the king held a televised speech, in which he – against the expectation of neutrality – was openly judgmental and accordingly accused of taking a side and of adopting 'the Spanish position' against the Catalan one. This promotion of an outspoken view on political matters goes beyond the king's constitutional position and one might conclude that he acted as a cultural broker instead of a neutral mediator in this case. In his speech, Felipe VI still frequently emphasized those values that the monarchy usually advocates, i.e. unity, solidarity, and stability. His speech was thus of cultural importance: On the one hand, the figurehead, officially meant to represent the Spanish nation, openly interpreted the event and thus manifested a concrete denotation appealing to a majority. On the other hand, this meaning-making process has the potential to further oppose the differing camps. In conflictual situations people often turn towards their head of state and the leading institutions of the nation. What is happening in Spain, however, raises the question for which 'nation' the king spoke.

In the case of the 2014 Scottish referendum, Queen Elizabeth II did not reveal any personal opinions, but she still made a political intervention – despite preserving neutrality – by encouraging people to carefully deliberate before voting. Her seemingly neutral speeches are often interpreted as constituting indirect comments on politics. In this regard, both her Christmas address 2018 as well as a speech she gave in January 2019 on the topic of finding common ground and respecting differing positions, were widely discussed as the queen's comments on the messy Brexit discussions in British parliament.[2] These cultural acts of the kings and queens in the face of crisis-like situations reveal how entangled the institution of monarchy still is with the *Realpolitik* of the day, even though it occupies a rather symbolic position.

Monarchies are not only political or historical instances, but confront us with cultural phenomena such as ritualistic actions and (invented) traditions, (fictional)

---

2 See, for example, the editorial article "The Guardian View on the Queen and Brexit" in *The Guardian*.

depictions of the monarchs' lives, or their entanglement with national and cultural concerns. Thus, it is necessary that the study of culture approaches these phenomena with the special qualities, methods, and perspectives it comprises. There are as many notions of culture as there are differentiations of studying its forms, such as (British) Cultural Studies, the study of culture, or the German Kulturwissenschaft(en). The theoretical, methodological, and conceptual ways of studying culture made use of in this volume are marked by a transdisciplinary approach to phenomena which encompass all aspects of human life.[3] Important to this volume's underlying notion of culture is Clifford Geertz's understanding of culture as a "web of significances," which generates meanings that the study of culture uncovers and analyzes. Geertz explains that

"[t]he concept of culture that I espouse [...], is essentially a semiotic one. Believing, with Max Weber, that man is an animal suspended in webs of significance he himself has spun, I take culture to be those webs, and the analysis of it to be therefore not an experimental science in search of law but an interpretive one in search of meaning." (1973: 5)

Based on these considerations we suggest to regard monarchies as this complex aggregate of meanings from the perspective of the study of culture and thus complement existing (prevailingly historical) studies on that topic. It is evident that the current cultural importance of monarchies cannot be grasped without the respective contexts and histories. In the following section of the introduction, we will therefore also very briefly draw on historical developments to contextualize the present volume, before moving on to describing its outline.

EUROPEAN MONARCHIES IN THEIR HISTORICAL CONTEXT: A BRIEF OVERVIEW

Monarchies have been the predominant state forms in Europe during the Middle Ages until the 19th century, when only France, San Marino and Switzerland were republics. They flourished and often developed into huge empires, especially England (later Britain) and Spain were among the largest empires in world history. However, most European monarchies were abolished after World War I and as of 2019, only twelve monarchies, most of them constitutional, remain in Europe: The

---

3   With this, we refer to Raymond Williams's famous notion of "culture as a whole way of life" (2008 [1958]: 83).

United Kingdom of Great Britain and Northern Ireland, Denmark, Norway, Sweden, the Netherlands, Belgium, Spain as well as the petty states of Andorra, Liechtenstein, Monaco, Luxembourg, and the State of the Vatican City. Those remaining monarchies, which survived crises of abolishment, abdications, revolutions, and decolonialization have to renegotiate their places between the institutions' histories and traditions on the one hand and (post-)modern political, social, and medial environments.

The present state of monarchies, which many of the articles focus on, cannot be understood as given and independent from history, but must be seen as the result of developments both of the institutions themselves and their political, social, and cultural contexts. These contexts were crucial in giving shape to monarchies' present position in society, including their functions and our understanding of them. While Richard Williams in his 1997 study of the British monarchy entitled *The Contentious Crown* claimed that 19th-century research mainly focused on the development of the British working and middle class, "what might be called 'the survival of the upper class' – the monarchy and aristocracy – was neglected" (1997: 1), this period is well researched nowadays (e.g. Giloi 2011, Paulmann 2000, Cannadine 1996 [1990], or Williams 1997).

In the 19th century and the beginning of the 20th century, European monarchies underwent severe changes. The 19th century was the time in which most nation states were formed in Europe, often as the results of nationalist movements such as in Germany or Italy. Monarchies partly took a crucial role in the process of nation building, but on the other hand also had to face changes with regard to the nations' and their own political situations and struggled for a survival of the institutions. Some European monarchies still were important imperial powers. While Spain already faced anti-colonial uprisings and the resulting losses of colonies, especially in America (e.g. Spanish-American War 1898), the British Empire flourished at the same time and Queen Victoria was proclaimed the Empress of India in 1876. Thus, transnational concerns and negotiating the monarchies' place in a changing European and imperial context were crucial for maintaining power (Banerjee/Backerra/Sarti 2017).

A great caesura concerning the international standing of most European monarchies was World War I. Many European monarchies were abolished and the situation of the remaining monarchies – at home and abroad – became increasingly difficult. After WWI, Europe suffered in great parts from unemployment and poverty which led to a general dissatisfaction. Not only the British King George V faced a loss of his power and had to fear a revolution. In Spain, local and municipal elections led to victories of candidates favoring an end to the monarchy and an establishment of a republic in 1931. King Alfonso XIII did not abdicate, but went into exile and Spain temporarily became a republic – the second time after 1873-1874. Sweden, which remained neutral in both World Wars, saw a breakthrough of parliamentarism in 1917, when the coalition government of liberals and social democrats was appointed. As with most other European monarchies, this meant that the sovereign's political influence was significantly reduced.

Following the Second World War, monarchies in Europe have faced an era of rapid change. Media developed as quickly as never before, global ties were strengthened and European networks such as the European Coal and Steel Community (ECSC as of 1951) or the European Economic Community (EEC as of 1958) as predecessors of the European Union were formed. With regard to the British context, historian David Cannadine called the time post World War Two "a period of unprecedented change" (1983: 139) – a development that has not ceased today. In their volume *The Windsor Dynasty 1910 to the Present*, Matthew Glencross, Judith Rowbotham, and Michael D. Kandiah show "the extent to which, amongst other things, flexibility or adaptability in the face of change has been one of key characteristics of the Windsor dynasty." (2016: 10) After WWII, the British Empire was slowly but surely transformed into the Commonwealth of Nations. Anti-colonial movements reached a new heyday in more or less all remaining European colonies, sometimes resulting in war, as in the cases of Britain, France, and Portugal, in general having the effect of a loss of the colonies. All British colonies were granted independence by 1968, and by the 1980s all remaining colonies in Africa had gained their independence. Nevertheless, imperial ties remain (albeit in new and changed forms).

With regard to this loss of (political) power at home and in the empires, a wholly new image of the monarchy had to be created, with the monarch being stylized as the people's sovereign, 'public servant,' and a national figurehead (cf. ibid: 4-5). One of the most striking examples might be the British King George VI, who visited miners and football games and became engaged in charitable causes. A strong emotional tie between monarchy and people was supposed to create support for the institution (cf. Owens 2016; Zweiniger-Bargielowska 2016). Special emphasis was placed on the monarchy's perseverance, continuity, and function as a means of group identification. As David Cannadine notes, "the monarchy appeared, particularly on grand, ceremonial occasions, as the embodiment of consensus, stability and community" (1983: 140; Kramer 2017).

The stylization of monarchies as families significantly contributed to the endearment of the monarch to the people (cf. Wienfort 2016). In Britain, this process already saw its beginning with Queen Victoria, Prince Albert, and their nine children (cf. Williams 1997: 7). With regard to the marriage of the then Prince of Wales, Walter Bagehot felicitously observed that "a *family* on the throne is an interesting idea," as it brings an air of ordinariness to the Crown and fosters emotional engagement (2009 [1867]: 41). The display of a family life gave subjects the opportunity to identify with the royal family. When King George V went on his regular outings and visits, he brought along his wife, Queen Mary, as well as their older children. A constant modernization of the monarchy took place, including a significant increase in public relations work, a strong focus on the relationship towards the people as well as upholding family and national values. In 1923, Prince Albert, later King George VI, was allowed to marry Elizabeth Bowes-Lyon although she was not of royal descent – at the time, this was a revolutionary decision and a sign of modernization of the institution, which paved the way for many similar developments to come. In many European monarchies, sovereigns and heirs to the throne are nowadays married to commoners with ordinary jobs. To name only a few, King Carl XVI Gustaf is married to Silvia Sommerlath, a German commoner who got to know the prince 1972 as Olympia-hostess in Munich, their daughter Crown Princess Victoria married the fitness coach Daniel Westling, and Mette-Marit, wife of the Norwegian Crown Prince Haakon has what is frequently called 'a controversial past.'

With the evolution of electronic mass media in the first half of the 20th century, monarchies increasingly turned to representational capacities, which go hand in hand with their new cultural presence and their visibility as royal celebrities. The 1930s meant the rise of the radio and the monarchy began to use it for its own ends. The first Christmas broadcast by the king was aired in 1932 and instigated the beginning of a tradition that is still upheld today, albeit on TV. Especially since Elizabeth II's coronation in 1953, which even sparked the sales numbers of TV sets, media developed as quickly as never before. Until today, the monarchies try to keep pace with it and partake as "active participants in this brave new media world. Conscious that their survival depends to a large part on popular support, they have embraced social media and the digital, and boast Facebook, Flickr and Twitter accounts." (Adams 2016: 282) Additionally, this development is flanked by unauthorized and fictional media representations of the sovereigns, their families, and their lives including crises and scandals.

In his pioneering study on the history of performing royal rituals between 1820 and 1977, David Cannadine concludes explaining that "[b]y definition, the period since the coronation [of Elizabeth II] in 1953 is too recent for detailed or satisfactory historical analysis" (1983: 155). While the 1980s slowly but surely move into the realm of research in newest historical studies, historical science more often than not shies away from researching contemporary phenomena.

The contributions in this edited volume offer insights into the developments of European monarchies since the 19th century as well as into their present condition, thus giving an impression of both continuities and changes of European monarchies. Royal families are permanently adapting to contemporary society with its challenges of contingency and rapid changes. Reflecting the modernization of monarchies including their recent developments, this volume aims at contributing to an adequate analysis of recent and contemporary royal phenomena, a subject area that has barely received scholarly attention so far. When it comes to contemporary phenomena, the study of culture is especially well equipped to provide a comprehensive perspective, taking into account the multifarious layers of cultural realities and their representations.

OVERVIEW OF THIS VOLUME'S THREE SECTIONS

As the previous sections have illustrated, European monarchies' pasts are widely researched nowadays, especially in historiography. However, the study of culture and related disciplines only recently started to approach this topic. All articles in this edited volume are dedicated to cultural concerns regarding monarchies. Their range of interest reaches from the 19th century until today, acknowledging that research on monarchies has to adapt to its object of research, which is itself in a constant state of flux, change, and modernization. As frequently the case with topics newly emerging in certain disciplines, these circumstances create both methodological chances and challenges, that are taken up and fructified in the book's three sections, which focus on diachronic as well as contemporary issues, national and transnational contexts, and various aspects concerning the intricate relationships between sovereigns, their subjects, and the media.

Royal Public Interactions and Trans/National Relations (19th-21st Century)

The first section sets the stage for the volume by contextualizing both national and transnational roles and challenges taken on by European monarchies from the 19th century until today. The contributions to this section offer diverse perspectives on remnants of imperial monarchical forms such as honors and decorations in (post)colonial societies, on 'royal residues' in and through exile, the sovereigns' use of technological innovations such as the radio in the 1930s, and their marketing strategies and self-fashioning through an updated family image in the 21st century. In this way, the section fruitfully explores the application of interdisciplinary approaches from historical studies to media analysis and marketing and paves the way for a multifaceted discussion of the roles monarchies play for contemporary European societies.

In their article on Meghan Markle's "Impact on the British Royal Family Brand," Pauline Maclaran and Cele C. Otnes explore the various ways in which Prince Harry's 2018 marriage to the African American actress Meghan Markle influences the perception of the British monarchy. They illustrate the paradox of an "accessible mystique" of the British royals, that is carefully negotiated as members of the royal family have to stay above other forms of celebrity. Based on their analysis of archival as well as ethnographic data such as interviews and participant observation, the authors suggest a conceptualization of the British royal family as a corporate brand, which is composed of five key elements that they identify as global, heritage, human, family, and luxury. Maclaran and Otnes elaborate on how Meghan Markle, as the newest addition to the British royal family, already has and will continue to contribute both positively and negatively to all of these five brand elements.

Deirdre Gilfedder is also concerned with developments that impact the royal image. Her historiographic article sets out to explore the early royal radio addresses, which she describes as the centerpiece of the BBC in its nascent years and which were instrumental in the corporation's strategy for its Empire service. Gilfedder discusses the decisive role of royal broadcasting for the advancement of what she describes as "a new 'media empire' of radio." She approaches the radio broadcasts as media rituals and communication events from a media theoretical perspective, drawing on works by John Durham-Peters, Nick Couldry, and Daniel Dayan. Gilfedder further discusses how these broadcasts returned the king to the imagined 'center' of society and thus contributed to a modernization of British royalty. With the example speeches she analyzes – George V's Christmas message of 1932, the 1936 abdication speech of Edward VIII, and George VI's rally to war speech of 1939 – she scrutinizes the imperial outreach of the British monarch's political communications.

Robert Aldrich and Cindy McCreery, equally concerned with the imperial complexities of the royal past, outline the creation and proliferation of European and colonial honor systems in the 19th century. Their contribution is concerned with the distribution of honors and decorations, individuals' complex affective relationship to them and what they stand for in 19th and 20th-century European states as well as throughout their colonial and postcolonial territories. Focusing on the examples of British knighthoods and colonial honors in India and beyond as well as honors in other European empires and their post-colonial legacies, Aldrich and McCreery's article shows that many of the post-colonial states adopted and adapted the honors systems established under colonial rule. Their contextualized and interpretive analysis provides a comprehensive approach to orders and decorations as a means of understanding colonial and postcolonial power dynamics in connection to monarchies.

With its focus on monarchs and royal families in exile, Torsten Riotte's article continues along the line of discussing power relations and the transnational dimensions of monarchies. He zooms in on the questions of how former sovereigns (and their families) survived dynastically, how they found financial support to live in exile, and under what circumstances they remained part of the exclusive group of European dynasties. Riotte's historiographic analysis mainly takes into account economic and legal documents and thus provides an innovative perspective on 'royal survival' and the adaptation processes European monarchs had to undergo when facing challenges of societal and political developments. He emphasizes the dimension of cultural negotiations when arguing that monarchs in exile had to make use of their social or cultural capital to negotiate their legal status in their new home countries.

Monarchy on Page, Stage, and Screen

The second section "Monarchy on Page, Stage, and Screen" discusses representations of former and current monarchs in films, on television as well as in theatre plays and biographies. The four case studies address questions of gender, power, cultural memory, and national identity by approaching the filmic, dramatic, and biographical texts from a literary and cultural studies perspective. They highlight not only the way the respective depictions inform their audience about the monarchs at their center, but also what these representations reveal about present views on society, politics, and the institution of the monarchy.

In her article on the remediation of Elizabeth I in Shekhar Kapur's *Elizabeth* (1998), Susanne Scholz investigates how this iconic queen is made sense of in contemporary filmic representations. The article's special focus is on Elizabeth I's relationship to the Earl of Leicester and its visualization in dancing scenes. Susanne Scholz' contribution scrutinizes royal dance as a language to visually represent the queen's 'political body' – which is essentially unrepresentable – and thus to render it intelligible for modern audiences. She places Kapur's fictitious depictions of the dancing Elizabeth in a historical perspective through a comparison with 16th-century representations of courtly dance. Scholz discusses issues such as romantic love, sexuality, gender (hierarchies), and a patriarchal order as well as questions concerning (fictional) remediations and cultural memory. The article thus reveals resemantizations of royal dance and discusses how these representations customized for a modern gaze reflect today's cultural concerns, desires, wishes, and anxieties.

The topic of cultural memory in the representation of a former sovereign forms the thematic core of Stefan Trajković Filipović's article on the Montenegrin Tsar Stephen the Little (1767-1773) and his filmic afterlife. Being a highly controversial figure during his lifetime, Stephen the Little gained literary attention since the late 18th century and became the focus of the films *Lažni car* (1955; *The Fake Emperor*) and *Čovjek koga treba ubiti* (1979; *Man to Destroy*). In his article, Trajković Filipović analyzes both films with respect to the sovereign's depiction as a beloved reformer, unifier, and alternative to internal feuds, corruption, and political hypocrisy. Trajković Filipović critically approaches the filmic representation of his reign as a short 'golden age' of Montenegro's history from the perspective of (media) memory studies and reviews them against the background of historical sources.

In her contribution to this volume, Marie-Theres Stickel discusses the question of how literary works may shape the public perception of a royal figurehead. She scrutinizes how Mike Bartlett's play *King Charles III* (2014) and Catherine Mayer's biography *Charles: The Heart of a King* (2015) represent Prince Charles' struggle with the political neutrality expected of the heir apparent. As both works toy with the idea of an outspoken (future) king meddling with political matters, Stickel's article elaborates on the evaluation of Charles' activist stance. Her literary studies perspective reveals how the works use their respective generic qualities to not only portray the heir, but also to imagine the future king and thus to contribute to political debates surrounding the monarchy.

The section's final article is dedicated to two fictional representations of Queen Elizabeth II in contemporary theatre texts, Peter Morgan's *The Audience* (2013) and Moira Buffini's *Handbagged* (2013). Both plays focus on the relationship between the queen and her prime ministers, depicting their confidential meetings and thus imaginatively filling the gap of what is known about the queen's personal opinions and her involvement in political matters. Against this backdrop, Eva Kirbach explores the construction of the queen's fictional character especially with regard to her gender and political power. Given that the sovereign nowadays lacks political 'hard power' and is supposed to refrain from expressing political opinions, the article demonstrates how the fictional queens use patterns of both male and female gendered behavior to exercise power and to wittily influence their prime ministers.

Royal Representations in Contemporary Popular Cultural Contexts

The book's third and concluding section "Royal Representation in Contemporary Popular Cultural Contexts" traces modes of representing royalty in comics, cult series, and concerts. The realm of popular culture is still often neglected in the study of culture as well as in royal studies. However, the analysis of the popular in regal contexts allows for promising insights into how monarchies' (unofficial) representations change over time and how 'bottom-up' approaches to the monarchy might subvert the images carefully constructed and conveyed by official sources. The section uncovers various ways in which the contemporary British monarchy enjoys a popularity that permeates fictional and factual representations, thus reproducing the royals' special celebrity status.

Natalie Veith's article is dedicated to an examination of neo-Victorian comics, which form part of a popular cultural counter discourse to conventional heritage culture surrounding Britain's (monarchical) history. Through a close reading of Alan Moore and Eddie Campbell's *From Hell* (1989-1996), Grant Morrison and Steve Yeowell's *Sebastian O.* (1993), and Sydney Padua's *The Thrilling Adventures of Lovelace and Babbage* (2015), Veith analyzes the depictions of Queen Victoria in neo-Victorian comics, which experiment with anachronistic, intermedial, and metafictional scenarios. Although Queen Victoria seems to be a marginal figure in these comics, Veith argues that the queen's relevance lies in her apparent insignificance, as the monarch is used to dramatize and negotiate contradictions within the stories, e.g. concerning power, knowledge, gender, and agency.

The focus of Marie Menzel's contribution on the remediation of kings and queens in the famous science fiction TV-series *Doctor Who* (1963–) is how monarchy functions as an embodiment of Britishness in popular culture. Interweaving fact and fiction, the program integrates both past and future kings and queens into its fantastical narrative, illustrating the sovereigns' importance for issues like cultural memory and collective identity. Approaching the series from the perspective of media cultural studies, the article uncovers how *Doctor Who* represents, remediates, and imagines British queens as sites of memory, which invoke a sense of Britishness and national identity. Menzel thus shows how the depicted sovereigns' mythologies and symbolic as well as mnemonic powers are used in the serial narrative to represent satirical versions of the past rather than to take a critical or evaluative stance towards the monarchy.

Christina Jordan's article focuses on Elizabeth II's Jubilee celebrations in the new millennium and scrutinizes the cultural functions of the concerts *Party at the Palace* (2002) and the *Diamond Jubilee Concert* (2012). Pop concerts and parades of 'the people' have become central constituents of the latest large-scale royal events and can thus be regarded as part of a new generation of invented royal traditions. The article shows how the concerts help to modernize the monarchy by inviting public participation in royal celebrations and creating a new layer for the royal image. Jordan delineates how popular cultural events thus add to (seemingly) historic royal traditions and activities and help to shape a modernized image of the monarchy.

While contemporary monarchies are often considered to be rather "post-political" (Higson 2016: 360), Imke Polland's concluding afterword exemplarily shows that European monarchies currently regain political importance. She reflects on the press's appraisal of the British monarchy's role in the context of the Brexit negotiations. By analyzing public reactions to Queen Elizabeth's speeches and the ambassador function of the royal heirs, Polland elaborates on the subtle involvement of British royals in debates about national independence and their symbolic power in maintaining ties with other nations at times of crises.

This serves as an example of the wider cultural(-political) functions performed by contemporary European royalty. While conflicting demands for European integration on the one hand and nationalist movements on the other hand shape the current political landscape and media discussions in Europe, it should be a focus for future research on monarchies to scrutinize how the institutions and their traditions are instrumentalized in the far-reaching incisions and processes of transformation in Europe. Their continued importance is reflected by the recent wave of interdisciplinary studies on monarchies. While this book contributes to this renewed academic interest in monarchies by adding literary, media, historical, and cultural perspectives, there are many more fruitful trajectories for future research.

In 2019, Swedish King Carl Gustaf's decision to remove five of his grandchildren from the line of succession and 'slim down' the monarchy to the core family testified to a wider trend in royal 'family politics.' Officially, this gesture offers his offspring the possibility to lead ordinary lives and follow careers of their own, but it also goes hand in hand with a withdrawal of both their titles as royal highnesses and their royal duties. Prince Charles, too, is known to be planning a similar 'cutting-back' for the British royal family upon his succession to the throne. It will be interesting to scrutinize in how far this will affect royalty's performance of charitable tasks and what changes it will bring for the royal image.

The Duke and Duchess of Sussex, Prince Harry and Meghan, also decided to renounce the title of HRH for their son Archie. Their particular take on the role of royal heirs provides an intriguing case study to analyze the ongoing reconceptualization of royal status. In addition, their strategic use of social media platforms provides an interesting example of royal 'activism' and communication. The press has already observed that "The Royal-Related Action Is Now Happening on Instagram" (Duboff 2019: n. pag.) and generates its own headlines from royal statements made online. The transformations of royal celebrity effectuated by social media might be another fruitful field for studying contemporary monarchies.

Interestingly enough, young royals are increasingly open about their (mental) health issues. It was again Prince Harry, who publicly talked about personal problems, pressures, and psychological needs. Victoria, Crown Princess of Sweden's history of anorexia was also openly communicated. These confessions combined with royal support for charities dedicated to mental health issues are worth investigating. This new trend may lead to a form of 'personalized monarchism' as the public/private dichotomy continues to dissolve. It will be interesting to study how this affects people's relationship to the royals and public reception processes.

These are merely a few suggestions based on the most recent developments in the royal houses of Europe. As the articles in this volume show, monarchies were, are, and are likely to remain important phenomena within European cultural, historical, political, social, and medial landscapes and thus will continue to provide fruitful areas for interdisciplinary investigation.

WORKS CITED

Adams, Ruth (2016): "The Queen on the Big Screen(s): Outdoor Screens and Public Congregations." In: Mandy Merck (ed.), The British Monarchy on Screen, Manchester: Manchester University Press, pp. 264-287.

Bagehot, Walter (2009 [1867]): The English Constitution, edited by Miley Taylor. Oxford: Oxford University Press.

Banerjee, Milinda/ Backerra, Charlotte/ Sarti, Cathleen (eds.) (2017): Transnational Histories of the 'Royal Nation', London: Palgrave Macmillan.

Blain, Neil/O'Donnell, Hugh (2003): Media, Monarchy and Power. Bristol and Portland: University of Chicago Press.

Cannadine, David (1983): "The Context, Performance and Meaning of Ritual: The British Monarchy and the 'Invention of Tradition', c. 1820-1977." In: Eric Hobsbawm/Terence Ranger (eds.), The Invention of Tradition, Cambridge and, New York: Cambridge University Press, pp. 101-164.

Cannadine, David (1996 [1990]): The Decline and Fall of the British Aristocracy. London: Papermac.

Couldry, Nick (2001): "Everyday Royal Celebrity." In: David Morley/Kevin Robins (eds.), British Cultural Studies: Geography, Nationality, and Identity, Oxford: Oxford University Press, pp. 207 – 219.
Duboff, Josh (2019): "The Royal-Related Action Is Now Happening on Instagram". In: Vanity Fair May 2, 2019, accessed December 15, 2019 (https://www.vanityfair.com/style/2019/05/meghan-markle-prince-harry-princess-charlotte-instagram-message).
Geertz, Clifford (1973): "Thick Description: Toward an Interpretive Theory of Culture". In: The Interpretation of Cultures. Selected Essays, New York: Basic Books, pp. 3-30.
Giloi, Eva (2011): Monarchy, Myth, and Material Culture in Germany 1750-1950, Cambridge and New York: Cambridge University Press.
Glencross, Matthew/ Rowbotham, Judith/Kandiah, Michael D. (eds.) (2016): The Windsor Dynasty 1910 to the Present. 'Long to reign over us'?, London: Palgrave Macmillan.
Higson, Andrew (2016): "From Political Power to the Power of the Image: Contemporary 'British' Cinema and the Nation's Monarchs." In: Mandy Merck (ed.), The British Monarchy on Screen, Manchester: Manchester University Press, pp. 339-362.
Kramer, Jürgen (2017): "'Mystic in Its Claims' and 'Occult in Its Mode of Action'? Reflections on the Popular Appeal of the British Monarchy." In: Anette Pankratz/Claus-Ulrich Viol (eds.), (Un)Making the Monarchy, Heidelberg: Universitätsverlag Winter. pp. 21-40.
Laing, Jennifer/Frost Warwick (eds.) (2019): Royal Events: Rituals, Innovations, Meanings, London and New York: Routledge.
Merck, Mandy (ed.) (2016): The British Monarchy on Screen, Manchester: Manchester University Press.
Minier, Márta/Pennacchia, Maddalena (eds.) (2014): Adaptation, Intermediality and the British Celebrity Biopic, Farnham: Ashgate.
Müller, Frank Lorenz/Mehrkens, Heidi (eds.) (2016): Royal Heirs and the Uses of Soft Power in Nineteenth-Century Europe, London: Palgrave Macmillan.
Nairn, Tom (2011 [1988]): The Enchanted Glass. Britain and its Monarchy, London and New York: Verso.
Owens, Edward (2016). "Love, Duty and Diplomacy: The Mixed Response to the 1947 Engagement of Princess Elizabeth." In: Frank Lorenz Müller/Heidi Mehrkens (eds.), Royal Heirs and the Uses of Soft Power in Nineteenth-Century Europe, London: Palgrave Macmillan.
Pankratz, Anette/Viol, Claus-Ulrich (eds.) (2017): (Un)Making the Monarchy, Heidelberg: Universitätsverlag Winter.

Paulmann, Johannes (2000): Pomp und Politik. Monarchenbegegnungen in Europe zwischen Ancien Régime und Erstem Weltkrieg, Paderborn: Schöningh.

Plunkett, John (2003): Queen Victoria. First Media Monarch, Oxford and New York: Oxford University Press.

"The Guardian View on the Queen and Brexit: a Crisis in the Making." In: The Guardian January 25, 2019, accessed February 7, 2019 (https://www.theguardian.com/commentisfree/2019/jan/25/the-guardian-view-on-the-queen-and-brexit-a-crisis-in-the-making).

Widholm, Andreas/Becker, Karin (2015): "Celebrating with the Celebrities: Television in Public Space during Two Royal Weddings." In: Celebrity Studies 6/1, pp. 6-22.

Wienfort, Monika (2016): "Dynastic Heritage and Bourgeois Morals: Monarchy and Family in the Nineteenth Century." In: Frank Lorenz Müller/Heidi Mehrkens (eds.), Royal Heirs and the Uses of Soft Power in Nineteenth-Century Europe, London: Palgrave Macmillan. pp. 163-179.

Williams, Raymond (2008 [1958]): "Culture is Ordinary." In: Neil Badmington (ed.), The Routledge Critical and Cultural Theory Reader, London et al.: Routledge, pp. 82-94.

Williams, Richard (1997): The Contentious Crown. Public Discussion of the British Monarchy in the Reign of Queen Victoria, Aldershot: Ashgate.

Woodacre, Elena/Dean, Lucinda H.S./Jones, Chris/Martin, Russell E./Rohr, Zita Eva (eds.) (2019): The Routledge History of Monarchy. London and New York: Routledge.

Zweiniger-Bargielowska, Ina (2016): "Royal Death and Living Memorials: the Funerals and Commemoration of George V and George VI, 1936–52." In: Historical Research 89/243, pp. 158–75.

Royal Public Interactions and Trans/National Relations (19th-21st Century)

"We'll Never be Royals" – or Will We? Exploring Meghan Markle's Impact on the British Royal Family Brand

Pauline Maclaran and Cele C. Otnes

The ubiquitous chorus of singer-songwriter Lorde's 2013 hit single "Royals" is a pointed reminder that gaining entry into the elite but evaporating monarchic clans around the globe is likely to be an elusive option for most listeners. This gap between aspiration and attainment emanates from and reinforces the ascribed hereditary status distinguishing members of monarchies – including the world's most visible, the British royal family – from other celebrities (cf. Rojek 2001; Thomson 2006).

Yet on May 19, 2018, the newest member to join what we elsewhere explicate as the *Royal Family Brand Complex* (hereafter RFBC; cf. Otnes/Maclaran 2015) seemed exactly the type of aspirational commoner Lorde might assume would find her message salient. On that day, Meghan Markle wed Prince Harry in St. George's Chapel at Windsor Castle. People have been interested in royal rituals – and especially the spectacle of royal weddings – since at least the Renaissance (cf. Butterfield 2018). Yet in this age of media saturation, with its instant social-media feeds and uploads, people's interest levels are incessant and insatiable. For while the first royal wedding to be televised in 1960 – that of Princess Margaret and Antony Armstrong-Jones – attracted 20 million viewers (cf. Frost 2017), over two billion people around the world engaged through some form of technology to view the newly-titled Duke and Duchess of Sussex's ceremony and post-nuptial procession in Windsor (cf. Kelly 2018). Importantly, this wedding also made salient a chronic challenge for St. James's Palace – the moniker for the RFBC's public relations staff tasked with managing the royal image (cf. Bedell Smith 2012). Simply put, the entry of an American, biracial, (minor) celebrity divorcée whose family of origin has proved problematic from a brand-image perspective once again reinforced the tightrope act of balancing the mystique of the monarchy with the accessibility its public expects (and indeed, demands). In fact, we assert that this balancing act represents the foremost strategic challenge royal brand managers have faced since the marriage of Prince Charles to Camilla Parker-Bowles in 2005.

In this chapter, we explore this paradox of 'accessible mystique' that those managing the RFBC must negotiate, as members of this monarchy attempt to retain their status of being 'above celebrity.' In doing so we also recall Walter Bagehot's pertinent quote when referring to royalty, "[i]ts mystery is its life. We must not let in daylight upon magic" (Bagehot 1873 [1867]: 76). Their royal status (the "magic" in Bagehot's terms) stems from their symbolic links to world heritage, their dynastic lineages, and even their assertions that God has chosen them to reign (cf. Otnes et al. 2011). As such, royalty's pre-eminence is very different to that of other celebrities, deeply encoded as the apex of a hierarchical social system (cf. Couldry 2001). We think through some of these implications in relation to consumer culture, specifically articulating the latest challenges the RFBC faces because of the addition of Meghan Markle. Building upon the work of Balmer and colleagues that conceptualizes monarchies as corporate brands (cf. Balmer et al. 2006; Balmer 2011), in our book *Royal Fever* we conceptualize the RFBC as comprising five key types of brands: family, global, heritage, human, and luxury (cf. Otnes/Maclaran 2015). We have since come to argue that it is the heritage component, stemming from roots in dynastic, historic, geographic, and religious domains, that differentiates this complex brand from other 'celebrity/family' brands – even those enjoying immense fame and a relatively long run in the limelight (e.g. the Kennedys).

We also assert that a key challenge for managers of the RFBC is considering how to strategically adjust and assess the interplay between these brand components for the different consumer segments who engage with the brand by purchasing products, services, and experiences. Specifically, we explore these questions: How might the former Meghan Markle (now Meghan, Duchess of Sussex) – the newest 'brand extension' within the RFBC – influence the five brand components that we assert comprise the RFBC? To which of these is she most likely to contribute in building and maintaining mystique? Alternatively, which might she diminish or perhaps even damage, as the brand attempts to remain 'above celebrity' and delicately balance the accessibility demanded by consumer culture with the retaining of its mystique? To ground our discussion within contemporary understandings of complex brands, we first discuss in detail the notion of brand culture, and explicate how consumers may interpret brands in multiple ways. Next, we elaborate upon the five key brand components of the RFBC we identify above, and their particular salience to consumers. We then explore how Meghan Markle has already influenced these five elements, might do so in the future, and the challenges these trends pose to the RFBC's marketing staff.

Our discussion draws upon our nine-year ethnographic investigation into the machinations of the RFBC. We interviewed retailers, curators, and consumers of royal memorabilia and other royal-related experiences, and immersed ourselves in the study of past, present, and future royal events. We explored archival data, conducted hours of observations, and monitored commentary in traditional and social media (cf. the appendix in Otnes/Maclaran 2015 for details).

BRAND CULTURE AND THE MONARCHY

In essence, branding involves firms' strategic efforts to manage customer perceptions both of an organization (e.g. the Apple corporate brand as a whole), and its individual products and services. Branding involves much more than creating a clever logo or strapline (e.g. "Think Different" that evokes Apple's rebel ethos). Rather, it entails coordinating many strategic experiences surrounding the brand (e.g. the buzz Apple creates on social media and instore around its latest iPhone or iPad, and how this contributes to consumers' perceptions of the values and beliefs that undergird a brand and its firm).

Hence, within the ecosystem of contemporary consumption and marketing practices, scholars and practitioners talk of brand culture; that is, of the meaning systems brands evoke and the collective perceptions they engender among consumers (Schroeder/Salzer-Morling 2006). A robust stream of research now affirms people construct and perform their identities in collaboration with brand culture, using brand values to enhance their own self-concepts (cf. e.g. Arnould/Thompson 2005; Cheng et al. 2012). Thus, the monarchy is interpretable not just as a vestigial political institution, but also as a corporate brand that provides specific tangible benefits for consumers (Balmer et al. 2006). For example, in offering a shared symbol of nationalism that combines a sense of longstanding tradition and history, it offers security, and for some even perceived stability, in an increasingly uncertain world.

A cultural perspective on branding expands meaning-creation processes to include not only those created intentionally by producers (e.g. the image and market positioning), but also those emanating from consumers, employees, intermediaries, and of course, the media (cf. Holt 2004). Myriad brand interpretations may be salient to different stakeholders, and may vary according to cultural codes, ideological discourses, and personalized meanings. Thus, with respect to the RFBC, although palace officials may try to dictate public perceptions of its image, ultimately a broader range of influencing factors eludes their control. Simply put, consuming this brand spans a vast variety of touchpoints – from engaging in touristic experiences to memorabilia collecting, fashion, and film. In addition, sometimes people go to great lengths to achieve authentic connections with the brand. For example, Andrew Lannerd, a self-professed obsessive of the RFBC, states his favorite royal elements to 'collect' are personal encounters with the queen and her family (cf. Otnes/Maclaran 2015).

Besides the human additions the RFBC accumulates through birth and marriage, it also has generated several royal spin-off brands, such as the Windsor Farm Shop and Highgrove, Prince Charles's country home (open to the public). Furthermore, Queen Elizabeth II, Prince Philip and/or Prince Charles have awarded several other (typically British) brands such as Fortnum & Mason, Weetabix and Heinz Tomato Ketchup a 'Royal Warrant.' This designation represents the willingness of these RFBC members to affirm that the brand is of such high quality that at least some members of the royal household (the staff that serves the monarchy), and perhaps even some of the family members themselves, use it. In addition to Royal Warrants, some brand associations with the royal family (e.g. tours at Buckingham Palace and Windsor Castle; the design and production of commemoratives by the Royal Collection) are within the RFBC's control, while others decidedly are not. For example, the monarchy cannot dictate social-media conversations about errant actions by the individual royals.[1] Nor can it control the creation of 'Republican' or resistant memorabilia such as "Royal Wedding Sick Bags" (cf. "Lydia Leith Art & Design"). Nevertheless, it is also the case that uncontrollable brand depictions can actually benefit the RFBC. In fact, some would assert that films such as *The Queen* (2006) and series like *The Crown* (2016–) – that depict the human, emotional side of Elizabeth II and her family – have done more to help the monarchy win the hearts and minds of people in Britain and beyond than all the efforts of the St. James's Palace public relations team combined (cf. e.g. Pankratz 2017).

As we note above, we conceptualize the RFBC as a composite of five different types of brands – global, heritage, human, family, and luxury. Each taps into different aspects of this brand complex, and each offers the potential to contribute to

---

[1] On March 4, 2019, new social media guidelines were published on the royal family's website. These allow the website hosts to edit or delete comments that are deemed inappropriate, leaving more room for influencing content (social media community guidelines 2019: n. pag.).

the balancing act between mystique and transparency, helping to create a charismatic "aura" for the brand (Dion/Arnould 2011). We unpack each element below, and revisit our questions pertaining to Meghan Markle's contribution to the RFBC for each. First, we provide a short overview of reactions to Meghan Markle's entry into 'the Firm,' as Prince Philip calls the RFBC, alluding to its corporate-like dimensions.

MEGHAN MARKLE: THE NEW BRAND VARIANT

Given the still-compelling narrative of Edward VIII's abdication from the throne in 1936, when news of Prince Harry's relationship with the *Suits* actress became public, some observers immediately began to compare Markle to that former king's paramour-turned-spouse Wallis Simpson. Both were divorced Americans in their 30s; both rose from modest upbringings to mingle in circles of privilege (Markle attended Northwestern University; Simpson married a shipping magnate who socialized with the British aristocracy).

The comparison is important because the starkly different reactions to their status as divorcées among royal circles aptly capture how dramatically that dimension has been destigmatized. Essentially, both Edward VIII's family and Parliament forbade him from marrying Mrs. Simpson, and he chose to relinquish the throne to do so. In the contemporary royal family, where three of the queen's children are themselves divorced, Markle's marital status generated barely a mention within or outside of the monarchy. Nor was her profession questioned, although within the royal family, actresses traditionally had been considered excellent choices for mistresses, but certainly not for wives (e.g. the actress Lillie Langtry's stint as mistress of the Prince of Wales – later Edward VII; cf. Ridley 2012).

Much more significant in the discourse about Markle's suitability were questions about her underlying motives for marrying Prince Harry (e.g. the 'gold-digger' stereotype), and of course, her biracial heritage. Yet the fact that Prince Harry posted a letter requesting that journalists refrain from criticizing Ms. Markle's ethnicity indicates a key shift in the discourse of assessing the suitability of a royal bride. Simply put, the RFBC now represents an entity where potential royal spouses endure much less scrutiny with regard to suitability. This is especially so for family members relatively far down in the line of succession such as Prince Harry. Rather, it is now the external stakeholders of the brand who offer up the norms and strictures governing appropriateness – especially the royal watchers and pundits, often through relentless and even ruthless social-media commentary.

Indeed, critics found plenty of fodder to mention and meme – and as the world became more familiar with the facets of Markle's own brand (e.g. her problematic family), it became apparent her transition into the RFBC might not be particularly smooth. Moreover, while some argued her unique ethnicity would help reinvigorate the royal family, others satirized her relatives, her family, and her ethnocentric wedding elements. For example, the Gary Janetti Prince George meme on Instagram relentlessly pokes fun at Meghan with many classist allusions; and the British comedy TV series *The Windsors* (2016–) mercilessly parodies the royal couple, including frequent satirical portrayals of Meghan's US background and family history.

THE RFBC: THE GLOBAL ELEMENT

The RFBC is most certainly a global brand. The queen is sovereign of the United Kingdom and fifteen other realms, as well as Head of the Commonwealth of Nations. She has long bolstered the heritage aspect of its global dimension by engaging in regular, ritualized Commonwealth tours. Prince Charles and his sons (of the generation dubbed the 'Young Royals') took over this aspect of royal ambassadorship after the queen decided to curtail foreign travel after her 90th birthday. These tours aim to ensure that the popularity of the RFBC remains undiminished in far-flung corners of the world.

In addition, the burgeoning growth of the middle classes in the BRIC countries (Brazil, Russia, India, and China) – representing 40% of the world's population – affords new opportunities for touristic growth within Britain, with royal sites and events high on the priorities of many visitors. As noted, global media figures for royal events often reach huge audiences and generate significant revenues for British retailers. It is estimated that the royal wedding of Prince William and Kate Middleton in 2011 contributed over £620 million to the British economy (cf. Brand Finance 2012). Indeed, it is hard to imagine a brand that has more truly global appeal to so many different demographic segments than the RFBC.

The best brands weave compelling narratives that engage and enchant consumers. A key dimension that fuels the global fascination with the RFBC is the fairy-tale narrative of Prince Charming finding his Princess. This narrative is globally sustained primarily through the machinations of the Disney Corporation, since it issued its first 'underdog-to-princess' film, *Snow White*, in 1937. Of course, the pervasiveness of repeat-viewing technologies such as videos, DVDs, and streaming, as well as support by Disney's massive global merchandising efforts, only bolster the appeal of these narratives. They are especially compelling because they typically feature heroines (sometimes heroes) rising above their 'commoner' status to fulfil their destinies as virtuous "brand underdogs" (Paharia et al. 2011).

Recent royal romances such as those between Prince Charles and Lady Diana Spencer, Prince William and Catherine Middleton, and now Prince Harry and Meghan Markle reinforce and resonate with this underdog-to-princess global narrative. Yet one critical aspect within the sphere of the RFBC is that unlike the plots of Disney films and their sourced storybooks, the transformation from underdog to princess now occurs with the assistance of myriad viral social-media technologies. As a result, this identity shift is now subject to intense scrutiny, meaning consumers around the globe now cocreate the myth. In other words, they pass judgment on whether the underdog does in fact possess the iconic qualities worthy of the transformation to royal status. Furthermore, they often include the 'villains' that the underdog has to overcome; in Princess Diana's case, when Camilla Parker-Bowles was revealed to be Prince Charles's mistress prior to the breakup of this royal marriage, Diana leveraged her underdog status by stating famously in her television interview with Martin Bashir, "[t]here were three of us in this marriage, so it was a bit crowded" (*Panorama* 1995).

In the case of both Diana and Catherine, much of the value they bring to the brand came about through their production of photogenic, publicly-shared 'heirs and spares' that will ostensibly perpetuate the monarchy, and contribute to the dynastic aura of the brand by literally keeping it alive. For Meghan Markle, it is unlikely that her future progeny will enjoy that kind of status, given the number of royals ahead of them in the line of succession. So will Meghan Markle be able to make powerful contributions to the RFBC as well? As a commoner, Catherine Middleton reinforced the powerful essence of the 'underdog myth' that even – within hierarchically rigid Britain – virtuous, hard-working people can move up the economic and social ladder. Markle also is a commoner; in addition, she stems from a nation long gripped by Anglophilia, because of America's roots as a British colony (cf. Prochaska 2008). Although Meghan's national heritage ensures a built-in fan base from 'across the pond,' the issue of her biracial background has spurred much ongoing diverse commentary and discussion.

Racism is one of the most inherent social tensions in much of the world, as problems such as civil wars, ethnic cleansings, refugee displacement, and discourses affecting daily life attest. The rise of the far right in Europe and Britain and the 'othering' that accompanies its philosophy is reinforcing such negative discourses (cf. Lazardis et al. 2016). It remains to be seen whether Markle's racial heritage, coded by many as a welcome symbol of diversity but by others as egregious (the *Daily Mail* described her as "straight outta Compton," a stereotypically poor black area of Los Angeles; Alibhai-Brown 2018) will contribute to her enhancing the aura of the RFBC on the global stage. Cynics would say that un- (and under-) articulated racist beliefs in cultures should mean her heritage might be a liability. More liberal commentators assert that her biracial heritage serves to update the monarchy for the 21st century, and serves as a compelling symbol of its adaptation to a multicultural global environment.

THE RFBC: THE HERITAGE ELEMENT

As one of the world's most famous heritage brands, the longevity of the British royal family – with its lineage traceable to the Battle of Hastings in 1066 – plays a paramount role in symbolizing British tradition, values, and identity. In this respect, the many cultural rituals surrounding the RFBC afford opportunities to engage people at an emotional level, whilst simultaneously reasserting the pervasive presence of the monarchy in British culture. Even daily rituals like the Changing of the Guard at Buckingham Palace or Windsor Castle lend a sense of pomp and circumstance. The RFBC stages eye-catching spectacles to delight a continuous stream of tourists throughout the year, engendering emotional participation by facilitating touristic experiences and commemorative purchases (cf. Gopaldas 2014). Other, more infrequent rituals such as coronations and jubilee celebrations mark pivotal points in a monarch's reign, and serve as causes for national (and global) emotional contagion, especially with the influence of social media. One of the most engaging rituals of all is most certainly a royal wedding, with its spectacular trappings, formal processions, religious rites, and romantic connotations.

Royal rituals often contain traditional elements that help them reach back into the past (e.g. royal coaches, uniforms). Yet they also change and evolve over the years, through what Cannadine (cf. 1983: 101) refers to as 'invented traditions,' whereby new processes of formalization and ritualization are introduced. For example, Charles and Diana initiated the now familiar balcony kiss at royal weddings and Harry and Meghan's wedding is further evidence of these processes at work. Some pundits noted the ceremony bestowed "a modern glow" upon monarchic British pageantry (Gross 2018). In fact, the wedding did introduce several new and unanticipated elements into this longstanding royal rite. Once again, Markle's heritage – in particular, her desire to include influences from African-American culture into the church service – accounted for many transformations. This infusion of black culture was surely nowhere more pronounced than in the fiery and impassioned sermon delivered by Reverend Michael Bruce Curry, the first presiding black bishop of The Episcopal Church, to a somewhat stunned royal audience (as press shots of Camilla, Kate, Andrew and Queen Elizabeth attest). A black gospel choir's vibrant rendition of 'Stand by Me,' and a performance by 19-year-old black cellist Sheku Kanneh-Mason, ensured Meghan's black heritage was focal in the formal proceedings. She seemed to assert it was a heritage she would likely include in future RFBC rituals (e.g. births and christenings).

Another first for a royal wedding ceremony was the fact that Meghan walked herself down the aisle to the quire of St. George's Chapel; Prince Charles then escorted her for a short distance, as her father did not attend. Significantly, Charles did not 'give her away,' standing back as she made the final steps to Prince Harry on her own. Widely lauded as a feminist act, Meghan signaled she was establishing herself as an independent woman willing to challenge traditional patriarchal values.

How will both of these aspects of her heritage and identity – the racial and the feminist – contribute to the RFBC as remaining 'above celebrity?' Simply put, people often exhibit mixed emotions about products, services, experiences, or brands emanating from one culture, but incorporated in another. That is, they may demonstrate "cultural ambivalence" (Otnes et al. 1997) about products rooted in black culture. Consider black pop music, it appeals to people of many races; on the other hand, racial prejudice might keep people from attending concerts or inviting musicians from this same genre to perform at key venues. Although Meghan Markle delights crowds on her walkabouts with Prince Harry, the question remains whether this is a novelty effect, or whether her racial heritage will actually allow the RFBC to move the dialog about racial issues and tensions forward on a broader stage.

THE RFBC: HUMAN AND FAMILY ELEMENTS

All family brands are comprised of human beings, but not all human brands include other family members. Compare, for example, the actress Sandra Bullock – a single 'human brand' – to other 'acting families' (e.g. the Baldwin brothers). Of course, things become more complicated for family dynamics when some members are extremely strong and visible, and the success of other family members may vary or diminish over time.

This unevenness typifies the family dimension within the RFBC. The queen is clearly the focal and most powerful human brand, through her status as monarch. Moreover, she has achieved significant historical influence since becoming the longest-reigning monarch in the entire lineage on September 9, 2015. She has kept the 'brand promise' she made when she dedicated her life to her British subjects in a radio address on her 21st birthday. Although her political power is technically nil, she strategically wields power within the brand itself – making her preferences known to other family members regarding their actions and aesthetic choices.

What are Meghan Markle's distinguishing features as a human brand? The most obvious is her celebrity status derived from her acting career, one that resonates strongly in a global culture obsessed with celebrity. Yet the royals are very different from other celebrities (cf. Otnes/Maclaran 2015). They do not have to star in films, perform music, or complete any other feats to acquire fame; they merely have to be born. Historically when spousal choices for princes and princesses were limited to only-royal candidates, the issue of demarcating between royalty and celebrity was moot. Now, however, the persona that a non-royal spouse must create is paramount to the survival of the brand.

In fact, Meghan Markle's celebrity status may well diminish the sheen of royal pomp and pageantry, locating her main contribution around engaging in star-studded spectacles with world-class celebrities, rather than reinforcing the cultural power of the crown. This was indeed the flip side of her wedding, where appearances by Oprah Winfrey, the Clooneys, the Beckhams, and a host of other Hollywood-rated actors and actresses (not least, many of her former co-workers from *Suits*) eclipsed everyone but herself, Harry, and the queen. Certainly, while celebrities have been frequently seen at other royal weddings, they have not occupied such a prominent place as was the case at Meghan and Harry's wedding. To this end, we see an increasing emphasis placed on Meghan's humanitarian work by palace publicists, no doubt in an effort to tone down what some might perceive as a garish celebrity patina.

Social justice is thus the second key characteristic of Meghan as a human brand, one traceable to her successful challenge of what she perceived to be a sexist commercial for a dishwashing liquid by Proctor & Gamble at the age of eleven. Since that time, she has established an impressive record of philanthropic projects, including promoting the international children's charity World Vision, and her work as a UN Women ambassador. With respect to this role, her rousing UN speech in 2015 on International Women's Day firmly established her as a champion of women's rights with the oft-quoted phrase, "I am proud to be a women and a feminist." Of course, whether the social justice aspects of her brand can co-exist comfortably with her other elements – especially her love of *haute couture* (addressed below) remains to be seen. Interestingly, the fact that *Suits* garnered relatively modest ratings no doubt made it easier for St. James's Palace to help reposition her from actress to duchess. If her *Suits* character had been more firmly embedded within popular culture, and if she had developed a more identifiable celebrity persona, no doubt St. James's Palace would have found her image more difficult to reshape.

As we have just demonstrated in relation to Meghan, each individual human brand has its own set of values – and in marketing terms – its own set of differentiating characteristics. Family brands are based on kinship networks, engaging the public through the personalities that comprise them, and the relational dynamics between these personalities. Managing the natural gifts, goals, needs and personalities of these individuals can be tricky. Furthermore, the different distribution of these attributes means some human brands will by nature garner more attention than others, and some will be more naturally charismatic and attract followers. This situation may lead to jealousy and tension within the family brand, especially if some members have more power within the matrix. The way Princess Diana's popularity eclipsed Prince Charles is an example of the type of "soft power" (Müller/Mehrkens 2016) that individual royals may wield.

Anyone entering an established, prestigious family brand must find a comfortable place within it, synchronizing his or her own values with those of other family members while simultaneously carving out a unique path. One understanding that Meghan Markle seems to demonstrate is that the key to achieving recognition by the other powerful individuals within the RFBC is to demonstrate how her values and interests align with theirs. For example, her love of dogs resonated instantly with the queen – and with the royal corgis themselves. Prince Harry reported about this rapport: "I've spent the last 33 years being barked at, this one walks in... [to meet the queen...the dogs are] just wagging tails, and I was like, 'Argh.'" (Thorbecke 2017: n. pag.)

Moreover, powerful individuals within a family brand obviously can champion and defend others in the brand complex, even if the aura associated with an individual remains firmly his or her own. In that vein, the queen has already signaled her firm endorsement of Meghan, recently selecting her as a companion and coambassador on a trip to the city of Chester.

Meghan Markle thus seems adept at harmonizing with the queen and other family members. However, the situation is very different within her own kinship network and for many royal-watchers (and no doubt for those embedded within the RFBC itself) this aspect of the 'Markle family brand' is seen as detrimental. The one exception to this categorization is Meghan's mother, Doria Ragland, the only family member to attend the wedding. Otherwise, Meghan Markle has disengaged with her family of origin. Family brands provide rich templates for the creation of narratives around them; often, these are outside the control of the individual members themselves. In the case of Meghan's family of origin, many media stories highlight their various undesirable actions. In particular, her father admitted staging photo shoots for money prior to the wedding, her brother submitted a letter for publication warning Prince Harry not to marry her, and her stepsister Samantha Markle has vocally criticized Meghan, and is publishing an autobiography entitled *The Diary of Princess Pushy's Sister*. In addition, her former sister-in-law Tracy Dooley arrived in England with her two sons to act as special correspondents for the highly popular *Good Morning Britain* during the wedding. Mysteriously ditched at the last minute from the program, they nevertheless offered many opinionated media interviews, despite not having spoken to Meghan for many years. In short, most of Meghan's family appear determined to milk their tenuous connections to the new duchess, while undermining her in the process.

In truth, it is the family brand dimension that is likely to be most problematic for Meghan Markle, in terms of her contributing to the RFBC. This is because by shunning her family of origin (even rightfully, as many argue), Meghan violates a sacred sociological norm of many cultures – that family should stick together through thick and thin. The supreme irony here is that historically, the 'family brand' aspect of the royal family has been rife with glaring examples of family dysfunction, ranging from public fighting to murder. Nevertheless, their place at the pinnacle of the social hierarchy has diffused the impact of painful family narratives – especially in the days when the RFBC determined political and economic fates. The dilution of that power, coupled with the age of the autonomous consumer who constantly monitors the foibles of *any* brand on social media, now means that renowned human/family brands must respond to criticism, and quickly.

THE RFBC: THE LUXURY ELEMENT

Jean-Noël Kapferer (2018), a renowned scholar of luxury brands, recently observed that these represent desirable indulgences that bring pleasure and pride to their owners. Furthermore, he argues that historically, luxury goods have been elusive and unattainable for most people in the world. However, luxury brands that stem from America are actually much more accessible than those from Europe, where the vestiges of vertically-stratified social structures still influence the luxury market. In that regard, Meghan Markle behaves much more like a 'European luxury brand' than her sister-in-law Catherine, who still often wears brands that are from High Street, off-the-rack retailers.

Another way to conceptualize Meghan Markle's luxury-brand contribution is that she emulates two very American segments – the *nouveaux riche* and the classic Hollywood starlets. With respect to the first, since her marriage Meghan Markle has selected brands she found less attainable on her actress's salary. In particular, she chose the French brand Givenchy to design her wedding gown (albeit with a British woman at the helm of the house). Although her choice of one of the most iconic *haute couture* brands for her wedding day is perhaps understandable, her preference for it and others (e.g. Carolina Herrera, Prada, Dior, and two favorite British brands in Stella McCartney and Burberry) has contributed to herself being 'branded'– as extravagant. Indeed, she spent almost a million dollars on her wardrobe in her first month of marriage alone (cf. O'Neill 2018).

With respect to the second point of dressing like a classic starlet, Meghan Markle's Los Angeles upbringing and choice of profession no doubt helped school her in the fashion choices made by the world's most famous Hollywood actresses. In fact, she has stated that her fashion role model is Audrey Hepburn – an iconic beauty, if not quite a royal one (she was the daughter of a Dutch baroness). Hepburn's aristocratic roots, as well as her collaborations with some of Hollywood's most famous costume designers, may have contributed to her fondness for *haute couture*. By emulating many of Hepburn's signature touches (from her bateau neckline to her eyebrows), Meghan Markle seems to be positioning herself in the orbit of the iconic style-starlets from the golden age of Hollywood (e.g. Hepburn, Vivien Leigh, Elizabeth Taylor), even as she has given up her acting career. It is yet undetermined how this strategy can coexist with her other persona – that of a modern woman who declared prior to her marriage that she would henceforth be known for her humanitarian work with her husband.

CONCLUSION: MEGHAN'S ROYAL FUTURE

As we have shown in this chapter, Meghan Markle's present and future contributions, both positive and negative, stretch across all five facets of the RFBC. In terms of its *global* element, she is likely to contribute a broader appeal for the RFBC due to her biracial nature that makes for a more inclusive image in our post-migrant times. Her potential contribution to the *heritage* aspects are more ambiguous. On the one hand, the choices in her wedding clearly demonstrate that she wants her African-American heritage to be a visible component of her identity, a component that is likely to be very popular with many members of the British Commonwealth. However, this heritage may not resonate enough with British people, even with its increasingly diverse population. Furthermore, in an America that has seen issues related to race become much more sensitive and even strident, it is not clear that trumpeting her race will increase her appeal, even among citizens of her country of origin.

As an *individual brand*, Meghan Markle has the opportunity essentially to start over in this sphere; her celebrity status was never so established as to overshadow any persona she may choose to create. In short, she is free to emphasize her professed love of social-justice causes, and her professed desire to change the world for good with Prince Harry. It seems her natural charisma has already endeared her to several important members of the brand (namely, the queen), and Prince Charles's somewhat double-edged nickname of 'Tungsten' for her already supports a brand personality that is strong-willed and steely.

However, in relation to the overall *family brand*, Meghan cannot contribute members of her own family as a support system for the RFBC. In fact, this is her weakest link; with the exception of her mother, her own family members are actually working to undermine her, and to rattle the foundation of her own human brand, supporting the persona of Meghan as the manipulative gold-digger. However, this threat is likely to diminish with the arrival of Meghan and Harry's first child, Archie Harrison Mountbatten-Windsor, born on May 6, 2019. As they produce their own entrants into the 'family brand,' it is likely her blood relatives will only be salient for her (and for St. James's Palace) as a thorn in their side.

Finally, with regard to the *luxury brand*, it is unclear whether Meghan's clearly expensive and elitist tastes can coexist with the other dimensions of the human brand she and St. James's Palace strategically emphasize. Her unabashed extravagance in this arena could give rise to tensions around issues pertaining to new- versus old-money values, or even American versus British norms of wealth display. From our analysis of the discourse around this issue, we expect her childhood aspirations to channel the movie stars she wishes to emulate (not to mention her reported admiration for Princess Diana as an icon both of fashion and of social justice) is winning out over a need to appear judicious in spending. In short, it seems Meghan is more interested in contributing to this dimension of the RFBC than Kate and other young royals (except Princess Eugenie, who announced prior to her wedding in 2018 that her ceremony would resemble Meghan and Harry's in location and scope). The way Meghan chooses to create her component as a luxury brand may simply serve to heighten the increasing divide between the 'haves' (e.g. the RFBC and the wealthy in Britain) and the 'have-nots' (the increasing numbers of British below the poverty line). It is likely to evoke pertinent debates about the cost of the RFBC, and how well it serves Britain. These issues are becoming increasingly salient in an era when the queen, the strongest human brand in the RFBC, is winding down her duties and bringing other members of the family to the forefront.

WORKS CITED

Alibhai-Brown, Yasmin (2018): "Britain in Black and White." In: Newsweek May 11, pp. 20-29.
Arnould, Eric J./Thompson, Craig J. (2005): "Consumer Culture Theory (CCT): Twenty Years of Research." In: Journal of Consumer Research 31/4, pp. 868-882.
Bagehot, Walter (1873 [1867]): The English Constitution, London: H. S. King.
Balmer, John M. T. (2011): "Corporate Heritage Identities, Corporate Heritage Brands and the Multiple Heritage Identities of the British Monarchy." In: European Journal of Marketing 45/9/10, pp. 1380-1398.
Balmer, John M. T./Greyser, Stephen A./Urde, Mats (2006): "The Crown as Corporate Brand: Insights from Monarchies." In: Brand Management 14/12, pp. 137-161.
Bedell Smith, Sally (2012): Elizabeth the Queen: The Life of a Modern Monarch, New York: Random House.
Brand Finance (2012): "Understanding the Value of the British Monarchy as a Brand." In: Brand Finance Journal Special Jubilee Issue, June.
Butterfield, Lanisha (2018): "A Renaissance Royal Wedding." In: University of Oxford Arts Blog April 17, accessed April 14, 2019 (http://www.ox.ac.uk/news/arts-blog/renaissance-royal-wedding-0#)
Cannadine, David (1983): "The Context, Performance and Meaning of Ritual: The British Monarchy and the 'Invention of Tradition' c. 1820-1977." In: Eric Hobsbawm/Terence Ranger (eds.), The Invention of Tradition, Cambridge: Cambridge University Press, pp. 101-164.
Cheng, Shirley Y. Y./Barnett White, Tiffany/Chaplin, Lan Nguyen (2012): "The Effects of Self-Brand Connections on Responses to Brand Failure: A New Look at the Consumer–Brand Relationship." In: Journal of Consumer Psychology 22/2, pp. 280-288.
Couldry, Nick (2001): "Everyday Celebrity." In: David Morley/Kevin Robins (eds.), British Cultural Studies. Oxford: Oxford University Press, pp. 221-234.
Dion, Delphine/Arnould, Eric (2011): "Retail Luxury Strategy: Assembling Charisma through Art and Magic." In: Journal of Retailing 87/4, pp. 502-520.
Frost, Katie (2017): "Looking Back at Princess Margaret's Wedding Day." In: Town&Country December 10, accessed March 19, 2019 (https://www.townandcountrymag.com/society/tradition/a12265404/princess-margaret-wedding-to-lord-snowdon/).
Gopaldas, Ahir (2014): "Marketplace Sentiments." In: Journal of Consumer Research 41/4, pp. 995-1014.

Gross, Jenny (2018): "Prince Harry and Meghan Markle's Royal Wedding Gives British Pageantry A Modern Glow." In: The Wall Street Journal May 19, accessed April 14, 2019 (https://www.wsj.com/articles/britain-puts-on-a-royal-spectacle-for-prince-harry-and-meghan-markles-wedding-1526714332)

Holt, Douglas B. (2004): How Brands Become Icons: The Principles of Cultural Branding, Boston, MA: Harvard University Press.

Kapferer, Jean-Noël (2018): "Pursuing the Concept of Luxury." Keynote Speech June 22, European Association for Consumer Research Conference, Ghent, Belgium.

Kelly, Helen (2018): "Royal Wedding 2018 Viewing Figures: How Many People Watched Meghan Markle Marry Harry?" In: Express May 20, accessed March 19, 2019 (https://www.express.co.uk/showbiz/tv-radio/962610/Royal-Wedding-viewing-figures-Meghan-Markle-Prince-Harry-kiss-David-Beckham).

Lazardis, Gabriella/Campani, Giovanna/Benveniste, Annie (2016): The Rise of the Far Right in Europe: Populist styles and 'Othering', London: Palgrave Macmillan.

"Lydia Leith Art & Design", n. d., accessed March 19, 2019 (https://lydialeith.com/collections/work/products/sick-bags).

Müller, Frank/Mehrkens, Heidi (2016): Royal Heirs and the Uses of Soft Power, London: Palgrave Macmillan.

O'Neill, Grace (2018): "This is How Much Meghan Markle Has Spent on Clothes Since Marrying Prince Harry." In: Elle Australia July 3, accessed March 19, 2019 (https://www.elle.com.au/fashion/meghan-markle-clothing-cost-post-marriage-17954).

Otnes, Cele C./Crosby, Elizabeth/Maclaran, Pauline (2011): "Above Celebrity: Maintaining Consumers' Experiences of Heritage-Based Fame." In: ACR North American Advances 38.

Otnes, Cele C./Maclaran, Pauline (2015): Royal Fever: The British Monarchy in Consumer Culture, Berkeley: University of California Press.

Otnes, Cele C./Lowrey, Tina/Shrum, L. J. (1997): "Toward an Understanding of Consumer Ambivalence." In: Journal of Consumer Research 24/1, pp. 80-93.

Pankratz, Anette (2017). "'That's Entertainment': Monarchy as Performance." In: Pankratz, Anette/Claus-Ulrich Viol (eds.), (Un)making the Monarchy, Heidelberg: Winter, pp. 41-64.

Paharia, Neeru/Keinan, Anat/Avery, Jill/Schor, Juliet B. (2011): "The Underdog Effect: The Marketing of Disadvantage and Determination through Brand Biography." In: Journal of Consumer Research 37/5, pp. 775-790.

Prochaska, Frank K. (2008): The Eagle And The Crown: Americans And The British Monarchy, New Haven and Connecticut: Yale University Press.

Ridley, Jane (2012): The Heir Apparent: A Life of Edward VII, the Playboy Prince, New York: Random House.
Rojek, Chris (2001): Celebrity, London: Reaktion Books.
Schroeder, Jonathan E./Salzer-Morling, Miriam (eds.) (2006): Brand Culture, London: Routledge.
"Social Media Community Guidelines", March 4, 2019, accessed June 12, 2019 (https://www.royal.uk/social-media-community-guidelines?fbclid=IwAR3X4Tdmp-PqIoZI4n5U6pasTVJhzeykyFqC9_2keHfZZcrfFQxG-EYatTI).
Thomson, Matthew (2006): "Human Brands: Investigating Antecedents to Consumers' Strong Attachments to Celebrities." In: Journal of Marketing 70/3, pp. 104-119.
Thorbecke, Catherine (2017): "Queen Elizabeth's Corgis Immediately 'Took To' Meghan Markle, Prince Harry Says." In: ABC News November 28, accessed March 19, 2019 (https//abcnewsgo.com/Entertainment/queen-elizabeths-corgis-immediately-meghan-markle-prince-harry/story?id=51418394).

Films and Television

Panorama. "An Interview with HRH the Princess of Wales." November 20, 1995. BBC1.
Snow White and the Seven Dwarfs. Directed by David Hand. 1937. Walt Disney Productions.
Suits. Created by Aaron Korsh. 2011–. USA Network.
The Crown. Created by Peter Morgan. 2016–. Netflix.
The Queen. Directed by Stephen Frears. 2006. Paris: Pathé.
The Windsors. Created by George Jeffrie/Bert Tyler-Moore. 2016–. NOHO Film and Television.

Your Media Majesty:
Three Kings and Radio in the Inter-War Years

Deirdre Gilfedder

In the nascent years of the British Broadcasting Company Limited (BBC) the founder and director Lord Reith chose to use royal radio addresses as the centerpiece of the company's broadcasting programming in its bid to establish a national presence in the United Kingdom, but also in his more ambitious strategy of developing the new BBC Empire Service. Between the wars three British monarchs spoke on the BBC numerous times with three celebrated royal broadcasts particularly marking the period: King George V's live broadcast Christmas message of 1932; the abdication speech of Edward VIII in 1936 and George VI's rally to war speech in 1939 – made famous in the Tom Hooper film *The King's Speech* of 2010. The content of these addresses was of immense importance in tumultuous times and aimed to create social and imperial cohesion. The broadcasts were also historic media events that characterized and established a role for radio in the British Empire while simultaneously, as Briggs (1965) has argued, effecting a modernization of British royalty. This paper seeks to outline what kind of communication model was applied for royal broadcasts, to study how royal broadcasts functioned as media rituals (cf. Couldry 2003) and events (cf. Dayan/Katz 1992) and to question the established notion of a modernized monarchy in a declining 20th-century British Empire. Through this study, the political communication of British monarchs will be approached as relating not only to the United Kingdom but as having an imperial outreach and role. Conversely, the British monarchs' new presence in broadcasting also played a role in the branding of a new 'media empire' of radio.

Transformations in media technology in the 20th century were instrumental in helping certain European monarchies to survive political upheaval, after a 19th century during which revolt and republicanism displaced monarchies' hold. Republican associations had even appeared in Britain during Queen Victoria's reign.

Yet as David Cannadine (1983) has shown, the rise of the illustrated press was instrumental in bolstering her popularity later in her reign. Between the world wars, in the 20th century, the British kings, in a similar way to politicians, could use developing media outlets to communicate to their people in a way not possible in the 19th century. Radio was seen by the BBC as a means of transmitting the monarch's power that befitted modern notions of an 'imagined community' experienced through media simultaneity (cf. Anderson 1993 [1983]). Through radio broadcasts the king could speak to the absent body of the nation or Empire. In doing so the monarch emerged as an incorporeal presence and exploited the 'magic of transmission' to distribute royal presence and figuratively enter peoples' homes. While the hope was that the medium would create proximity between monarch and people through this *ersatz* intimacy, the British royals nonetheless employed a model of 'dissemination' through broadcasting during the Great Depression. This could be compared with Franklin D. Roosevelt in the United States, for example, who simulated intimate dialogue through his 'fireside chats' on the NBC.

The 1930s were, of course, an intense period of political mass communication engaging new theories of mediated power. As of 1933, Joseph Goebbels considered radio as the greatest instrument to spread propaganda for the Nazi government due to its low cost and high distribution potential and its established model of unifying audiences (cf. Lacey 2002 qtd. in Hilmes/Laviglio 2002: 34). Mussolini equally laid emphasis on radio to enforce a grid of fascism in a country where literacy rates limited the power of the press and he developed an international reach for Italian radio. In countries like Mexico, the government attempted to disseminate what was seen as a national culture through state broadcasting throughout the 1930s. The BBC, originally a commercial consortium of radio manufacturers, soon found its ambitions tied in with the state agenda. Receiving a royal charter in 1927, the medium was conceived as a tool for managing the public and exercising moral authority. While the BBC always denied using propaganda, royal broadcasts in the British context might be regarded as constituting ideological symbolic power. Indeed, they strove to influence not only a sense of national community[1] but also imperial soft power, just when the Empire was being challenged by events in Ireland, the Statute of Westminster and growing nationalism in dependent colonies such as India.

---

1   David Cannadine demonstrates how the Christmas broadcast cast George V as the 'Father of the nation,' yet this role was to be far more international (cf. 1983: 142).

This paper approaches both the history and philosophy of broadcasting in the United Kingdom in the 20th century through a transdisciplinary cultural perspective on media events. Emphasis will be placed on the first example, as the Christmas message initiated and encapsulated the imbrication of media majesty in the 20th century. As Cannadine (1983) shows, the message 'invented' a modern tradition, and carved out a place from which the monarch was to speak, one that Edward VIII and George VI learned to occupy.

The following seminal studies have provided historical material as well as media theory for this essay: Simon Potter's research on the history of the BBC Empire Service traces the chronology of the BBC's rise to become a public service with imperial ambitions. Volume II of Asa Briggs' definitive Oxford history of British broadcasting (1995 [1965]), written with the help of the BBC, offers detailed information on radio in the inter-war period. Applying the concept of media events as introduced by Daniel Dayan and Elihu Katz in their work published in the early 1990s, this paper will explore how a monarch crosses media thresholds and structures social communication. Nick Couldry (2003) furthered the concept of a media event by theorizing media rituals. The work of John Durham Peters (1999) on the earlier years of radio explores the history of ideas behind the radio as medium. Furthermore, as witnessed by the film *The King's Speech* (2010), radio evokes the king as voice and body both concomitant with and distinct from the political role of the monarch. Ernst Kantorowicz's (2016 [1957]) concept of the two bodies of the king, centered on the medieval and early modern history of European monarchy, places a particular emphasis on the case of Britain. His conceptualization will therefore allow us to see how the notion of the king as body, voice, speech, or political idea structured relations in a period seen by Kantorowicz himself as the end of European tradition, namely the early 20th century.

THE CHRISTMAS MESSAGE 1932: SPEAKING TO IMPERIAL SUBJECTS

The idea of a Christmas message from the king to the people of the United Kingdom and the Empire was conceived by John Reith, the head of the BBC, who wrote to King George V in 1923 suggesting a broadcast. The king as a conservative was suspicious of modern technology and reportedly lacked confidence over his oratorical skills, so he initially declined. Reith's idea was to use radio to disseminate a 'personal message of the king' – not the king's institutional speech but the king as himself. Reith's motivations were largely to do with both national and imperial ambitions. The king on radio would foster British identity as well as constitute a powerful advertisement for BBC radio sets. As media historian Kate Lacey has pointed out, the Depression era was "pivotal in providing a spur to the production of radio both as consumer good and one of the vehicles available for the production of *needs*" (Lacey 2002 qtd. in Hilmes and Laviglio 2002: 23). Though the BBC prided itself on an anti-commercial philosophy, after the United States, Britain had the highest concentration of radio sets in the inter-war period and license ownership increased exponentially through the 1930s, which benefitted the BBC monopoly. The number of homes with wireless sets rose from 4.5 million in 1931 to almost 8 million in 1939 (cf. Potter 2012: n. pag.). However, broadcasting King George V as emperor would be an even more significant event in freedom-seeking colonies and dominions such as Australia and Canada, who had been resisting introducing the BBC into their airwaves. Long-distance radio technology had not been developed and Australia for example was restricted to the 'sealed-set' system.[2] Yet radio consumption also boomed in Australia where by 1938 67 per cent of households owned sets. According to Simon Potter (2012), in the 1920s, both Canada and Australia were more interested in having US-style commercial radio than an elitist public broadcaster along the lines of the BBC model or the BBC itself. Potter's history of the BBC Empire Service shows that its officers perceived the Americanization of broadcasting around the world, and particularly within the British world, as a potential threat. Spreading the British model overseas was seen by Lord Reith as a way to perpetuate British cultural influence, and contain Americanization. Reith strongly believed in the importance of the British Empire to world order and a BBC Empire Service could only enhance its strength in the context of anti-imperial rebellion, the rise of fascist powers in Europe and the power of the United States. An empire service might maintain 'sentimental ties' (in the words of Reith) with the dominions and colonies and project Britain overseas. Focusing attention on the king's voice would in theory mediate him as center and symbolic focal point of this Empire.

It was notably the beginnings of decolonization that sparked the royal Christmas broadcast. In the Irish Free State De Valera's Fianna Fail ended all land payments to Britain at the beginning of the 1930s, triggering an economic war, while in India the civil disobedience movement was initiated by Gandhi in March, 1930. Following the Balfour report and in the wake of large colonial losses in the Great War, the Statute of Westminster also redefined the Empire. In 1931 The Statute of

---

2   Sealed sets were radios that could only receive transmission from channels for which they were licensed. It was suited to the earliest British and Australian systems which were government controlled.

Westminster legally established both autonomy and equality between the United Kingdom and a number of dominions, abolishing their status as colonies and creating the British Commonwealth. In fact, George V had attempted to exclude the laws of royal succession from the provisions of the Statute of Westminster. However, the equality between Britain and former colonies promised by the 1926 Balfour report, was supposed to be bound by 'common allegiance to the crown,' the principle that had given an aura of feudal loyalty to imperial subjects in the past. British imperial citizenship was conjugated as subject-hood, with personal allegiance to the king as the defining tenet until well into the 20th century. During the First World War, the definition of a British subject was not only one born under the king's dominion, but also 'one who owes allegiance to the king,' as the oath taken by colonial soldiers during the war reveals, in a 'debt of gratitude' for the sovereign's protection. With the Statute of Westminster dominions that had separate legislations would constitutionally need to ratify the law to integrate the monarch into their systems. The king would thus reign from within these multiple legislations and this would guarantee equality (rather than subordination to Great Britain) in the new British Commonwealth. Much later in the Australia Act in 1986, the British monarch became inscribed in fully independent legislation as Queen of Australia, whereas in Canada, Elizabeth II became Queen of Canada via the constitutional patriation of 1982.

Back in Britain in 1932, Labour Prime Minister Ramsay MacDonald convinced George V that in the context of new imperial relations, the monarchy was pivotal for maintaining unity in the Empire and a broadcast would enhance its role and make a decisive contribution. MacDonald also assuaged the king's fear of broadcasting by suggesting that the noted imperialist poet Rudyard Kipling write the text of the message (cf. Glencross 2013). At this time the BBC was determined to create the Empire Service, but ran into a number of technical difficulties broadcasting across long distances. Financing the scheme was also challenging: programming on the service was initially allocated 10 pounds a week and was restricted to simplified messages and retransmissions of some very basic British content. For the Christmas broadcast, short-wave technology was employed through the General Post Office's transmitters. The BBC had the government's support for the establishment of an Empire Service and at the Colonial Conference of 1927 representatives of colonies and dominions had expressed enthusiasm for the scheme (cf. Briggs 1965: 360). The first broadcasts were to Australia and New Zealand, and then Canada, Eastern, Western, and South Africa, India, Egypt, and the West Indies. Six days after the service opened, the king was to deliver his Christmas message.

The speech was anticipated in the dominions, and advertised beforehand in one Australian newspaper as "proof of the innate solidarity of Empire" (Potter 2012: n. pag.). According to records, at least 20 million people listened to the message across the world (cf. Briggs 1965: 363). The king's voice, experienced simultaneously, could create the larger imagined community that Benedict Anderson (1993 [1983]) argued was always created by media. Indeed, Anderson stressed the superiority of radio in "summoning into being an aural representation of the imagined community where the printed page scarcely penetrated" (ibid: 54). The Christmas message would additionally perform Reith's notion of disseminating British authority.

The significance of the king on radio at the time should be understood within the functioning terms of the United Kingdom's constitutional monarchy, the result of a long history of democratic developments. Ernst Kantorowicz, an expert on Frederick the Great of Prussia, devoted his attention to the British monarchy in his work on *The King's Two Bodies* (Kantorowicz 2016 [1957]) where he wrote of the medieval British concept of *curia regis,* the great officers of the king's court which constituted the predecessor of parliament. Executive authority came to be exercised through the notion of the-king-in-council, advised by the Privy Council, and through orders that sealed parliamentary laws. Kantorowicz quoted the 15th-century English judge John Fortescue and medieval jurists who theorized that the king had two bodies – one natural, and one political. While these bodies may be indivisible in the king's person, (the dignity of the king's person depends on it), judicially they are separate and there is no doubt the social, political body of the king is superior to his natural self. In Britain a constitutional monarchy formed over centuries of devolution of statehood from the monarch's political body to the parliament, originally known as the 'king-in-council' thus further splitting the king's political body into constitutional crown and parliament. The two bodies of the king, one that grows old and dies, and one that is immutable and that "never dies," as Kantorowicz puts it, are thus perhaps best formulated by the British monarchic and democratic tradition. By the time Walter Bagehot was writing on the British monarchy in the 19th century, he commented that "a republic has insinuated itself beneath the folds of monarchy" (2012 [1867]: 44). Thus Britain, sometimes conceived of as a 'crowned republic,' had practically severed the natural body of the king from the body politic. While British politics operated for and against the king, the gravitas of monarchy was arguably borne into the 20th century by the Empire where the monarch played the central role in imperial citizenship and subjecthood. Indeed, something of the ancient aura of the king survived in his ability to reign over global domains, symbolized by the attribute of the orb that featured in royal portraiture.

From the body of the king comes forth his speech. Yet in Britain the 'queen's speech' or the 'king's speech' is also devolved from the natural speaking body, as what the king or queen says is highly regulated. The official "king's speech" is not the kind of address George V, George VI, and others gave on the radio, but rather a formal enunciation made to parliament, and indeed is nowadays written by the government. In the 20th century, the king was the mouthpiece of the government and it was rare for the king to speak personally as his natural body. Certainly before the 1920s, most of his subjects had never heard his voice. When King George V spoke over the radio for the first time at Wembley in 1924, his voice bore the trace of the king's body, though disassociated from its corporeal source and deterritorialized. Live broadcasts invoked the royal presence, distributed by what was seen as the magic of electronic transmission into lounges around the world and forced attention onto the king as symbolic center of society. There was something reminiscent of a survival of a more ancient and sacral notion of monarchy in the radio broadcasts – the notion of an immortal and redemptive presence of the king.

The text of the Christmas address spoken by the king in person, evokes the power of radio, imagined as the numinous in modernity: "Through one of the marvels of modern Science, I am enabled, this Christmas Day, to speak to all my peoples throughout the Empire....To men and women so cut off by the snows, the desert or the sea, that only voices out of the air can reach them..." ("First Empire Address by King George V" 1932: n. pag.).

While Asa Briggs argued that radio modernized the monarch in the 1930s, the king speaking on it could also be regarded as rather more ancient and ritualistic, containing a measure of Benjamin's 'numinous aura' through its uniqueness and authenticity (cf. 1969). Distance in the Empire is seen as collapsing through mechanized proximity with the king, a meeting of king and subjects experienced simultaneously by an imperial community: "I take it as a good omen that Wireless should have reached its present perfection at a time when the Empire has been linked in closer union. For it offers us immense possibilities to make that union closer still," (First Empire Address 1932: n. pag.) says the king at a time of burgeoning decolonization and a divisible monarchy. In some ways the Statute of Westminster had split the king's body further into divided legislations across the realms. "If the British decided to chop off the king's head, mused Charles Dixon in 1936, how many times would it have to be done? Once for Australia? Again for Canada? Again in New Zealand?" (Twomey 2017: 34). Radio offered a means to aggregate a 'closer union.'

Daniel Dayan and Elihu Katz have explained their notion of the media event as interrupting routine and focusing on the event with ceremonial reverence. As such it involved reimagining the sacred: "the origin of media events is not in the secular routines of the media but in the 'sacred centre' that endows them with the authority to preempt our time and attention." (Dayan/Katz 1992: 32) The idea that a mediated king could 'hold the Empire together' and that mediation could seal the corporate body of state, meant that the broadcast was staged as an 'historic event.' For Dayan and Katz the media event, while ostensibly modern, "renews the centre, confirming traditional authority," (Couldry/Hepp 2010: 4) as such it can "reinforce the status of leaders," (Dayan/Katz 1992: 201) precisely through a notion of enhanced aura. As Nick Couldry points out, the media itself occupies a mythic center through its own mystifying rituals (cf. 2003: 42). Thus the broadcast is an event, the center of the center, that became a media ritual.

The Christmas broadcast employed a model of communication that in many ways followed an idea of imperial structure. The king's message was disseminated rather than communicated in the terms discussed by John Durham Peters' work on early broadcasting. For Peters (1999), technologies such as the telegraph and radio appeared following a line of dreaming about communication, telepathy and the 'sharing of consciousness.' Communication was philosophically pursued as an idea during the 1920s with the hopes and fears of its informing role in 'mass society.' Peters explores the dissemination model of communication where reciprocity is suspended and reception is invisible and imagined. As in the parable of the sower, broadcasting is "a mode of communication that is democratically indifferent to who may receive the precious seeds [...]" (ibid: 52). Dissemination is, on the one hand, conceived of as unidirectional and an expression of power. On the other hand, it seeks virtual equality in reception. This model fit the king's political communications perfectly. King George V was "speaking into the air" (Peters 1999) to an invisible audience rather than a point-to-point dialog. At the same time the service hoped to close the gap of the disembodiment of radio and connect the king with listeners, restoring honor to an institution that in other countries was losing its legitimacy. Debate raged in the early 1930s over whether British audiences should wear hats when the king spoke (cf. ibid: 66). Yet this important communication act also helped to define the radio as participating in the public sphere. Following the broadcast, Reith was surprised at the number of listeners who responded by letter, and in 1933 the governments of the countries who were to receive the message (New Zealand, Australia, Canada, India, South Africa, Kenya) prepared their own messages to the monarch to be sent by telegram, creating a limited measure of dialogical communication.

Peters also explains that radio audiences were united in imagination rather than location, and radio dealt with the mutual absence of bodies by creating a sense of closeness through sound effects and other techniques (cf. ibid). In 1933, Franklin

D. Roosevelt simulated an intimate dialogue by addressing the American public as 'my friends' with the accompanying sound effect of a crackling fire during his 'fireside chats.' For royal ceremonies and parades the BBC held a microphone close to the bells on the horses' harness. As of 1940, the brass-band musical theme that introduced the news, 'Imperial Echoes,' resounded in homes in West Africa and India creating a signature for BBC news. Meanwhile, the king, like Walter Benjamin's film actor (cf. 1969: 11), was to be disembodied through technology, and yet unlike film, radio conveyed liveness, not dead reproduction. For Peters (1999), radio emerged in an epoch fascinated by a revival in spiritualism after the losses of the First World War. Radio was seen by some as communication between souls through the ether, somewhat like a spiritualist séance. It seems that radio inventor Marconi, for example, had participated in a royal séance in London with Queen Alexandra, and King George V himself was a reader of the spiritualist magazine *Psychic News*. Lord Reith was one of the first to employ the ether as a metaphor for airwaves, writing in 1924 that "[w]ireless is manifestly dependent for its functioning on the universal ether – a fascinating, but illusive and probably incomprehensible medium" (ibid: 103).

For Peters, media at this time was not that far from the notion of a medium and much of the discussion around electro-magnetic waves tapped into imaginative spiritualist discourses inherited from the Victorian age (cf. 1999). Thus the king as radio presence confirmed utopian ideas about communications, conjured up the pseudo-spiritual realm of the media event while conveying Victorian ideas about global power.

KING EDWARD VIII'S ABDICATION SPEECH, 1936: HIS MAJESTY VERSUS THE MEDIA

The abdication crisis was also an imperial crisis. Since the Statute of Westminster the dominions had to be consulted as to questions of the succession. In November 1936, Stanley Baldwin approached dominion governments with a question about a morganatic marriage (a solution which would enable the king to remain in office while, however, his wife would not be queen) it was seen as a compromise that had also been put to the British government. The prime ministers of South Africa, Australia, and the Irish Free State all objected to Wallis Simpson being queen, as well as to a morganatic solution and advocated an abdication as the lesser of evils, with only the Prime Minster of New Zealand supporting the idea of a morganatic marriage. Baldwin had thus garnered support from the Empire, now equal partners in the Commonwealth, and used this to pressurize the king to abdicate.

The abdication crisis was a struggle between the office of king (crown and councillors) and the natural king, a man in love. It was also a major media event. Already the subject of the prince's affair with Wallis Simpson had led to battles in the press. While rumors of the affair emerged in papers in the United States, the British media baron, Lord Beaverbrook, who ran the *Daily Express*, the paper with the largest circulation in the world throughout the 1930s, acquiesced to pressure from the Prince of Wales to keep the story out of his papers (cf. Fairbanks 1966). This 'gentlemen's agreement' on a blackout was extended across the Commonwealth to Canada and Australia. The sensationalist dailies that appeared during the late Victorian and Edwardian periods and had – according to David Cannadine (1983) – exalted the monarch, remained largely obsequious to royal authority between the wars. However, as of 1936, the British press did begin to churn out headlines (including the *Express*) about the king and Mrs. Simpson and what had become a constitutional crisis. The newspaper *The Times* and the BBC then fought over how the decision would be conveyed to the public. Sir John Reith, a convinced monarchist and apparently dismayed by the king's association with an American (cf. Potter: n. pag.), quickly introduced the king's broadcast on the Empire Service made shortly after he had signed the abdication papers.

In his speech Edward VIII refers to the indivisibility of the two bodies of the King:

"At long last I am able to say a few words of my own. I have never wanted to withhold anything, but until now it has not been constitutionally possible for me to speak. There has never been any constitutional difference between me and them [the ministers of the Crown] and between me and Parliament. Bred in the constitutional tradition by my father, I should never have allowed any such issue to arise." ("Edward VIII Abdication Speech" 1936: n. pag.)

In reality, Edward VIII had hoped to strengthen the power of the king and reduce that of parliament and had planned another broadcast where he would have announced that he was remaining king (cf. Davies et al. 2003: n. pag.). King Edward had already been praised by *The Radio Times* of 1936 as an excellent broadcaster (cf. BBC Archive) and the planned broadcast had been seen and tweaked by Winston Churchill (who in fact was against abdication). It could have been a convincing event for the ambitions of the king, but it was rejected by Baldwin as unconstitutional, for speaking directly to his subjects through radio would mean to act against the wishes of his constitutional advisers. The last time this had happened was with King Charles I in 1642 (cf. Briggs 1995). We can see that broadcasting involved a complexity for the crown between body, voice, and corporate notion of state and people. The abdication was made real to the Commonwealth through the speech act of a broadcast, thus sealing the BBC Empire Service as a seat of authority that even had the power to manage monarchy.

GEORGE VI ON THE EVE OF WAR: RE-CENTERING THE EMPIRE

George VI's adventures and misadventures with radio were fictionalized in the Oscar-winning film *The King's Speech* of 2010, based on the diaries of the Australian speech therapist Lionel Logue. George VI's speech impediment, his brother's abdication and the context of approaching conflict on the continent were more dramatic than the film's representation of history would lead us to believe. Once again, the BBC required a speaking king to bolster their Empire Service that was vying against German and Italian radio broadcasts in English and other languages. Despite Reith's insistence on impartiality and balance in journalism, it became increasingly important to counter propaganda from the countries adhering to the axis whose modern technology, in particular in short wave broadcasting, outstripped the BBC. Their programs included negative and distorted versions of events in Britain, and the Germans had even sent questionnaires to British colonies and dominions asking for evaluation on the quality of their broadcasting. This critical situation was the impetus behind the introduction of foreign language broadcasting at the BBC with the beginnings of the first Arabic service, the Palestine Broadcasting service in 1936, in collaboration with the Colonial Office (cf. Briggs 1995: 374). In 1938, the son of the King of Yemen launched the official Literary Arabic Language Service, showing once again how royalty could attract attention and authority on this supposedly non-propagandistic public service.

The struggle on the airwaves for influence in Egypt, India, and as far as Australia brought the BBC closer to the colonial office. For Briggs the policy had changed from "talk of 'sentimental ties' to talk of 'protecting England'" (1995: 366). Empire listeners were caught up in the political maelstrom, even though most actually tuned in to the BBC for its variety of programs. On September 3, 1939, three years after the abdication speech, Britain declared war on Germany and King George VI was called upon to perform another momentous task. His short speech employed all the rhetorical techniques to convince British listeners of the necessity to fight the Nazi regime and it was once again addressed to a widespread but invisible Empire.

"In this grave hour, perhaps the most fateful in our history, I send to every household of my peoples, both at home and overseas, this message, spoken with the same depth of feeling for each one of you, as if I were able to cross your threshold and speak to you myself..." ("King George VI Addresses the Nation" 1939: n. pag.)

As his father before him, the king evokes the medium of radio as a quasi-magical device to abolish distance between the king's body and those of his listeners. The king's spectral presence penetrates into the homes of those across the seas who could tune in to the improved short wave transmission. By 1939, BBC Empire Service listeners included around 100.000 wireless sets in the 47 colonies, with around 1 million each in Australia and Canada and over 200.000 in New Zealand. The speech was of course heard beyond the Empire and though the king speaks of "the peoples of the world," he concentrates specifically on his subjects, who are the "we": "For the second time in the lives of most of us, we are at war." Further in the message he states, "the freedom of our own country and of the whole British Commonwealth of nations would be in danger...." The purpose of the broadcast was to enjoin imperial subjects once again to participate in war: "It is to this high purpose that I now call my people at home, and my peoples across the seas, who will make our cause their own." (ibid)

George VI's radio address resurrects the chivalrous contract between king and subject: to fight and die for king and Empire. This traditional notion of citizenship, drawn from medieval and Greco-Latin roots of *pro patria mori*, was thus cast into the air for the last time in the Empire's history. In Australia, the conservative Prime Minister Robert Menzies, responded to this injunction the very same day with a broadcast on the Australian Broadcasting Commission, the ABC, calling the country to war as vassals of Empire, in his famous address: "Fellow Australians. It is my melancholy duty to inform you officially that in consequence of a persistence by Germany in her invasion of Poland, Great Britain has declared war upon her and that, as a result, Australia is also at war." (Prime Minister Robert G. Menzies 1939: n. pag.)

New Zealand's Prime Minister Michael Joseph Savage also responded on the National Broadcasting Service with a declaration of intense loyalty to Britain: "Where she goes, we go. Where she stands, we stand. We are only a small and young nation, but we are one and all a band of brothers and we march forward with union of hearts and wills to a common destiny." (1939: n. pag.)

The Empire Service had encouraged listeners to tune into a radio realm where Britain was firmly the authorized center. While the early success of the service had been compromised by fragile technology and low funds, by the 1940s it became the international voice of Britain, contributing significantly to the war effort, and operating with the ministry for information. The kings' broadcasts as centerpieces in the BBC's program, were not so much reflections of a political reality, but speech acts that organized imperial relations. The BBC Empire Service, while ostensibly informing and entertaining dominions and colonies, helped to redefine a structure with center and periphery at a time of freedom struggles, dominion nationalisms and growing American influence. At the heart of this imbrication between the media service and political power was the monarch, distributing his powerful aura to all his subjects in a pact that resembled medieval chivalry more than modern democracy. This is not to diminish the radio's democratic usefulness, as the abdication crisis demonstrates, 'speaking into the air' gave overseas British subjects access to events at the center. Yet while the development of mass media was supposed to bring the monarchy closer to the people, in many ways it sealed the media as a new 'sacralized' realm.

WORKS CITED

Anderson Benedict (1993 [1983]): Imagined Communities: Reflections on the Origin and Spread of Nationalism, New York: Routledge.
Bagehot, Walter (2012 [1867]) : The English Constitution, Cambridge : Cambridge University Press.
Benjamin, Walter (1969): "The Work of Art in the Age of Mechanical Reproduction." In Hannah Arendt (ed.), Illuminations, translated by Harry Zohn, New York: Shocken Books, pp. 217-251.
Briggs, Asa (1995 [1965]): The History of Broadcasting in the United Kingdom – the Golden Age of Wireless 1927-1939 Vol II., Oxford: Oxford University Press.
Cannadine, David (1983): "The Context, Performance and Meaning of Ritual: The British Monarchy and the 'Invention of Tradition', c.1870-1977." In: Eric Hobsbawm/Terence Ranger (eds.), The Invention of Tradition, Cambridge: Cambridge University Press, pp.101-164.
Couldry Nick (2003): Media Rituals: A Critical Approach, London: Routledge.
Couldry, Nick/Hepp, Andreas (2010): "Media Events in Globalised Media Cultures." In: Nick Couldry/Andreas Hepp/Friedrich Krotz (eds.), Media Events in A Global Age, Abingdon: Routledge.
Davies, Caroline/Tweedie, Neil/Day, Peter (2003): "Edward VIII's Unspoken Abdication Speech." In: The Daily Telegraph January 30, accessed March 20, 2019 (https://www.telegraph.co.uk/news/uknews/1420505/Edward-VIIIs-unspoken-abdication-speech.html).

Dayan Daniel/Katz, Elihu (1992): The Live Broadcasting of History, Cambridge, MA: Harvard University Press.

Fairbanks, George (1966). "Australia and the Abdication Crisis 1936." In: Journal of Australian International Affairs 20/3, pp. 296-302.

Glencross, Matthew (2013): "The First Christmas Speech." In: History of Government Blog, No 10 Guest Historian Series, April 24, accessed March 20, 2019 (https://history.blog.gov.uk/2013/04/24/the-first-christmas-speech/).

Hilmes, Michelle/Lavilgio, Jason (2002): Radio Reader: Essays in the Cultural History of Radio, New York: Routledge.

Kantorowicz, Ernst (2016 [1957]): The King's Two Bodies: A Study in Medieval Political Theology, Princeton: Princeton University Press.

Lacey, Kate (2002): "Radio in the Great Depression: Promotional Culture, Public Service and Propaganda." In: Michele Hilmes/Jason Loviglio (eds.), Radio Reader: Essays in the Cultural History of Radio, New York: Routledge.

Peters, John Durham (1999): Speaking Into the Air: A History of the Idea of Communication, Chicago: University of Chicago Press.

Potter, Simon (2012): Broadcasting the Empire: the BBC and the British World, Oxford: Oxford University Press. Digital Version.

Twomey, Anne (2017): "Royal Succession, Abdication and Regency in the Realms: the Crown in the 21st Century." In: Review of Constitutional Studies 22, pp. 33-54.

Films and Television

The King's Speech. Directed by Tom Hooper. 2010. See-Saw Films/The Weinstein Company/UK Film Council.

Archival Sources

Australian War Memorial, accessed June 19, 2019, updated October 24, 2017 (https://www.awm.gov.au/articles/encyclopedia/prime_ministers/menzies).

BBC Archive (1936): "The New King as Broadcaster." In: The Radio Times, January 24, accessed March 20, 2019 (http://www.bbc.co.uk/archive/edward_viii/12950.shtml).

"Edward VIII Abdication Speech", December 11, 1936, In: History of the BBC, accessed February 1, 2017 (https://www.bbc.co.uk/programmes/p04hd10t).

"First Empire Address by King George V", December 25, 1932. In: History of the BBC, accessed February 1, 2017 (https://www.bbc.co.uk/programmes/p027m2xp).

"King George VI Adresses the Nation", September 3, 1939, accessed June 19, 2019 (https://www.bbc.co.uk/archive/king-george-vi-addresses-the-nation/zky9f4j)

"Prime Minister Robert G. Menzies: Wartime Broadcast", September 3, 1939 In: Savage, Michael Joseph (1939): Sound Archives. Reference Number 31615, September 5, accessed March 20, 2019 (https://ngataonga.org.nz/collections/catalogue/catalogue-item?record_id=206464).

European Royals and their Colonial Realms: Honors and Decorations

Robert Aldrich and Cindy McCreery

MEDALS, SASHES AND BADGES: THE GIVING AND RECEIVING OF ROYAL HONORS

Honors and decorations – membership in medieval chivalric orders like Britain's Order of the Garter or newer orders like France's Legion of Honor – may seem mere sideshows to the main business of 19th and 20th-century royal (or 'royalesque') European government.[1] Many people today, including historians, tend to dismiss such decorations as simple baubles, prized only by vain subjects keen to display shiny medals, bejeweled stars and silken sashes on formal court dress or uniforms. Yet up through the 19th and for much of the 20th century (and, in some places, the 21st century), in both European states and their overseas colonies, honors mattered greatly. In a deferential society, where differences in social status and class were carefully measured and visible, the award and display of honors was both a source and expression of enormous pride – individual pride as well as pride in the larger nation and empire. It could also be a source of jealousy, and, for political opponents, one of anger at the regime's attempts to 'buy' support. Conferring titles of nobility, orders of chivalry and decorations was an important prerogative of the monarch as the *fons honorum*.[2] Even in societies which explicitly

---

[1] This article presents some preliminary findings from our new collaborative research project on monarchies, decolonization and royal legacies. It focuses primarily on civilian rather than military honors, though it should be noted that many orders (e.g. the OBE) were awarded for both civilian and military service.

[2] The 'fount of honor' (from the Latin *fons honorum*) refers to the individual in a state (or head of a dynasty) who claims the exclusive right to confer titles of nobility or

rejected their royal pasts and embraced republican or communist ideals, honors became a key method for the state to reward individual as well as group 'heroes.' In short, the distribution and display of honors and decorations reveal the complexities of individuals' relationships with the ruler, both within 19th and 20th-century European states and throughout their colonial and postcolonial territories.

Much research on orders of chivalry has focused on the Middle Ages, but Antti Matikkala's *The Orders of Knighthood and the Formation of the British Honours System* argues that medieval orders retained their significance as coveted markers of royal esteem and acknowledgement of status and achievement throughout the early modern period and beyond (cf. Matikkala 2008, 2014). The iconic French Order of the *Légion d'Honneur,* created by Napoleon in 1802 and the model for many later state honorary orders, has legitimately attracted the attention of a number of historians (Tulard, Monnier and Échappé 2004; de Chefdebien and Flavigny 2017). Scholars of the 19th century have investigated the creation of new orders and the 'inflation' of the honors system, for example in France and Germany, in the context of economic development, nationalism, democratization and even a 'grey economy' of the marketing of honors (cf. Ihl 2004; Thompson 1994). A sociological approach to honors has been provided in a wide-ranging study by Samuel Clark, looking at honors across Western Europe (and elsewhere) from Antiquity to the present (cf. Clark 2016). Clark considers various social science theories – including behaviorist psychological theory, rational-choice theory and organizational theory – to analyze (both qualitatively and statistically) honors and their relationship to social structures and power. Specialists in law and constitutional history have also examined the 'honors prerogative' of rulers and the legal standing of title-holders, including the validity of imperial titles in overseas territories (cf. Cox 1997 and 1998). Honors have featured, too, in scholarly works on material culture (including museum exhibition catalogues) as well as antiquarian publications (cf. McClenaghan 1996).

Yet the role of honors in European colonialism remains understudied. This article makes the case for taking honors and decorations seriously as a means of understanding the nuances of colonial and postcolonial power dynamics within (as well as outside) monarchies. It compares existing scholarship on honors (especially in the British Empire) with examples from the French and some other European empires, to suggest that honors and decorations formed a fundamental, if contested, aspect of colonial and post-colonial rule. Comparative scholarship on

---

knighthood or award honors and decorations. This was normally the prerogative of a reigning monarch, although the privilege is now also exercised by republican and other heads of state (and is also still claimed by some heads of deposed dynasties).

honors and awards in colonial situations is patchy. Most scholars have focused on a single nation or empire; but even here research has been limited by a lack of full official records on the process of granting honors. Historians such as David Cannadine in his signal *Ornamentalism*, published in 2001, have provided influential overviews of the political use of honors within the 19th- and early 20th-century British Empire. More recently, Tobias Harper and Karen Fox have examined the system in 20th-century Britain and in the former Dominions of Australia, Canada and New Zealand (cf. Harper 2014, 2015 and 2017; Fox 2010 and 2013). John McLeod and Jesse S. Palsetia have done valuable work on the British honors system in India, and in responses in Britain and India to the award of a baronetcy (in 1857) and a peerage (in 1919) to two prominent Indians (cf. McLeod 1994 and 1997; Palsetia 2003). For a more global view, however, we need to consider sources beyond mainstream academic scholarship (cf. Duckers 2008; Mulder and Purves 1999). Indeed, while 'official' scholarship on colonial orders is often thin on the ground, popular accounts of honors and awards are flourishing, particularly on the web. As well as useful overviews on government websites, online encyclopedias, popular history sites such as Royal Ark, and commercial marketplaces such as Medal Hound and eBay provide often detailed and well-illustrated accounts of both well-known and more obscure honors and decorations. In turn they point to (ongoing) public interest in honors and decorations. Indeed, phaleristics – the study and collecting of insignia of orders of chivalry and of merit, medals and other decorations – is a thriving area of interest. *The Musée de la Légion d'Honneur et des Ordres de la Chevalerie* in Paris and the Tallinn Museum of Orders of Knighthood in Estonia, as well as, among others, St Petersburg's Hermitage Museum and London's Imperial War Museum, offer major collections of decorations from around the world for public view. There are active societies of phaleristics in numerous countries, many with their own websites and bulletins. In addition, dedicated shops (including antique dealers) and manufacturers of decorations, and such fairs as the semi-annual Britannia Medal Fair in London testify to popular fascination by connoisseurs and collectors. It is time that historians caught up by providing further contextualized and interpretive analyses of honors and decorations. The present article represents an exploration of the phenomenon of honors in European colonial empires. After an overview of the history and practice of awarding honors by European monarchs, it will examine knighthoods in the British Empire (particularly in the settler societies) and the colonial honors in

India and elsewhere; finally, we briefly discuss honors in other European empires and in several independent non-European states.[3]

EUROPEAN MONARCHIES AND HONORS

From at least the early modern period until the end of the First World War, almost all European states, like the vast majority of states throughout the world (other than France, Switzerland, San Marino, and the republics in the Americas), were monarchies, and in this period most of the major powers conquered extensive overseas empires. In the period of heightened nationalism and the creation of new nation-states through unification or secession, as well as the parallel expansion of overseas empires in the late 19th and early 20th centuries, monarchs (as well as republican rulers) developed new systems of national and now also colonial honors and decorations. These often emulated in form and design chivalric honors originally created in the Middle Ages.

For centuries European monarchs regularly ennobled subjects at home, granting titles (duke, marquess/marquis, earl or count, baron) that were generally hereditary, and the British sovereign also created hereditary baronetcies.[4] The British monarch appointed elite men, often aristocrats, to orders of chivalry, such as the Orders of the Garter, the Thistle and the Bath, the most prestigious of the orders. These orders specified a strict limit on membership (for example, the Garter was and remains limited to 24 living members) which helped to maintain their high status. In the 19th century these often accompanied senior political appointment, and many an ambitious Victorian cabinet member looked forward to joining the exclusive club. If they missed out on these distinguished chivalric orders, British men could be given an 'ordinary' knighthood, i.e. made a Knight Bachelor.

Monarchs of other European countries also awarded titles of nobility at home and, though much more rarely, in the colonies and abroad. Portuguese and Spanish kings, who oversaw the creation of massive maritime empires, granted patents of nobility to explorers, *conquistadores* and governors. In the early 16th century the Portuguese Vasco da Gama was made Count of Vidigueira (and bore the resounding if rather meaningless title of Admiral of the Seas of Arabia, Persia, India, and

---

[3] Space is lacking here for extensive discussion of a number of issues that merit further research and analysis, including issues of gender and ethnicity in the disbursement of honors, the production and iconography of insignia, the reciprocal conferring of awards between royals, and the popular understanding of honors systems in the past and today.

[4] The term 'marquess' is used in Britain; 'marquis' in France.

all the Orient), and Afonso de Albuquerque was created Duke of Goa; the Portuguese sovereign also awarded titles of nobility in colonial Brazil (cf. Monteiro and Corrêa de Silva 2018; Schwarcz 2018). French monarchs of the *ancien régime* ennobled a few subjects in New France (what is now eastern Canada and parts of the USA), or elevated expatriates who already possessed noble titles to higher ranks. There is today one extant French barony in Canada, created by Louis XIV and now recognized in the British honors system (cf. Ruggiu 2009 and 2011).

Nineteenth-century French monarchs created further noble titles, including those for military commanders who distinguished themselves in colonial campaigns – their titles frequently taken from battles won (cf. Dumons and Pollet 2009; Ihl 2000). For example, Thomas Robert Bugeaud's service in the conquest of Algeria earned him the title of Duc d'Isly and the dignity of marshal in the French army from King Louis-Philippe. Similarly, ennoblement (or promotion to a more senior title) was *de rigueur* for military officers who won key battles in the British Empire, as well as for British viceroys of India, many governors-general and senior colonial officials in London. Examples include the Marquess of Wellesley (India) in the early 1800s, Baron Lugard (Governor-General of Nigeria) in the early 1900s, and Second World War hero Viscount Slim, who also served as Governor-General of Australia.

European monarchs themselves sometimes took on titles alluding to their imperial roles – Queen Victoria famously became Empress of India in 1876 – and sovereigns for long had also bestowed civilian (as distinct from military) honors on those who rendered services to the colonial state. Their creation was a way of affirming imperial (and often monarchical) power over distant domains and of honoring subjects who labored in far-flung possessions. But not all subjects were treated equally within this system, and indeed the racial, class, and gender division of honors reflected broader inequalities within and between individual colonies, as well as between colonies and the European metropole.

KNIGHTHOODS IN THE BRITISH EMPIRE

The numbers of colonists who received knighthoods in the 'white' settler colonies of Australia, Canada, New Zealand, and South Africa (which by the early 20th century, following self-government, came to be known as the Dominions) remained relatively modest. This reflected imperial caution as well as some local opposition and/or ambivalence to British titles. Honorees were often drawn from elite social, business, and conservative political circles. To take the Australian case: Stanley Bruce, a former Australian prime minister, was made a baron and in

1947, as Viscount Bruce of Melbourne, became the first Australian to sit in Britain's upper parliamentary chamber, the House of Lords (cf. Radi 2011 [2004]). In 1953 Clive Baillieu, whose distinguished career in business and as a British government advisor was favored by his privileged Melbourne family and educational background, became a baron (cf. Potter 2004). In 1963 Prime Minister Robert Menzies was the first Australian to be awarded the Order of the Thistle, an honor in which he (and the nation) took great pride; he is shown wearing the mantle and insignia of the order in one notable image.

Figure 1: Sir Robert Menzies, c. 1963-4

Source: 2014.17, Unknown artist, colour process lithograph (Courtesy of the National Portrait Gallery, Canberra, Australia).

Brisbane-born Richard Casey, Liberal Party politician, diplomatist and later governor-general of Australia, was made a baron in 1960 and nine years later became the first Australian to be created a Knight of the Garter (cf. Bridge 2011). The first Aboriginal Australian to be knighted, in 1972, was community leader, pastor and footballer Douglas Nicholls, who later served as Governor of South Australia (cf. Broome 2012). Australian Labor Party politicians remained more wary of knighthoods than their counterparts in the conservative Liberal Party, but occasionally accepted them. Similarly, in New Zealand, politicians, especially those with an imperial bent, such as Sir Joseph Ward, who was created baron in 1911, were overrepresented among those granted top honors. Some Maori leaders were also rewarded with knighthoods for their service to New Zealand and in particular the

Maori people. The first Maori to be so honored, James Carroll, was made a Knight Bachelor in 1911, while, to take a female example, in 1970 the Maori Queen Te Atairangikaahu became a Dame Commander of the British Empire (cf. "Overview of the New Zealand Royal Honours System").

Until the last quarter of the 20th century, culturally traditionalist and politically conservative Australians and New Zealanders – most of whom were still of British and Irish ancestry, though that was rapidly changing with migrations from other parts of the world – remained wedded to a notion of British heritage, loyalty to the Crown and an affinity with the old British Empire (now as the Commonwealth of Nations). In the mid-20th century, the British sovereign's role as Head of State in Australia and New Zealand was rarely contested; "God Save the Queen" remained the national anthem. There was indeed no separate Australian or New Zealand citizenship until 1948. The conferral of a knighthood by the monarch on his or her distant subjects represented, for many, the most esteemed acknowledgement to which they could aspire. Consequently, such awards were feted in the press, through civic receptions and by the treasuring of insignia as family heirlooms; the titles visibly differentiated an elite within society.

By contrast, in 1919 Canada asked the British government to cease awarding honors, other than military medals, to Canadians. This reflected public anger with a 'cash for honors' political scandal that had embarrassed the David Lloyd George government in Britain and had allegedly led to some Canadians whom compatriots considered unworthy being honored. Although not all Canadians, especially those with a conservative and pro-empire bent, agreed with their government's request, there was sufficient support for this measure that it remained in place (cf. Harper 2014; McCreery 2005). Similarly, in 1925 the Nationalist government of South Africa, Britain's other Dominion, reflecting the views of its Afrikaner (the descendants of Dutch settlers) support base, stopped the conferment of British civil titles and orders.

BRITISH COLONIAL HONORS: INDIA

Throughout the 19th-century British Empire, policy towards colonial honors reflected broader political and racial views about particular colonial communities (cf. Dirks 1993; Keen 2013: 185-192). British belief in Indian rulers' desire for honors, combined with their commitment to defusing local opposition following the 1857 rebellion (misleadingly referred to as the 'mutiny'), led the British to create a unique system of Indian honors during the reign of Queen Victoria (cf. Taylor 2018: 174). In 1861 the Order of the Star of India was established – it is arguably the most ornate of the British awards, its badge including a hand-carved cameo of the monarch, surrounded by diamonds (cf. Duckers 2008).

Figure 2: Order of the Star of India, badge of Knight Commander (c. 1900, United Kingdom)

Source: The exhibition of the Tallinn Museum of Orders of Knighthood, Estonia ("Wikimedia Commons" 2017a)

In 1878, after Victoria assumed the title Empress of India, the Order of the Indian Empire and the Order of the Crown of India (the latter reserved for women) were created. While the East India Company had been thoroughly discredited following the 1857 rebellion, its Order of British India (established in 1837 and granted mostly to native Indian military officers for 'long, faithful, and honorable service') was incorporated into the British government's Indian honors system and was briefly resurrected by the Viceroy, Robert Bulwer-Lytton, in time for the imperial durbar of 1877 (cf. Harper 2014; McClenaghan 1996).

As with British honors, the Indian honors were hierarchical, with various ranks – knight grand commander, knight commander, or companion in the case of the Star of India (which mirrored the ranks within some metropolitan orders) – carefully calibrated to reflect the status of the person honored. The insignia of the order avoided the imagery of the Christian cross in deference to the Hindu, Muslim or other non-Christian faith of most Indians; thus the badge of the Order of the Indian

Empire comprised a red-enameled rose, which gave rise to its nickname, the 'Jam Tart' (cf. Duckers: 2008 45-46).

The assumption was that giving such awards would reward Indian loyalty to the British monarch and state, and guarantee future support in the face of growing nationalist opposition to British rule. Such honors reflected and reinforced existing social hierarchies within both Indian and British society. Most of the highest awards given to Indians went to high-ranking princes, who were also distinguished by the number of gun salutes they received. Often the award was less a recognition of actual service than of the prince's social and political status. High-ranking princes received more prestigious ranks of awards (e.g. Knight Grand Commander) than lesser-ranking ones. Many maharajahs collected both of the orders for men, the more commonly awarded Order of the Indian Empire and the more prestigious Star of India.

Figure 3: The Maharajah Ganga Singh of Bikaner, c. 1930

Source: Carl Vandyk, photograph ("Wikimedia Commons" n. d.)

Yet the process was not always a rubber stamp; the British government could show displeasure with the public or private life of one of the feudatories by delaying an appointment, or giving a prince a lesser honor that one he might consider his due. In turn Indian princes felt entitled to lobby actively for awards (and, in particular, promotion to higher-ranking degrees), for themselves but also for their subjects.

In 1942 the Maharajah of Bikaner suggested that imperial honors would be very helpful to ensure his people's continued support for the war effort (cf. Harper 2014: 107). Bikaner himself was awarded numerous honors, as seen in one photograph where he wears the breast plaques of the Order of the Star of India, the Order of the Indian Empire and the Hessian Order of Philip the Magnanimous.

Appointments to the Indian orders were occasionally also made to those outside of the Indian Empire, as when the British appointed the king of a newly unified Bhutan, Ugyen Wangchuk, a knight in 1907. The monarch continued awarding the Indian knighthoods right down to the dying days of the Raj, but ceased making new appointments to the orders after the independence of India and Pakistan in 1947. The last Knight of the Indian Empire died only in 2010.

When the same awards were given to British personnel in India as to Indians, they explicitly rewarded seniority and distinguished service (as assessed by civil service superiors) in the British administration. Yet again status played a major role in determining who received which version of which award. The higher-ranking civil servants received more prestigious awards than more junior colleagues (cf. Harper 2014: 187). Crucially, and this was true across all 19th-century honors systems, few women received honors. When they did, they came from a separate and more rarely awarded order, e.g. the Order of the Crown of India.

Occasionally Indians received honors from the domestic British honors system, which was viewed as a remarkable privilege. The sole peerage created by the monarch during the colonial era for an Indian, in 1919, honored Satyendra Sinha, first Baron Sinha of Rajpur. He was a London-educated barrister, Advocate-General of Bengal (the first Indian to hold such a position), governor of Bihar and Orisha (the first Indian to hold a governorship) and Indian representative at the Versailles peace conference at the end of the First World War. The title is currently held by his great-grandson (cf. McLeod 1997).

The monarch did concede a few hereditary baronetcies to Indians, the first, in 1857, given to Sir Jamsetjee Jejeebhoy, a Parsi businessman and philanthropist from Mumbai, followed in 1890 by Sir Dinshaw Petit, a textile merchant (cf. Palsetia 2003). Of the paltry seven baronetcies created for Indians, three are extant. The extreme scarcity of hereditary titles given to non-white British subjects during the imperial age reflects British racial and, as David Cannadine reminds us, class prejudices (cf. Cannadine 2001).

BRITISH COLONIAL HONORS BEYOND INDIA

British ambivalence about the conferment of honors on 'native' subjects is well illustrated by the case of Australia. Common in colonial Australia, especially in the 19th century, was the award of metal 'kingplates' or 'breastplates,' often adapted from British military officers' gorgets (metal badges), to loyal Aboriginal men. Governor Lachlan Macquarie introduced the practice in 1814 to identify 'chiefs' who would serve as intermediaries between a 'tribe' and the government. Such identification of 'chiefs' was seen as crucial by colonial administrators keen to present Aboriginal society in European hierarchical terms, and to mark and reward loyalty to colonial rule. Other 'badges of merit' were given to indigenous people who helped the colonists. Hundreds or possibly thousands of breastplates were awarded up until 1946. But such designations, while they delighted not only the individuals honored but their wider communities and descendants, were regularly mocked by colonial settlers (Troy 1993; Kaus n. d.). Moreover, as Karen Fox points out, official honors and decorations proved problematic for many indigenous leaders in 20th- and 21st-century Australia and New Zealand (cf. Fox 2014b: 499). Did their acceptance of such honors imply support for the imperial project, one which had so disadvantaged indigenous people – or did it provide recognition of these leaders' work and indeed the efforts of the communities they represented in seeking to remove such disadvantage? Awarding honors, to indigenous people as indeed to others, thus involved not just individual recognition, but propaganda for the colonial state (and for those groups whose members were honored) and an effort to secure collaboration in the pursuit of imperial objectives.

Throughout the empire, the granting or acceptance of honors and decorations in the case of indigenous people and nationalists raised complex political and moral issues. Residents of Ireland, formally part of the British state in the 19th and early 20th centuries, could be awarded the 'Order of St Patrick' (though it was rarely conferred), as well as other imperial honors, but nationalists there objected to the acceptance of British decorations. It is significant that the Republic of Ireland chose to establish no system of honors when it eventually became independent in the mid-20th century, while Northern Ireland, which remains part of the United Kingdom, naturally retains the British honors system (cf. Smith 1998).

Other parts of the British Empire proved more responsive to honors, and indeed imperial honors proliferated in the 19th and early 20th centuries. Beyond the British chivalric orders and the separate Indian orders given to Indians and Britons working in India, in the 19th century the British government awarded growing numbers of honors to colonials, and to Britons for colonial service, firstly through the Order of St Michael and St George. The order was created in 1818 particularly for services to Britain in the Ionian Islands and Malta, but its regulations were revised in 1868, by which time the British Empire had expanded enormously, so that the order could be given to those who 'hold high and confidential offices within Her Majesty's colonial possessions, and in reward for services rendered to the Crown in relation to the foreign affairs of the Empire' (cf. Harper 2014: 20). For most of the second half of the 19th and the early 20th century, the Order of St Michael and St George was the most commonly conferred order for colonial service beyond India. During the eight-month 1901 British Empire Tour of the Duke and Duchess of Cornwall and York (the future George V and Queen Mary), for example, the Duke conferred six Knight Grand Cross (GCMG), fifteen Knight Commander (KCMG) and forty-four Companion (CMG) honors as well as eight ordinary knighthoods on colonial officials. (cf. Wallace 1902: 480-485). At the end of the 19th century the Royal Victorian Order (1896) and the even more exclusive Royal Victorian Chain (1902) were established to allow the monarch to personally reward distinguished service to the Crown and royal family (cf. Duckers 2008: 47). While the Royal Victorian Chain was primarily given to Britons, from time to time it was seen as a suitable honor for visiting foreign royalty.[5]

In 1917, a century after the creation of the Order of St Michael and St George, and in the wake of a domestic 'cash for honors' scandal involving political donors in Britain, a new, 'untarnished' order was deemed necessary. George V created the Order of the British Empire (OBE) for those who carried out notable civilian service (though it could also be given for military service). Remarkably, this order was, from the start, intended for both men and women (cf. Harper 2014: 33-84). The First World War had provided opportunities – indeed, created the necessity for – incorporation of women into non-traditional positions in public and private life in Britain, and the new order (as well as the extension of the vote to some women in 1918) was an acknowledgement of war service. This also represented rapidly changing norms and perspectives about the place of women in society in general during the early 20th century. Nevertheless, women have never achieved parity with men, neither in Britain nor in other countries, in the award of honors.

The OBE was given out generously during the First World War, indeed many felt too generously, and as Tobias Harper (2014) notes, there were widespread concerns that the award was 'cheapened' by this practice. At the end of the war

---

5   In 1907, for example, Britain's Foreign Office recommended that Edward VII give the Royal Victorian Chain to King Chulalongkorn of Siam instead of the Order of the Garter. Chulalongkorn, however, politely refused the Chain and in the end received no decoration. This episode forms part of a an on-going research project by Cindy McCreery on 19th and early 20th-century British honors and foreign royals.

the British government determined to emphasize its significance by avoiding 'inflation' through setting strict quotas as to who could receive the honor, and at which of the five grades. Social class continued to play a role – those from the upper classes often being made 'members,' 'officers,' 'companions,' or 'knights' of the order, and working-class people mainly restricted to the lower 'medal.'

The Order of the British Empire continues to be awarded in Britain and in a certain number of Commonwealth realms (though it has been superseded or entirely replaced by local honors in others). As Harper has demonstrated, the OBE has been domesticated – it is now not awarded for service to the British Empire but service to the particular country where it is given. Despite the nomenclature of the order, today's recipients, of course, have no direct connection with the extinct institution of the British Empire. Discussions about changing the name of the order nevertheless have come to nought because of the continuing value attached to receiving an 'OBE' (cf. Harper 2014: 212-214).

Harper's thesis, which provides the most comprehensive account of 20th-century British honors (especially the OBE) and the political and social implications of their disbursement, demonstrates that these quotas were linked to assumptions about a colony's 'civilized' status, with a distinction between the 'civilized' self-governing Dominions and the 'less civilized' 'Crown' or dependent colonies, i.e. territories with predominantly non-white populations, in the rest of the empire. By the 1960s and 1970s it was becoming embarrassingly obvious that more, and higher-level honors went to people in the Dominions than the Crown colonies: by 1976 far more people in New Zealand, for instance, received senior honors than in Papua New Guinea (PNG), despite having similar population levels. While PNG's less developed, geographically isolated status undoubtedly played a role in the disparity, the same held true for highly urban and populous Hong Kong, which received relatively few honors. While protests produced some small gains, the overall system of honors continued to favor Dominion populations (cf. ibid). Yet even there, honors received a mixed reaction. As Karen Fox notes, the discourse of egalitarianism, the idea that colonial society is more democratic than in Britain, has played a powerful role in Canadian, New Zealand, and Australia debates over honors, but with varied results – for example, Canada established its own honors system (and withdrew from British honors) decades before New Zealand and Australia (cf. Fox 2014a).

With the move to full independence from Britain in the 20th century, former British colonies had to decide how, or whether at all, to incorporate honors in their new incarnations. The answers varied considerably between states, as well as over time. Australia, Canada and New Zealand, which, as Harper (2014) notes, tended to have 'gentler' overall experiences of colonialism than colonies in Asia and Africa, and whose white populations were thus relatively sympathetic to Britain, often adopted British-style honors. But even here, individual variations between Dominions reflected their particular histories and constituencies (cf. ibid: 217).

Canada, which since 1919 had eschewed British honors, as previously mentioned, finally created its own Order of Canada in 1967 but retained the British monarch, in the role of Queen of Canada, as the fount of honor. Australia and New Zealand followed the Canadian model – albeit more slowly. The Order of Australia was not established until 1975 and the Order of New Zealand not until 1987 (cf. "Department of Prime Minister and Cabinet"). Controversies continue. A Canadian newspaper magnate long-resident in Britain, Conrad Black, was determined to accept a British life peerage offered in 2001, and successfully pursued the matter through the law courts despite the opposition of the Canadian government. The prestige of the Order of Australia, created by Labor Party Prime Minister Gough Whitlam, was undoubtedly limited by the fact that traditional imperial honors also continued to be awarded in Australia. In 1976, under the (conservative) Liberal Party Prime Minister Malcolm Fraser, the grades of knight and dame were added to the Order of Australia. Those grades were no longer awarded after 1986, following the election of another Labor government. However, in 2014, the conservative, monarchist and Anglophile Prime Minister Tony Abbott, following on from a 2009 New Zealand precedent, revived knighthoods and damehoods within the Order of Australia. The public and press greeted the initiative (and particularly the prime minister's nomination of Queen Elizabeth's husband Prince Philip as a Knight of the Order of Australia) with ridicule and derision; Abbott confessed that he had not consulted the cabinet on this matter. No further appointments were made after 2015, though other grades in the Order of Australia (companion, officer and member, as well as medal) continue to be given. Karen Fox and Samuel Furphy cite this episode as a telling example of the complexity of Australian post-colonial identity (cf. Fox/Furphy 2017).

In 1952 the nationalist South African government, which had come to power in 1948 claiming a mandate for radical change, created its own honors system, and from the 1960s, with the establishment of the republic and withdrawal from the British Commonwealth, South African honors expanded and were revised several times. The system was rationalized in 1994 following the end of the apartheid era and the development of a majority-rule democratic government. In South Africa, unlike the other former Dominions, but like other republics, the president, not the queen, is the fount of honor (cf. "Department of Arts and Culture").

The evolution of the honors system in Canada, Australia, New Zealand and South Africa offers much insight into the changing relationship between these erstwhile Dominions and the old 'mother country.' Though at different times and circumstances and varying degrees, each of these countries has distanced itself from Britain by developing new symbols of national identity, such as honors, anthems, flags, royal titles, and oaths of citizenship. Ongoing transformations in these former British colonies and in Britain's own position in the world – such as immigration of people with more diverse backgrounds, an alteration of trade partnerships, the succession of new generations without ancestral ties to a British 'homeland' and political interest – has meant the severing or effacement of traditional links between these countries and the United Kingdom. Imperial honors are now only very exceptionally and controversially awarded in the former Dominions, countries once considered bastions of 'overseas Britishness.' Yet local honors, such as the Order of Canada, Order of Australia, and Order of New Zealand, are still awarded in the name of the queen.

Beyond the Dominions, former British colonies adopted a variety of honors systems. Some, as in Jamaica, retain the British monarch as Head of State and thus the fount of honor, while elsewhere, for example in India, there is a wholly separate order, whose highest honor, the Bharat Ratna, is notable for its exclusivity. As Harper points out, however, the Indian order has not escaped some of the accusations of political interference which characterized the 19th-century British Indian orders (cf. Harper 2014: 205-206). The Order of the British Empire (OBE) continues to be awarded, both in Britain and in some of the smaller Commonwealth countries such as the Bahamas, Barbados, Papua New Guinea and the Solomon Islands which maintain close ties to Britain, and whose modest resources do not permit the establishment of local honors (cf. Harper 2017).

Colonial subjects (and citizens of former colonies) avidly sought knighthoods and other honors, though leftists and nationalists often refused honors, or in a few cases accepted but later renounced them. The Indian National Congress recommended that nationalists decline British imperial honors, and the great Indian writer and Nobel Prize-winner Rabindranath Tagore renounced his knighthood after the 1919 Amritsar massacre. Chin Peng, the leader of the Malayan Communist Party, was granted an OBE for fighting with the British against the Japanese in World War II. The honor was withdrawn after he fought against the British in the Malayan Emergency following the war.

Indeed, in India the issue of honors, so central to the British administration of the Raj, became a divisive topic during the negotiations over Indian independence. Jawaharlal Nehru, leader of the nationalist movement, remained adamant that Britain must cease distributing honors in India in 1946 – that is, the year prior to independence – but British officials in India remained determined to keep them as long as possible. After acrimonious debate Britain acceded to the new Indian government's demands, to the bitter dismay of local British administrators. Yet the last British Indian honors were only announced in the monarch's New Year's list of 1948, several months after the independence of India and Pakistan. (cf. Harper 2014: 196-205). Elsewhere British honors remain sensitive. The last Chief Executive of Hong Kong, Donald Tsang, was given a knighthood hours before the 1997 handover of the Crown Colony to the People's Republic of China, but has never used the title of 'sir' that accompanies it.

The investiture ceremonies of orders, decorations and other honors in the British Empire were often highly ritualized, public acts intended to strengthen colonial control (cf. Taylor 2018: 201).[6] Such ceremonies and accompanying festivities were intended not only to celebrate honored individuals and their achievements but also functioned as a kind of propaganda. They reinforced the primacy of the monarch, the role of viceregal representatives and indeed the whole colonial regime. Those decorated had proven their loyalty to the colonial state and were generally not likely, once honored – at least the authorities hoped – to participate in subversive activity. Even more importantly, they served as influential examples to fellow colonials of the rewards of imperial service. The decoration pinned to a colonial settler or indigenous person's chest was meant to attach that person – and more broadly his family and community – firmly to the colonial power. It also created a personal link, even if only a nominal one, with a distant sovereign. The hope of receiving some honor or emolument could be a powerful inducement to service and allegiance. From knighthoods awarded to worthy settlers to breastplates given to Aboriginal leaders, honors were meant to recognize and safeguard those who had made obeisance to the imperial sovereign. They were men and women whom the metropolitan officials and viceregal administrators regarded as useful interlocutors and intermediaries, and models for the masses of indigenous and migrant populations to emulate. The granting of such honors also provided a royal acknowledgement of the 'respectable' elite of a dominion or colony, a particularly valued mark of esteem when overseas subjects of the monarch, as in Australia, wanted to prove that colonists were far more than transported convicts, dubious adventurers and second-raters. The creation and awarding of knighthoods and other honors theoretically drew a parallel between elites in the metropole and

---

6   Orders awarded to Indian women were often, in accordance with cultural practices, presented in private, or even sent by post (cf. Taylor 2018: 201).

colonies. As David Cannadine has argued, such honors demonstrated the recognition – or at least, the selective recognition – of the British monarch and government for subjects in the empire (cf. Cannadine 2001).

COLONIAL HONORS IN OTHER EUROPEAN EMPIRES

This article has focused on the British Empire, especially India and the settler Dominions, but it is important to realize that the British case was not unique. A key dimension of our argument concerns the interrelationship between the European rule of colonies and the deployment of expanded honors systems as a technique of imperial governance in the late 19th and 20th centuries. Extension of a European-styled honors system was part of an international and transnational phenomenon in an epoch when great power status necessitated the conquest and rule of colonial territories, a shared discourse and practice understood throughout the 'concert of nations.' The following overview also reveals some of the significant differences among European nations in policies concerning the distribution of honors to colonial Europeans and indigenous populations.

Although continental European monarchies with overseas colonies generally did not award patents of nobility in the modern colonies (and the British imperial system of knighthoods with 'Sir' and 'Dame' prefixed to individuals' names did not have an exact equivalent elsewhere), the other colonizing powers also honored colonial public servants and military, as well as civilian colonists. France (even after it became a republic) provides an example. The *Ordre National de la Légion d'Honneur* was (and remains) the most prestigious French decoration, given not only to residents of the *métropole* but to those in foreign countries, and in the (ex-)French colonies. The sovereigns of 'protected' states in the French overseas empire, such as the King of Cambodia and the Emperor of Vietnam, were regularly decorated with the Legion of Honor, as were senior public servants and other *notables*. The French also awarded other national honors, including orders and medals given by individual government ministries, to those overseas. However, particularly significant were the *ordres coloniaux*, established in the French protectorates (the fully-fledged colonies – that is, areas annexed by France – had no separate honors systems). These were often given, even to those who had completed no service whatsoever, and had no links, to the protectorate whose order they received, as a general mark of recognition for service elsewhere in the French Empire (cf. Emering 2003; "Chancellerie de la Légion d'Honneur").

One particular difference between the British orders and the French ones awarded by both 'protected' rulers and the French state was their design. British insignia designed imperial orders, such as the three Indian orders, incorporated no indigenous symbols, though a cross, traditional in European insignia, was not part of the design of honors given primarily to non-Christians. The *ordres coloniaux* of the French Empire, however, included prominent indigenous motifs.

Figure 4: Order of the Dragon of Annam, badge of Grand Cross, 1896-1946

Source: The exhibition of the Tallinn Museum of Orders of Knighthood, Estonia ("Wikimedia Commons" 2017b)

For example, the insignia of the Ordre du Dragon d'Annam, instituted by the Vietnamese Emperor in 1886, featured a little dragon, perched at the bottom of a ribbon or surmounting a crown with a central medallion inscribed in Chinese seal script with the name of the order's founder, Emperor Dong Khanh, surrounded on the planchet by a star with rays. The dragon represented a central motif in Vietnamese iconography, a benign creature that symbolized the heavens and the emperor, who was, in Confucian belief, the son of heaven. The dragon was omnipresent at the Vietnamese court, figuring on the emperor's seal and robes, on silver incense containers and porcelain tableware, and on gold-bound imperial rescripts (cf. Baptiste 2014). The order, somewhat paradoxically, was awarded (though with different colored ribbons) by both the Vietnamese Emperor and the French President – who had inherited the royal-style rights to bestow honors from his monarchical forebears.

The *ordres coloniaux* were doled out so generously – one expert, Olivier Ihl (2004), writes about an 'inflation' of honors in late 19th-century France in general – that they were disparaged as *médailles en chocolat* (bits of chocolate wrapped in shiny paper). They were somewhat devalued in the eyes of the public by the quantity awarded, and by being given to men without a connection to the protectorate from which they issued. Yet the *ordres coloniaux* and other colonial medals – for bravery, public service and many other particular contributions to public life – remained highly desirable for both European and 'native' recipients eager for recognition. Rare was the long-serving colonial soldier or public servant who retired home without some order or medal. Those ranking highest in the colonial hierarchy sported a whole chest of medals. Unfortunately, there seems no comprehensive record of how many of these honors were awarded.

Not all of the colonizing countries established colonial orders – neither Germany nor the Netherlands, for instance, issued specifically colonial decorations. Yet most did, as an extension of metropolitan honors systems in order to recognize feats linked to colonial conquest and administration, and the development of the empire. King Leopold of the Belgians created the Order of the African Star in 1888, three years after the setting up of the notorious Congo Free State, the personal colony over which he reigned as sovereign. This was intended to reward service to developing the Congo and 'African civilization.' The Royal Order of the Lion was created in 1891 and was often given to African chiefs and local leaders (cf. Duckers 2008: 20).[7] The Italian state began acquiring overseas colonies in 1882, and the king instituted the Colonial Order of the Star of Italy in 1911 to recognize colonial service. In Portugal the Military Order of the Tower and the Sword (1808) revived a 15th-century order and was designed to reward service in Brazil, although its terms of reference were later expanded. Similarly, the Order of Our Lady of Vila Viçosa (1819) was also primarily intended to reward service in Brazil. In Spain, the Order of Isabella the Catholic (1815) was mainly intended to recognize service in the South American colonies, but its use was later broadened to reward other types of service to the nation. In the 20th century, Spain's main colonial orders focused on service in its colonies in northwestern Africa. The

---

7   Because of scandals arising from atrocities, exploitation and abuse of African laborers, Leopold was forced to cede his personal colony to Belgium in 1908. He continued to reign over what was then the Belgian Congo.

Order of Mehdaui was created in 1926 and the Order of Africa, which rewarded service to Spanish-African causes more broadly, in 1933 (cf. ibid: 89 and 91).

Further research is needed to determine why various countries set up colonial orders exactly when they did, and to what extent their creation was related to political developments in both metropoles and colonies. It is notable that Portugal's Order of the Colonial Empire (1932) was created under the autocratic interwar regime of António de Oliveira Salazar and the 'New State,' not the Portuguese monarchy, which had been abolished in 1910. Spain's Order of Africa, mentioned above, was created under the new Spanish Republic (which had been proclaimed in 1931) relatively soon after the defeat of a rebellion in Spanish Morocco. It remains clear, if remarkable, that even new republics frequently assumed the monarchical prerogatives of old regimes, and that the creation or maintenance of overseas empires usually allowed the creation of honors for colonial service; monarchical forms of honors endured even after monarchies were abolished. The new orders were commonly created to recognize service and achievements by civilians (the Spanish decoration was, officially, the Civil Order of Africa), suggesting an attempt to galvanize and acknowledge support for colonialism among non-military colonists and personnel; military medals had always been available for those in the armed forces in the colonies. The colonial orders ceased to be awarded with the end of empire.

HONORS AS IMPERIAL PRACTICE AND POST-COLONIAL LEGACY

Many of the successor states to the European colonies adopted, sometimes with little change, the honors systems established in colonial times that find their antecedents in monarchical *anciens régimes*. Ex-colonies of Britain have created honors system that in form – award by the 'fount of honor' (whether the British or local monarch, or a president), investiture ceremonies, the design of insignia, grades of the order – are patterned on British awards. For example, since 1992 the President of Mauritius has invested recipients with the Most Distinguished Order of the Star and Key of the Indian Ocean. In Barbados the highest level of the Order of Barbados, exceptionally, is the appointment as Knight or Dame of St Andrew. The former colonies of France almost always have an honors system modelled on the Legion of Honor, such as the National Order of the Lion in Senegal. Some countries with more radical governments, however, often adopted different types of honor systems; for example, communist Vietnam names 'Heroes' – of Labor, Motherhood and the People's Armed Forces – on the old Soviet model of Hero of the Soviet Union, Hero of Socialist Labor and Mother Heroine. But honors systems most typically follow models established in Europe as far back as the Middle Ages. Indeed the system of 'orders' is one of the most long-lasting legacies of this age of chivalry, and a successful European export as a mechanism of recognition of a citizen by the state.

In such independent countries as Japan and Thailand (as well as the American republics), towards the end of the 19th century rulers created new orders of chivalry modelled on European orders though incorporating local motifs and symbolism. In Thailand, the king created the Order of the Nine Gems in 1851, followed by the Order of the White Elephant (1861), the Order of Chula Chom Klao (1873), and others. The Japanese Emperor instituted among others the Order of the Rising Sun in 1875, then the Supreme Order of the Chrysanthemum (1876), and the Order of the Paulownia Flowers (1888). The Japanese orders, like the Thai ones, continue to be conferred, though sometimes with changes in eligibility over the time since their creation. The alignment of these orders with European ones represented efforts by independent sovereigns or feudatory rulers to modernize or at least adapt the ceremonial of their realms and to place both themselves and their states on a par with Western rulers and states. Western and non-Western rulers also regularly awarded orders to each other as a ritual sign of recognition and gift exchange (cf. Breen 2019).

Today, orders, decorations, and medals are often still eagerly sought, those honored proud to sport a medal or ribbon or to append a postnominal such as OBE to their names. Monarchs and presidents, or their representatives, invest recipients with due ceremony. Press and public celebrate those who receive the awards, though with continuing debate about whether honors lists are truly representative in terms of gender, ethnicity or other categories. They remain, nevertheless, one of the legacies of the realms of royalty and of the empires over which royals have reigned.

Orders and decorations, as preserved in museums and private collections, constitute artefacts in the material culture of colonialism, ones possessing a particular aura because of their connection with famous recipients and the royal personages (or republican presidents) in whose name they were awarded. They often retained great value – historical, emotional and monetary – even long after the recipient had died or the insignia had been discarded. Some medals, usually after the death of recipients, were sold by families who no longer felt the need to hold on to such items. Museums eagerly acquired decorations, especially those that had been awarded to local heroes and favorite sons, displaying the sashes and stars alongside uniforms, writings, photographs or other memorabilia. Institutions including national and specialized museums, royal collections and war memorials display such honors as relics of individual lives and achievements. Such objects thereby take on something of a sacred aura because of their association with a distinguished figure, the reliquary aspects enhanced by the precious metals and colorful silk ribbons that often form part of the insignia. Private collectors, too, buy decorations, and colonial orders and medals now regularly appear for sale on websites – the higher the honor and the rarer the award, the greater the price, with sums that often rise into the thousands of pounds for the rarest decorations – a new type of market in medals and decorations. In this way, the medals and badges of the age of empire enjoy a post-colonial afterlife; royal honors and other decorations enter into a commercial market of colonial memorabilia with a combination of collectors' passions, financial interest, historical investment and no doubt a measure of colonial nostalgia.

LIST OF THE MAJOR ORDERS MENTIONED IN THE ARTICLE, ORGANIZED BY NATION OR EMPIRE:

Australia:	Order of Australia
Barbados:	Order of Barbados
Belgium:	Order of the African Star, Royal Order of the Lion
Britain:	Order of the Garter, Order of the Bath, Order of the Thistle, Order of St Patrick, Order of St Michael and St George, Order of the British Empire (OBE), Order of the Star of India, Order of the Indian Empire, Order of the Crown of India, Order of British India, Royal Victorian Order, Royal Victorian Chain
Canada:	Order of Canada
France:	Order of the Legion of Honor, Order of the Dragon of Annam
Italy:	Order of the Star of Italy
Japan:	Order of the Rising Sun, Order of the Chrysanthemum, Order of the Paulownia Flowers
Mauritius:	Most Distinguished Order of the Star and Key of the Indian Ocean
Portugal:	Military Order of the Tower and the Sword, Order of Our Lady of Vila Viçosa, Order of the Colonial Empire
Senegal:	National Order of the Lion
Spain:	Order of Isabella the Catholic, Order of Mehdaui, Civil Order of Africa
Thailand:	Order of the Nine Gems, Order of the White Elephant, Order of Chula Chom Klao

WORKS CITED

Baptiste, Pierre (2014): L'Envol du dragon: Art royal du Vietnam, Paris: Snoek/MNAG.
Breen, John (forthcoming): "Ornamental diplomacy: Emperor Meiji and the monarchs of the modern world." In: Robert Hellyer/Harald Fuss (eds.), The Meiji Restoration and Global Intersections, Cambridge: Cambridge University Press.
Bridge, Carl (2011): "Casey, Richard Gavin Gardiner, Baron Casey (1890-1976), Politician in Australia and Diplomatist." In: Oxford Dictionary of National Biography, Oxford: Oxford University Press, accessed July 30, 2019 (https://www.oxforddnb.com/view/10.1093/ref:odnb/9780198614128.001.0001/odnb-9780198614128-e-30907)
Broome, Richard (2012): "Nicholls, Sir Douglas Ralf (Doug) (1906-1988)." In: Australian Dictionary of Biography, Canberra: Australian National University, accessed July 31, 2019 (http://adb.anu.edu.au/biography/nicholls-sir-douglas-ralph-doug-14920).
Cannadine, David (2001): Ornamentalism: How the British Saw Their Empire, London: Penguin.
"Chancellerie de la Légion d'Honneur", n. d., accessed August 13, 2019 (https://www.legiondhonneur.fr/sites/default/files/les_ordres_coloniaux_-_france_doutre-mer_.pdf).
Chefdebien, Anne de/Flavigny, Bertrand Galimard (2017): La Légion d'honneur: un ordre au service de la nation, Paris: Gallimard.
Clark, Samuel (2016): Distributing Status: The Evolution of State Honours in Western Europe, Montreal: McGill-Queen's University Press.
Cox, Noel (1997): "The British Peerage: The Legal Standing of the Peerage and Baronetage in the Overseas Realms of the Crown with Particular Reference to New Zealand." In: New Zealand Universities Law Review 17, pp. 379-401.
Cox, Noel (1998): "The Dichotomy of Legal Theory and Political Reality: The Honours Prerogative and Imperial Unity." In: Australian Journal of Law and Society 15, pp. 1-42.
"Department of Arts and Culture", Republic of South Africa, n. d., accessed July 31, 2019 (https://www.dac.gov.za/national-orders).
Dirks, Nicholas B. (1993): The Hollow Crown: Ethnohistory of an Indian Kingdom, Ann Arbor: University of Michigan.
Duckers, Peter (2008): European Orders and Decorations to 1945, Oxford: Shire Publications.

Dumons, Bruno/Pollet, Gilles (2009): La Fabrique de l'honneur: les médailles et les décorations en France, XIXe-XXe siècles, Rennes: Presses universitaires de Rennes.

Emering, Edward J. (2003): Orders, Decorations, and Medals of the French Overseas and the Post-Colonial Periods, San Ramon, California: Orders and Medals Society of America.

Fox, Karen (2010): "Grand Dames and Gentle Helpmeets: Women and the Royal Honours System in New Zealand, 1917-2000." In: Women's History Review 19/3, pp. 375-393.

Fox, Karen (2013): "A Pernicious System of Caste and Privilege." In: History Australia 10/2: 202-226.

Fox, Karen (2014a): "An 'Imperial Hangover'? Royal Honours in Australia, Canada and New Zealand, 1917-2009." In: Britain and the World, No. 1, pp. 6-27.

Fox, Karen (2014b): "Ornamentalism, Empire and Race: Indigenous Leaders and Honours in Australia and New Zealand." In: Journal of Imperial and Commonwealth History 42/3, pp. 486-502.

Fox, Karen and Samuel Furphy (2017): "The Politics of National Recognition: Honouring Australians in a Post-Imperial World." In: Australian Journal of Politics and History, 63/1, pp. 93-111.

Harper, Tobias (2014): Orders of Merit? Hierarchy, Distinction and the British Honours System, 1917-2004, New York: Columbia University. Unpublished manuscript of PhD dissertation, accessed September 28, 2019 (https://doi.org/10.7916/D8G44NFZ)

Harper, Tobias (2015): "Voluntary Service and State Honours in Twentieth-Century Britain." In: The Historical Journal 58/2, pp. 641-661.

Harper, Tobias (2017): "The Order of the British Empire after the British Empire." In: Canadian Journal of History 52/3, pp. 509-532.

Ihl, Olivier (2000): "Une déférence d'État: la république des titres et des honneurs." In: Communications (École pratique des Hautes Études) 69, pp. 115-137.

Ihl, Olivier (2004): "Gouverner par les honneurs: distinctions honorifiques et économie politique dans l'Europe du début du XIXe siècle." In: Genèses 55, pp. 171-204.

Kaus, David (n. d.): "Aboriginal Breastplates." In: National Museum of Australia, accessed July 31, 2019 (https://www.nma.gov.au/exhibitions/captivating_and_curious/the_stories_behind_the_objects/aboriginal_breastplates)

Keen, Caroline (2013): Princely India and the British: Political Development and the Operation of Empire, London: I. B. Tauris.

Matikkala, Antti (2008): The Orders of Knighthood and the Formation of the British Honours System, 1660-1760, Woodbridge: The Boydell Press.

Matikkala, Antti (2014): "On the Concepts of 'Sovereign' and 'Great' Orders." In: Coat of Arms Third Series 10/227, pp. 9-22.

McClenaghan, Tony (1996): Indian Princely Medals: A Record of the Orders, Decorations and Medals of the Indian Princely States, New Delhi: Lancer Publishers.

McCreery, Christopher (2005): The Canadian Honours System, Toronto: Dundurn Press.

McLeod, John (1994): "The English Honours System in Princely India, 1925-1947." In: Journal of the Royal Asiatic Society Third Series 4/2, pp. 237-249.

McLeod, John (1997): "'Without Precedent': The Sinha Peerage Case." In: Southeast Review of Asian Studies 19, pp. 13-30.

Monteiro, Nuno Gonçalo/Corrêa da Silva, Isabel (2018): "Élites e nobreza na monarquia liberal portuguesa: um itinerário crítico." In: Rui Ramos/José Murilo de Carvalho/Isabel Corrêa da Silva (eds.), A Monarquia constitucional dos Braganças em Portugal e no Brasil (1882-1910), Afragide: Dom Quixote, pp. 321-351.

Mulder, C. Peter/Purves. Alex Arthur (1999): Bibliography of Orders and Decorations, Copenhagen: Ordenshistorisk Selskab.

"Overview of the New Zealand Royal Honours System", Department of the Prime Minister and Cabinet, New Zealand, n. d., accessed July 31, 2019 (www.dpmc.govt.nz/our-programmes/new-zealand-royal-honours/new-zealand-royal-honours-system/overview-new-zealand-royal).

Palsetia, Jesse S. (2003): "'Honourable Machinations': the Jamsetjee Jejeebhoy Baronetcy and the Indian Response to the Honours System in India." In: South Asia Research 23/1, pp. 55-75.

Potter, Simon J. (2004): "Baillieu, Clive Latham, First Baron Baillieu (1889-1967), Businessman and Mining Financier." In: Oxford Dictionary of National Biography, Oxford: Oxford University Press, accessed July 30, 2019 (https://doi.org/10.1093/ref:odnb/46581).

Radi, Heather (2011 [2004]): "Bruce, Stanley Melbourne, Viscount Bruce of Melbourne (1883-1967), Prime Minister of Australia." In: Oxford Dictionary of National Biography, Oxford: Oxford University Press, accessed July 30, 2019 (https://doi.org/10.1093/ref:odnb/32135).

Ruggiu, François-Joseph (2009): "Une Noblesse atlantique? Le second ordre français de l'Ancien au Nouveau Monde." In: Outre-Mers 96, pp. 39-63.

Ruggiu, François-Joseph (2011): "The Kingdom of France and its Overseas Nobilities." In: French History 25, pp. 298-315.

Schwarcz, Lilia Moritz (2018): "Aristocracia no Brasil: cara e coroa." In: Rui Ramos/José Murilo de Carvalho/Isabel Corrêa da Silva (eds.), A Monarquia constitucional dos Braganças em Portugal e no Brasil (1882-1910), Afragide: Dom Quixote, pp. 352-375.

Smith, Murray (1998): "No Honours Please, We're Republicans." In: Irish Student Law Review 7, pp. 112-134.

Taylor, Miles (2018): Queen Victoria and India, New Haven: Yale University Press.

Thompson, Alaistair (1994): "Honours Uneven: Decorations, the State and Bourgeois Society in Imperial Germany." In: Past & Present 144, pp. 171-204.

Troy, Jakelin (1993): King Plates: A History of Aboriginal Gorgets, Canberra: Aboriginal Studies Press for the Australian Institute of Aboriginal and Torres Strait Islander Studies.

Tulard, Jean/Monnier, François/Échappé, Olivier (2004): La Légion d'honneur: deux siècles d'histoire, Paris: Perrin.

Wallace, Donald Mackenzie (1902): The Web of Empire: A Diary of the Imperial Tour of Their Royal Highnesses The Duke & Duchess of Cornwall & York in 1901, London: Macmillan and Co.

"Wikimedia Commons" (2017a), accessed August 29, 2019 (https://commons.wikimedia.org/wiki/File:Order_of_the_Star_of_India_knight_commander_badge_(United_Kingdom_1900)_-_Tallinn_Museum_of_Orders.jpg).

"Wikimedia Commons" 2017b, accessed August 29, 2019 (https://commons.wikimedia.org/wiki/File:Order_of_the_Dragon_of_Annam_grand_cross_badge_(Annam_1896-1946)_-_Tallinn_Museum_of_Orders.jpg).

"Wikimedia Commons" n. d., accessed August 29, 2019 (https://commons.wikimedia.org/wiki/File:Ganga_Singh_c1930.jpg).

Between Politics and Dynastic Survival: 19th-Century Monarchy in Post-Revolutionary Europe (1815-1918)

Torsten Riotte

INTRODUCTION: ROYAL FAMILIES AND DYNASTIC FAMILY NETWORKS

The French historian Lucien Bély has offered an intriguing interpretation of monarchical life during the Early Modern period (cf. 1999: 410-535). In his study of the so-called 'society of princes' he argues that the social life of those belonging to European dynasties always comprised a political dimension. As Bély convincingly demonstrates, a dynastic wedding or visit, the staging of music and theater as well as dress and dining embedded representative elements that can be described as political. Pomp and politics were intertwined.

Although Bély's study pays only cursory attention to the period post-1815, much could be said in favor of a similar interpretation for the post-Napoleonic period. In fact, the transformation of the political public made monarchical lifestyle visible to a much greater audience than before (cf. Cannadine 1994; Paulmann 2000: 181-194). Queen Victoria, the historian John Plunkett has argued, should be seen as a media monarch (cf. 2003: 13-67). Similar observations have been made for the German Emperor William II and his fellow German monarchs (cf. März 2013: 95-147; Mergen 2005: 34-45). Based on the increase in representation of monarchical splendor, historiography has described the 19th century as a monarchical century (cf. Langewiesche 2013).

However, national media appearances and the hosting of state receptions remained the prerogative of a relatively small group of reigning dynasts. The German historian Silke Marburg has contended that a focus exclusively on sovereign rulers – those visible in the media – deals with the tip of a dynastic iceberg that proves substantially larger when looked at from a different angle (cf. 2008: 33-41). Europe's dynastic families consisted of a much larger group of representatives: siblings, children and other relatives also belonged to the society of princes. Marburg's research is based on the private papers of Johann King of Saxony. These papers reveal how far dynastic visitors to the capital of Dresden or other Saxon residences, correspondence partners as well as guests to feasts and receptions formed a network of substantial size. Many of them were far removed from the limelight of the national media and remained underneath the radar of public attention.

Why does considering the not-so-famous in a historical narrative of European dynasties matter? Marburg's interpretation can be contextualized as part of the discussion about a cultural history of politics. While many historians emphasize for the 19th century what Bély has argued for the Early Modern period, namely that royal representation should be examined in its political dimension such as the impact of "soft powers" on political decision-making (cf. Müller 2016), Marburg argues that despite the importance of the political we can identify a number of aspects of dynastic life that were supposed to remain behind closed doors. Put differently, 19th-century aristocracy did not live exclusively in the public eye. They also sustained a sphere of life hidden from the public. Avoiding the term "private," Marburg (cf. 2004; 2010) introduces the German phrase *Binnenkommunikation* to explain such activity. The term can roughly be translated as 'exclusive internal networking.' *Binnenkommunikation* included such activities as wedding negotiations, financial support for poorer members of the family and hosting fellow dynasts who had lost their crown.

With regard to the latter, it is striking that former sovereigns without sovereignty remained within dynastic circles and were treated as members of the society of princes. The Count of Chambord, Bourbon pretender and grandson to Charles X of France, married into the House of Hapsburg (cf. Montplaisir 2008: 214-233). Ernest Augustus, the Duke of Cumberland, heir to George V, the last King of Hanover, wedded Thyra, a Danish princess with close ties to the British, Russian and Greek royal families (cf. Riotte 2018: 106-113). Both princes in exile entertained a lavish court and participated in Austrian court life. Given the amount of splendor, ceremonial and etiquette, it can be argued that the two saw themselves as part of Europe's dynastic families. With reference to Marburg's search for a new and appropriate terminology efforts such as finding and financing a residence in exile, establishing a court and extensive dynastic networking could be described as attempts at dynastic survival (cf. ibid: 48-53).

As historiography has so far neglected monarchs in exile, this article aims at demonstrating the importance of analyzing dynastic life after sovereignty. Broadening the view from royal sovereignty to dynastic survival enlarges our knowledge in (at least) two directions. Firstly, it points to the remarkable fact that former sovereigns belonged to the network of European dynasties despite their loss of power. After 1815, this was true for the overwhelming majority of princes in exile. Thomas Biskup and Michael Kohlrausch have underlined that post-revolutionary European monarchy increasingly looked at its future as a political or constitutional entity (as opposed to the fate of individual dynasts) taking into account that fellow sovereigns might have to abdicate. The aim of such policies was to stabilize the monarchical system as a whole (cf. Biskup und Kohlrausch 2008). As part of this development, a substantial number of former sovereigns proved quite successful in remaining within dynastic circles despite their loss of sovereignty. This was possible due to the informal support they received from their fellow dynasts as well as the respective governments (cf. Riotte 2018: 51-52).

Secondly, a close examination of the not-so-famous princes and princesses with a focus on their lives in exile produces surprising results. Many dynasts without sovereignty were able to afford a lavish lifestyle. We still know very little about royal wealth. How did monarchs in exile pay for royal luxury? The main hypothesis of this article runs that a key lesson to be drawn from the French Revolutionary and Napoleonic Wars is that they entailed less political innovation but greater awareness of financial emergencies. In the aftermath of the military conflict, dynastic families transferred large sums of money to foreign countries, preferably to Great Britain. London as a European center of finance and the United Kingdom as the country that had withstood Napoleon's ambition for hegemony appeared to be the right place to deposit a royal fortune (cf. Riotte 2019: 42-44). The awareness of revolutionary emergencies is not only reflected in economic, but also in legal terms. International private law increasingly distinguished between public and private monarchical property and hence between the public and the private person of a prince (cf. Loening 1979 [1903]: 197-198). Despite such a distinction, extraterritoriality saved reigning heads from paying taxes in foreign countries and also from being persecuted or put on trial abroad. Surprisingly, such exemptions were also granted to former sovereigns (though with increasing difficulties in the course of the century) by their host countries (cf. Riotte 2018: 113-130). As will be demonstrated, Restauration and the following decades up to the end of the Great War proved to be a period of transition in Europe between a dynastic and a constitutional state, a period during which dynastic elites gained concessions that undermined the principles of international law.

ROYAL FORTUNES AND EMERGENCY FUNDS

In January 1793, Louis XVI was beheaded. Sentenced to death by a revolutionary tribunal, the French monarch was guillotined as "citoyen Louis Capet" and his head and body buried at the Madeleine Cemetery in Paris (cf. Schultz 2012: 285-313; Hesse 1993). His younger brother Louis, the Count of Provence had left French soil two years previously. Although he escaped capture and death, he suffered during the course of his escape. From the German city of Koblenz, where a substantial number of émigrés had gathered, he traveled via Verona, Blankenburg to Courland where he was staying at a palace of the Russian Tsar Paul. His journey continued to Warsaw, Stockholm, and in 1807 finally to Great Britain (cf. Mansel 2005 [1981]: 56-188; Mansel 2011). In retrospect, he described the almost 25 years in exile as a painful experience. Always in need of financial support and personal goodwill, he endured isolation and "ennui" (Mansel 2005 [1981]: 78). In contemporary art such as poetry, loyalists described royal exile as the martyrdom of the French prince. In a copper print of 1814 published in the *Journal de Paris*, Louis was depicted in a rural winter scene walking through deep snow. Leaning on his niece's arm, Madame Royal is the only support he enjoys in a cold environment (cf. Scholz 2006: 93). Could royal exile mean anything beyond poverty, desertion and isolation?

William of Hesse-Kassel's experience proved to be quite different (cf. Berghoeffer 1923:48-137; Ferguson 2000: 60-71). Known for his financial ambitions, the German prince had amassed a fortune before the French Revolutionary and Napoleonic Wars. He had loaned Hessian troops as subsidiary forces to foreign countries which brought him substantial revenues. Investments on the Dutch and British financial markets increased his wealth further. With the support of international banking houses (Rothschilds was one of them) his income generated large profits. The historian Christian Wilhelm Berghoeffer has described William as the most successful capitalist of the time (cf. 1923: 29).

When Napoleon's forces occupied Hessian territory, the elector fled via Denmark and North Germany to Austria. Prior to his departure, valuables were hidden, the stock and exchange bills packed in boxes and transported to secret storehouses in Hesse-Kassel or, alternatively, carried to the prince's destinations in exile. In those cases where the French authorities discovered and confiscated valuables, bribery and corruption helped to save a substantial part of the elector's wealth (cf. ibid: 49-64). Elector William of Hesse-Kassel was a rich man despite fleeing his country and despite Napoleon occupying and annexing the territory in part to the Kingdom of Westphalia and in part to the Grand Duchy of Frankfort.

William lived in exile for more than six years. His revenues proved sufficient to purchase property and to cover the expenses of his court in exile for the entire period from 1806 to 1813. After an initial period in Denmark at his brother's residence, he proceeded to Austria where he arrived in 1808. A few weeks in Karlsbad were followed by five years in Prague. The emperor of Austria had declared the Bohemian capital as the prince's destination. William bought a *palais* in Prague, a castle in the Bohemian countryside as a country residence as well as a representative farm house. Since 1809, the residence in Prague had been equipped with an Austrian guard of honor and William was introduced to the Hapsburg court (cf. ibid: 71-72).

The privileges granted by the Austrian emperor can be explained in categories of international law. William of Hesse-Kassel contributed to the Austrian war effort against Napoleon. In 1808 he stayed in Prague as a private individual (at least from a legal point of view). When the military conflict between France and the Hapsburg monarchy broke out in spring 1809, William paid for a foreign corps in the Austrian army using his own revenue and joined the alliance against Napoleon. The Hapsburg monarchy accepted William not only as a partner in the struggle against Napoleon, but, more importantly, as the head of a government in exile. In international law, an exiled monarch could be a private individual. He (or she) gained the status of a subject of international law only once his (or her) host country had recognized him (or her) as a government in exile (cf. Koberg 2005). Such recognition required the host country to have not recognized the successor state (in William's case the Kingdom of Westphalia and the Great Duchy of Frankfort) as a sovereign state.

Legal aspects did not play a major role for William's restoration. He returned to Hesse-Kassel in 1813 and was restored as elector the following year. For the French Prince Louis, however, such a distinction had an essential bearing on his finances. Louis returned from exile and acceded to the French throne as Louis XVIII in 1815. Prior to his return he had accumulated a substantial debt. The support of a court, of émigré policies and a network of loyalist protégés had cost a fortune. Soon after his restoration a large number of creditors approached him as well as his brother, the Count of Artois (the later King Charles X), who had similarly relied on benefactors and creditors during his life outside France (cf. Riotte 2018: 154-156). In 1815, the French dynasty refused to honor these obligations. Although the King of France was prepared to recognize his debts, he insisted that the outstanding sum including the accumulated interest should be met by public funds. In exile, so the argument went, the two princes had acted as exile governments, not as private persons. Already in 1791 Louis (as Count of Provence) had claimed to represent the de facto regent of France because the revolutionary movement prevented his elder brother from reigning freely. After Louis XVI's execution in 1793, he informed European sovereigns that he had acted as regent for the king's underage son. Finally, in June 1795, the dynasty and loyalists declared him the legitimate successor to the throne, after the young Louis XVII had died in prison (cf. Mansel 2005 [1981]: 56-76). The question of whether the two princes had borrowed money in their private capacity and hence had to repay from dynastic funds or whether public finances would step in because the reigning monarch had acted as sovereign (or his intermediate) was debated in the highest courts of France. The court did not reach a final verdict until 1830 when revolution caused the elder branch of the Bourbon family to leave France. The cases of the "*créanciers du roi*," i.e. 'the king's creditors,' remained unresolved (Riotte 2018: 156).

The matter was further confused as a large group of creditors were not French citizens suing the acting sovereign of France in a French court in order to enforce international private law. However, what becomes clear is that French law in the late 18th and early 19th century distinguished between different forms of royal property. In fact, all over Europe, monarchical possessions and revenues were categorized in different classes of property. During the 18th century the idea had prevailed that royal fortune and public fortune were identical. This changed in the decades around 1800 when governments of state increasingly distinguished between public property, the property of the monarch as private property and, as a third category, the monarch's property as familial or dynastic property (cf. Aretin 2008). While the latter was generally bound in long-term obligations, the other two were meant to cover the running costs of the royal household. Public property remained under the control of the state. The state might pay the monarch a civil list or other forms of financial compensation, but the aim of such payments was to enable the monarch to live in accordance with his position and not to increase the financial wealth of the dynastic family. In conclusion, it can be argued that in contemporary political theory monarchs were not meant to be investors (cf. Riotte 2019: 45-46).

The distinction between the different forms of property was closely connected to the rise of the modern state. In Prussia, the royal family was given a civil list as compensation for the transfer of public land and property (and the income it generated) from the dynasty to the Prussian state. Negotiating the public domain could be a controversial task. Monarchs often demanded increasing payments or compensation in the light of inflation or rising costs (cf. Klein 2007: 50-61; Hoffmann 2006: 12-31). Prussia repeatedly decided to raise the monarch's income so that, in 1910, William II could rely on an annual payment of 19.2 Million Marks in his capacity as King of Prussia and an additional payment of three Million Marks as head of the German Empire. This turned the German *Kaiser* into the person with the highest income in Germany prior to the Great War (cf. Riotte 2016: 80-85; Philippi 1990: 380-381; Röhl 1985: 241).

To add a final example to the list of dynastic families and their personal wealth, it is worth considering the Guelph dynasty (cf. Riotte 2019: 38-46). The electorate of Hanover entered the French Revolutionary Wars in 1793. Fairly early in the course of the military conflict, the danger of a foreign invasion became manifest. Both French and Prussian forces approached the North German electorate. In 1794, the government of Hanover decided to move the amount of 3.5 Million Taler to Britain and to invest the sum in form of foreign exchange bills (cf. Roolfs 2005). The banking house "Coutts & Co." in London conducted the investment for the "Lords of His Majesty's Royal Regency of Hanover," and informed the regency about the profits it earned (Riotte 2018: 166-171). This secret deposit remained in London after the end of the Napoleonic Wars. Some papers were liquidized and withdrawn. In 1830 the deposit still amounted to £600.000 (cf. Riotte 2009).

As part of the debate about a Hanoverian constitution during the 1830s the funds in London were declared to be part of the so-called *Krondotationskasse* and later the *Königliche Kronkasse*, i.e. funds that were considered as the monarch's private property. By this decision the earlier emergency funds were privatized. After Ernest Augustus had acceded to the throne of Hanover in 1837, negotiations about the civil list and the cost of the royal household re-emerged with new intensity. The wealth of the dynasty was debated anew. Ernest Augustus proved a tough negotiator and the Diet of Hanover had to accept making further payments from public treasuries (cf. Roolfs 2005: 130-138).

The deposit in London remained unaffected by these negotiations. In the course of the following decades, the British investments grew and they were handled as private property of the dynasty as a family. This explains why they were unaffected by the Prussian annexation of Hanover in 1867. Although public funds were confiscated by the new Prussian government, the monarch's private fortune including the London exchange bills remained in the monarch's possession (cf. Riotte 2018: 166-168). King George V of Hanover and his family moved to the Austrian Empire and a familiar pattern evolved. It was the London funds that enabled the House of Hanover to live in exile in representative style. Just like the Elector of Hesse-Kassel half a century earlier, the monarch bought property and invested in the capital markets. Ernest Augustus, the Duke of Cumberland and son to the last King of Hanover was rich enough to have a full neo-Gothic castle built in the Austrian town of Gmunden where he lived with a household of about one hundred persons receiving dynastic, consular and diplomatic representatives (cf. Steckhan 2008: 59-70; Schießer 2017: 34-92). Ernest Augustus also participated actively in the court life at Vienna such as royal ceremonies, publicly appearing at royal feasts and parades (cf. Riotte 2018: 53-65).

Looking at the examples of Hesse-Kassel and Hanover, it is fair to argue that there are many similar patterns of organizing life in exile. The revolutionary experience caused European dynasties to employ safety measures to ensure that there would be enough private revenue in case of revolution or abdication. At least some (I suspect the majority) of European dynasties invested capital sums in the international financial market. At least before 1918 a typical member of Europe's dynastic aristocracy belonged to the excessively rich and showed an increasing awareness of the challenges of how to administer, sustain, and increase a substantial economic fortune (cf. Riotte 2019: 38-46). The distinction between public and dynastic fortune helped to create the capital for global investment. However, the idea of monarchy and private property also created difficulties that become visible once we turn to the legal aspects of this development.

DYNASTIC LIFE AND THE LAW

Generalizing individual case studies poses a certain risk. Any typology in historical analysis will be most convincing if it can be explained not only as analytical tool but also as part of contemporary language or practice, as Moritz Alexander Sorg (cf. 2018) has demonstrated in his interpretation of new monarchies during the 19th century. Sorg argues that a monarchy under a foreign prince became the dominant idea in European state-building processes after 1815. In his paper he compares such different states as Belgium, Greece, Romania, Bulgaria, and Albania and points to international diplomatic correspondence that emphasizes the idea of setting up a foreign prince as the head of a new state to be the most reliable guarantee for a peaceful European state system (cf. ibid: 83-86).

This contribution has examined French, Hessian, Prussian, and Hanoverian monarchs. It would be possible to add Portuguese, Italian, Spanish or Swedish royal families in order to justify a comparative history of exiled monarchs (cf. Riotte 2018: 364-382). There is, however, an additional contemporary argument for such a typology. A substantial number of former sovereigns settled in Austrian territory. This led the Austrian government to consider exiled monarchs as a legal category. In 1851, the department of justice pointed out to the Austrian government that sufficient similarities existed between foreign princes resident in the Hapsburg monarchy, such as the Prince of Wasa, the Prince of Liechtenstein, and the Bourbon prince Henri, the above mentioned Count of Chambord, to describe them as a legal entity. The department of justice suggested that instructions should be set up according to which all princes in exile, former sovereigns, or their relatives should be treated alike (cf. ibid: 139-142).

According to international law monarchs in exile did not exist. Sovereignty was either existent or lost, but as the Austrian lawyer Vesque von Püttlingen wrote, it was in the power of a national government such as the Hapsburg monarchy to grant a legal status equivalent to such of a reigning sovereign (cf. 1860: 156). As shown by the subsequent example, this idea did not come out of the blue and it was intertwined with questions of royal debt.

In 1833 the Austrian Count Simon Pfaff of Pfaffenhofen sued the French monarch Charles X in a civil court in Austria. Pfaffenhofen had lent Prince Charles the sum of 160.000 Francs during the 1790s in order to support the exile policies of the French émigrés (cf. Riotte 2018: 130-133). Pfaffenhofen's efforts in the early 1830s go back to the years immediately after the Restauration. He belonged to the group of creditors who approached the French king and his brother after 1815. As has been mentioned above, French courts were reluctant to decide whether the monarch's debts were to be paid for by public or private funds. They continued to debate the dynasty's obligations over the death of Louis XVIII and the accession of Charles X and still did not come to a decision when the latter fled France after the Revolution of 1830.

The Austrian legal system proved less hesitant in enforcing the payment of debts. In 1818, an Austrian court declared that Pfaffenhofen was bound to pay back the amount he himself had borrowed to afford the royal loan. Adding interest for the period of 27 years the original sum rose to an enormous total of 400.000 Francs. Given the size of his debt it proved of little consolation that the French royal family offered the count a small pension. In the years that followed, Pfaffenhofen repeatedly approached the French government, at some point publishing his correspondence with the royal household, to no avail. In 1825 he heard from the French minister at the head of the *Maison du Roi* that the French crown was still unable to repay him as the matter remained undecided (cf. ibid: 132). Pfaffenhofen briefly considered approaching the British government when Charles X and his family left France after the revolution of 1830. He refrained from bringing the matter before a British court but as an Austrian citizen he seized his opportunity after the Bourbon dynasty had settled in Austria in 1832 and he decided to sue the House of Bourbon (cf. ibid: 133).

The Austrian government and particularly the Austrian state chancellor Metternich did not want a trial and approached the ministry of justice to find a way to resolve this problem. Metternich sent an enquiry to the Austrian President of Justice, Ludwig Patrick Taaffe, in order to find out whether the former French monarch could be sued before a civil court. Taaffe wrote that from a legal point of view there was no reason why the former monarch Charles X should not stand trial. The Bourbon prince had lost his crown. The Austrian government had recognized Louis Philippe as the king of the French and hence the successor state enjoyed full recognition. In international law, a former sovereign did not represent a sovereign with the right of extraterritoriality. To Taaffe, Charles X represented a private individual (cf. ibid: 133).

Metternich did not agree with Taaffe and tried to enforce a legal exemption for the former French monarch. The state chancellor argued that the Austrian President of Justice needed to consider the political dimension of a trial. He invited Taaffe to 'reconsider' his position and the President of Justice acted accordingly. Taaffe compiled a new statement arguing the opposite of what he had written earlier. In his revised statement, he pointed out that the numbers of former sovereigns had so far not been sufficiently numerous to justify a codification of legislation in international law. However, he now argued that a monarch who had abdicated could not represent a private person because his royal character was intrinsic to his person. The German phrase he used literally translates that majesty was glued to his body (*"angeklebte Majestät"*). Distinguishing between forms of active and of passive or inactive sovereignty he phrased the French term of *"un souverain en non-actualité de la puissance royale,"* a sovereign with suspended royal power (cf. Riotte 2018: 134-135, 369).

In this sense, every dynasty that had lost its title and settled in Austria could claim that sovereignty was an integral part of a royal's persona, and also, as later practice would show, that such quality was passed on to the following generations. This meant that every member of a disempowered royal family was exempted from taxation and could not be put to trial (cf. Vesque von Püttlingen 1860: 156; Riotte 2018: 138-142).

While Charles X and the Count of Chambord were granted a full extraterritorial status, other exiled dynastic representatives were exempted from civil legislation (Riotte 2018: 150-154). They were not in danger of facing a civil court. Instead, cases against dynastic representatives would be decided by the *Oberthofmarschallamt*; i.e. the royal household of the Emperor of Austria. There were individual protests against such exclusive jurisdiction by some lawyers (ibid: 144-147). However, until the end of the Great War the Austrian government did adhere to this practice.

Given Taaffe's first statement, it becomes obvious that he was fully aware that such exemptions contravened international law. Over the decades, resistance to grant full extraterritoriality to royalty grew in the Austrian Department of Justice. It had always described the partial treatment of dynastic residents as "exemption" or "prerogative" and not as extraterritoriality (cf. Riotte 2018: 136-137). On the other hand, it did not refuse to grant exemptions. To resolve the inherent legal tension of such practice, the department created the legal category of "*kleine Exterritorialität*," i.e. 'small extraterritoriality' in the course of the century. Aware of the lack of legitimacy in international law, the department defined a status exclusive to national law. While this might still have contravened international legal standards, the creation of this category modeled on national legislation could be applied by Austrian judges. Whether a person was legally entitled to the status of 'small extraterritoriality' could be decided by an Austria court. The respective national governments were to decide whether such a category was legitimate. This is why during the 1860s and 1870s the exiled monarchs became the focus of negotiation between the Department of Justice and the other Austrian ministries (cf. ibid: 137-142, 149-154).

It is remarkable that the Austrian government granted such special status. Particularly with regard to the private character of a sovereign, the 19th century showed very different tendencies. While Early Modern legal authorities had claimed that there was no law above a sovereign, we find increasing doubts about such a view in writings of the late 18th and early 19th century. The enlightened philosopher Christian Wolff had already made a distinction between a monarch as the ruler and the monarch as a private person (cf. Loening 1979 [1903]: 181). In legal theory of the time, an acting sovereign could be held liable in case he purchased private property in a foreign country. It needed to be shown that such property was for private use only and not meant for state purposes (cf. ibid: 189). Contemporary legal literature argued that it was during the 19th century that a distinction between the private property of a monarch and public property was enforced (cf. ibid: 197-198). In legal theory, it would have been possible to sue a foreign sovereign in Austria if he owned property in the Hapsburg monarchy (cf. ibid: 201) However, no such cases in legal practice are known. The above-mentioned exemption was granted to ensure that no such court case would happen. This practice did not change until 1918. Before that date, no reigning sovereign or any dynast resident in Austria was sued before a civil court. And the few cases that were discussed by the emperor's court did not lead to any sentence or punishment (cf. Heyking 1926: 125). It can be argued without any difficulty that the members of European dynastic families preserved a special status – at least in the Hapsburg monarchy. Although international law had few sympathies with former sovereigns, monarchy proved too important to the European nation states to allow a member of a dynasty to be treated in common, civil terms.

CONCLUSION: DYNASTIC SURVIVAL IN 19TH-CENTURY EUROPE

The cultural history of politics has emphasized that a major difference existed between the role of monarchy in the 18th and in the 19th century. Sovereigns traveled Europe (and in some cases beyond) much more frequently after 1815 than before, so much so that modern historiography applies the the term '*Reisemonarchie,*' i.e. 'travel monarchy' in order to describe such transition (cf. Paulmann 2000:56-78; Barth 2013: 9-24). Members of royal families visited different countries and were received officially in state receptions and unofficially as private visits. Such trends were noted by contemporary authors and the media (cf. Paulmann 2000: 181-194). The lawyer Edgar Loening wrote in 1903 that monarchs would increasingly spend days, weeks, and even months abroad (cf. Loening 1979 [1903]: 196). This trend has led modern historiography to identify the importance of such visits for political decision making. It has been argued that state receptions and official royal tours should be described as "soft power politics" or as cultural politics (cf. Müller 2016; Schönpflug 2013: 9-30). Historians stress – not without justification – that such policies often proved just as efficient as political negotiations or even military intervention.

This interpretation needs qualifying. Johannes Paulmann has argued that European state visits, their perception and effects could be described as the internationalization of monarchy (cf. Paulmann 2001). Such a trend did not, as he emphasizes, contradict the nationalization of monarchical institutions as part of the rise of the nation state during the second half of the 19th century. Instead, as representatives of their state in a European theater of monarchs, individual sovereigns enforced national sentiments such as pride and honor. However, Paulmann also convincingly argues that dynastic and inter-state relations were increasingly disentangled during the second half of the 19th century. State visits mattered to an international audience, however, less and less to the governments of the time (cf. ibid: 171-176).

This article adds some additional aspects to the cultural history approach. Although dynastic relations no longer translated into foreign policies, internationalizing the monarchy included implications that have often been overlooked in existing research. During the period after 1815, monarchs came to realize that there could be a life after sovereignty. Due to the experiences of many dynasties during the French Revolutionary and Napoleonic period they began to deposit money in foreign countries partly in order to be prepared for the worst, partly to increase their wealth. With the rise of the modern state, public funds were disentangled from royal fortune. The increasing importance of banking for the finance sector added to this development (cf. März 1968: 57-90). Despite such investments, members of Europe's society of princes did not become private individuals. At least the Austrian state granted a special status to all dynastic representatives, both sovereign and other members of the royal family. In this sense, dynastic survival depended on both continuity and change. The rise of the modern state had not yet eliminated aristocratic privilege. However, legal prerogative had been transformed into a practice of partiality by state authorities and the governments of the time. It thus created a realm of monarchy that had hitherto not existed and that proved essential for dynastic survival up to the Great War. While legal privileges disappeared after 1918, dynastic survival can point to the hard facts of aristocratic life that can be found behind much of the soft powers of royal splendor up until today.

WORKS CITED

Aretin, Cajetan von (2008): "Vom Umgang mit gestürzten Häuptern. Zur Zuordnung der Kunstsammlung in deutschen Fürstenabfindungen, 1918-1924." In: Thomas Biskup/Martin Kohlrausch (eds.), Das Erbe der Monarchie. Nachwirkungen einer deutschen Institution seit 1918, Frankfurt am Main and New York: Campus-Verlag, pp. 161-183.

Barth, Volker (2013): Inkognito. Geschichte eines Zeremoniells, München: Oldenbourg.

Bély, Lucien (1999): La société des princes XVIe - XVIIIe siècle, Paris: Fayard.

Berghoeffer, Christian Wilhelm (1923): Meyer Amschel Rothschild. Der Gründer des Rothschildschen Bankhauses, Frankfurt am Main: Englert & Schlosser.

Biskup, Thomas/Kohlrausch, Martin (2008): "Das Erbe der Monarchie. Nachwirkungen einer deutschen Institution." In: Thomas Biskup/Martin Kohlrausch (eds.), Das Erbe der Monarchie. Nachwirkungen einer deutschen Institution seit 1918, Frankfurt am Main and New York: Campus-Verlag, pp. 11-34.

Cannadine, David (1994): Die Erfindung der britischen Monarchie, 1820-1994, Berlin: Klaus Wagenbach.

Ferguson, Niall (2000): The House of Rothschild. Money's Prophets 1798-1848, London: Penguin Books.

Hesse, Michael (1993): "Revolutionsopfer als Glaubensmärtyrer. Die Chapelle Expiatoire und die Sühnemonumente der Restauration in Paris." In: Gudrun Gersmann/Hubertus Kohle (eds.), Frankreich 1815-1830 Trauma oder Utopie? Die Gesellschaft der Restauration und das Erbe der Revolution, Stuttgart: Franz Steiner Verlag, pp. 197-216.

Heyking, Alphonse de (1926): L'exterritorialité, Paris: Rousseau.
Hoffmann, Ronald (2006): Die Domänenfrage in Thüringen. Über die vermögensrechtlichen Auseinandersetzungen mit den ehemaligen Landesherren in Thüringen nach dem Ersten Weltkrieg, Frankfurt am Main and New York: Peter Lang.
Klein, Winfried (2007): Die Domänenfrage im deutschen Verfassungsrecht des 19. Jahrhunderts, Berlin: Duncker & Humblot.
Koberg, Alexander (2005): Die Exilregierung im Völkerrecht (= Schriften zum internationalem und zum öffentlichen Recht, 57), Frankfurt am Main et al.: Peter Lang.
Langewiesche, Dieter (2013): Die Monarchie im Jahrhundert Europas. Selbstbehauptung durch Wandel im 19. Jahrhundert, Heidelberg: Universitätsverlag Winter.
Loening, Edgar (1979 [1903]): Die Gerichtsbarkeit über fremde Staaten und Souveräne. In: Festgabe für Hermann Fitting. Unter Mitarbeit von Juristische Fakultät der Vereinigten Friedrichs-Universität Halle-Wittenberg. Hildesheim: Scientia Verlag, pp. 169-331.
Mansel, Philip (2005 [1981]): Louis XVIII, London: John Murray.
Mansel, Philip (2011): "From Exile to the Throne. The Europeanization of Louis XVIII." In: Philip Mansel/Torsten Riotte (eds.), Monarchy and Exile. The Politics of Legitimacy from Marie de Médicis to Wilhelm II, Houndmills et al.: Palgrave Macmillan, pp. 181-213.
Marburg, Silke (2004): "Hochadelige Binnenkommunikation als Voraussetzung für die Generierung von Hochadeligkeit. Das Beispiel König Johanns von Sachsen, 1801-1873." In: Günther Denzel/Markus Schulz (eds.), Deutscher Adel im 19. und 20. Jahrhundert (= Büdinger Forschungen zur Sozialgeschichte, 2002/2003), St. Katharinen: Scripta Mercaturae Verlag, pp. 301-318.
Marburg, Silke (2008): Europäischer Hochadel. König Johann von Sachsen (1801-1873) und die Binnenkommunikation einer Sozialformation, Berlin: Akademie Verlag.
Marburg, Silke (2010): "Adlige Binnenkommunikation. Moderne in Nordwestdeutschland und Sachsen." In: Maarten van Driel/Meinhard Pohl/Bernd Walter (eds.), Adel verbindet – Adel verbindt. Elitenbildung und Standeskultur in Nordwestdeutschland und den Niederlanden vom 15. bis 20. Jahrhundert (= Landschaftsverband Westfalen-Lippe. Forschungen zur Regionalgeschichte, 64), Paderborn et al.: Ferdinand Schöningh, pp. 217-227.
März, Eduard (1968): Österreichische Industrie- und Bankpolitik in der Zeit Franz Josephs I., Wien: Europa Verlag.

März, Stefan (2013): Das Haus Wittelsbach im Ersten Weltkrieg. Chance und Zusammenbruch monarchischer Herrschaft, Regensburg: Pustet.

Mergen, Simone (2005): Monarchiejubiläen im 19. Jahrhundert. Die Entdeckung des historischen Jubiläums für den monarchischen Kult in Sachsen und Bayern, Leipzig: Leipziger Universitätsverlag.

Montplaisir, Daniel de (2008): Le Comte de Chambord. Dernier Roi de France, Paris: Perrin.

Müller, Frank Lorenz (2016): "Stabilizing a 'Great Historic System' in the Nineteenth Century? Royal Heirs and Succession in an Age of Monarchy." In: Frank Lorenz Müller/Heidi Mehrkens (eds.), Sons and Heirs. Succession and Political Culture in Nineteenth-Century Europe (= Palgrave Studies in Modern Monarchy), Basingstoke: Palgrave Macmillan, pp. 1-16.

Paulmann, Johannes (2000): Pomp und Politik. Die Monarchenbegegnungen in Europa zwischen Ancien Régime und Erstem Weltkrieg, Paderborn: Ferdinand Schöningh.

Paulmann, Johannes (2001): "Searching for a 'Royal International.' The Mechanics of Monarchical Relations in Nineteenth-Century Europe." In: Martin H. Geyer/Johannes Paulmann (eds.), The Mechanics of Internationalism. Culture, Society, and Politics from the 1840s to the First World War Press (= Studies of the German Historical Institute London), London and Oxford: Oxford University, pp. 145-176.

Philippi, Hans (1990): "Der Hof Kaiser Wilhelms II." In: Karl Möckl (ed.), Hof und Hofgesellschaft in den deutschen Staaten im 19. und beginnenden 20. Jahrhundert (= Büdinger Forschungen zur Sozialgeschichte 1985 und 1986, 18), Boppard am Rhein: H. Boldt, pp. 361-394.

Plunkett, John (2003): Queen Victoria. First Media Monarch, Oxford: Oxford University Press.

Riotte, Torsten (2009): "Der abwesende Monarch im Herrschaftsdiskurs der Neuzeit. Eine Forschungsskizze am Beispiel der Welfendynastie nach 1866." In: Historische Zeitschrift 289, pp. 627-667.

Riotte, Torsten (2016): "Macht- und Prachtentfaltung? Hof und Hofgesellschaft unter Wilhelm II." In: Friedl Brunckhorst/Karl Weber (eds.), Kaiser Wilhelm II. und seine Zeit, Regensburg: Verlag Schnell & Steiner, pp. 67-86.

Riotte, Torsten (2018): Der Monarch im Exil. Eine andere Geschichte von Staatswerdung und Legitimismus im 19. Jahrhundert (= Veröffentlichungen der Historischen Kommission für Niedersachsen und Bremen, 295), Göttingen: Wallstein Verlag.

Riotte, Torsten (2019): "Dynastie und Reichtum. Was wissen wir über das Vermögen des (ehemals) regierenden Hochadels im 19. und 20. Jahrhundert?" In:

Lu Seegers/Anne Kurr/Eva Maria Gajek (eds.), Reichtum in Deutschland. Akteure, Netzwerke und Lebenswelten im 20. Jahrhundert, Göttingen: Wallstein, pp. 35-56.

Röhl, John Charles Gerald (1985): "Hof und Hofgesellschaft unter Kaiser Wilhelm II." In: Karl-Ferdinand Werner (ed.), Hof, Kultur und Politik im 19. Jahrhundert. Akten des 18. Deutsch-französischen Historikerkolloquiums, Darmstadt 27-30 September, 1982 (= Pariser Historische Studien, 21), Bonn: Röhrscheid, pp. 237-289.

Roolfs, Cornelia (2005): Der hannoversche Hof von 1814 bis 1866 (= Quellen und Darstellungen zur Geschichte Niedersachsens, 124), Hannover: Hahn.

Schießer, Heinz (2017): Die Welfen am Traunsee. 130 Jahre Schloss Cumberland, Göttingen: MatrixMedia Verlag.

Scholz, Natalie (2006): Die imaginierte Restauration: Repräsentationen der Monarchie im Frankreich Ludwigs XVIII., Darmstadt: Wissenschaftliche Buchgesellschaft.

Schönpflug, Daniel (2013): Die Heiraten der Hohenzollern. Verwandtschaft, Politik und Ritual in Europa 1640-1918, Göttingen: Vandenhoeck & Ruprecht.

Schultz, Uwe (2012): Der König und sein Richter. Ludwig XVI. und Robespierre: eine Doppelbiographie, München: C. H. Beck.

Sorg, Moritz Alexander (2018): "From Equilibrium to Predominance. Foreign Princes and Great Power Poliitcs in the Nineteenth Century." In: Journal of Modern European History 16/1, pp. 81.

Steckhan, Peter (2008): Welfenbericht. 150 Jahre Familiengeschichte der Herzöge zu Braunschweig und Lüneburg dokumentiert in Photographie und Film, Göttingen: MatrixMedia Verlag.

Vesque von Püttlingen, Johann (1860): Handbuch des in Oesterreich geltenden internationalen Privatrechtes, Wien: Braumüller.

Monarchy on Page, Stage, and Screen

Who's Queen?
Elizabeth I in Contemporary Culture

Susanne Scholz

Miranda Richardson's impersonation of Elizabeth I in the Blackadder series of 1986, from which this article borrows its title, is probably one of the most iconic (and certainly the funniest) remediations of the so-called 'Virgin Queen' in the 20th century.

Figure 1: 'Good Queen Bessie' from the Blackadder series

Source: *Blackadder* (1986)

Turning Elizabeth into a figure of pop culture, she represents the queen as a rather wayward, sometimes childish young woman, who enjoys her power to rule those around her. This whole-hearted embrace of her royal might, we might somewhat pompously call it a *jouissance* of power, is not conceded to other, more serious actualizations of Queen Elizabeth I in the present, e.g. to the heroine of Shekhar Kapur's feature films, *Elizabeth* (1998) and *Elizabeth. The Golden Age* (2007). Riven between a desire for domestic contentment and a suffocating sense of their regal duty, latter-day Elizabeths seem to suffer from the burden of power more than to enjoy its pleasures.

Investigating the afterlives of a 16th-century queen raises a number of methodical and ideological issues. Foremost among them is certainly the question of mediation and cultural memory, and the problematic relation of historical source narratives and contemporary perception horizons – what *they* saw and what *we* can see. How we remember and how we *see* the monarch is closely interwoven with our own wishes, desires and anxieties, with contemporary perspectives on monarchy in general and female queens in particular. Adding to that, we are all embedded spectators, what we see is inflected by the visual regimes and conventions of our own time (cf. Dillon 2010). In addition, we must consider the phantasmatic nature of the representations, which demands that we read them as contemporary cultural symptoms and not as fanciful variations on some historical reality that is no longer accessible. If, as Michael Dobson and Nicola Watson claim, Elizabeth is still 'on progress' through the cultural psyche, it will be rewarding to trace "how she comes to occupy that locus of popular desire and adoration" (2002: 262), and how and following which desires modern spectators imagine that locus at the end of the 20th and beginning of the 21st centuries (cf. also Bronfen/Straumann 2009 and 2016; Burt 2001; Doran/Freeman 2003; Walker 2004; Scholz 2016).

Drawing on the representation of the so-called 'Virgin Queen' in Kapur's *Elizabeth* (1998), this article will investigate the ways in which Elizabeth as a historical monarch is made sense of, and maybe even made use of, in the context of contemporary societies, and how modern remediations of the queen transport something of what David Cannadine has called the "secular magic of monarchy" (1989: 102) into the present. I will focus on the representation of royal dance in order to do so, since dance features prominently in current representations of the queen while in early modern times it constituted a symbolic practice to make royal transcendence visible on earth. In this context, Kapur's versions of Elizabeth prove promising because he is trying to find a visual language for the representation of something that is, in our time and age, essentially unrepresentable, namely the 'political body' of the queen. The notion of the 'political body' of the monarch draws on Ernst Kantorowicz' magisterial study on medieval concepts of kingship which were resuscitated in the 1560s in order to explain (and legitimize) Elizabeth's exceptional status (Kantorowicz 1997 [1957]). In what he calls "medieval political theology," the monarch has two bodies, one of them his mortal and fragile 'body natural' and the other his sacrosanct 'body politic,' which is often symbolically troped in the image of 'the crown.' The political body of a reigning monarch is thus incorporated with the natural body, but not tainted by its shortcomings, such as gender, sickness, or age. It is a transcendental corporation which is materialized in the body of the highest representative of the royal blood line, but is in itself a metaphysical entity which lifts the respective monarch out of the sphere of mortal humans. It is this metaphysical component of the royal person, I contend, which is no longer conceivable in modern times, but which might hold some (maybe nostalgic, or mystic) attraction to contemporary audiences. Since transcendence is even in pre-modern times only visualizable by symbolic means, early modern political discourse had recourse to a number of practices and rituals in which to (temporally) make the royal aura visible to beholders (cf. Dillon 2010). One of the symbolic practices used to medialize the monarch's sacrosanct body in pre-modern times is royal dance.

ROMANCING THE QUEEN: IMAGES OF ELIZABETH I FOR MODERN AUDIENCES

Elizabeth I's passion for dancing looms large in the cultural imaginary of the 20th and the 21st centuries. No film version of Elizabeth's life and early reign can do without a scene in which the queen dances, frequently with her alleged favorite, Robert Dudley, the Earl of Leicester (cf. the BBC-Series *Elizabeth R* 1971, Kapur's *Elizabeth* 1998, the BBC-Series *The Virgin Queen* 2005). It is a well-established fact that Elizabeth danced, but it is also obvious that she did not use the symbolic capacities of dance as part of her political iconography. On the contrary, from the symptomatic evidence of some poetic representations of queens refusing to dance, we can assume that she carefully avoided being seen as the female partner in courtly dance, though there is evidence of her dancing in circles, and with other women (cf. Scholz 2013). So why is this image so pertinent? In the following, I want to venture some speculations about our fascination with the dancing queen. Starting from Shekhar Kapur's *Elizabeth* (1998), I will have a look at the notion of royal dance and place it in historical perspective. Since the dance has become the iconic image by which we 'remember' Elizabeth's 'romance' with the Earl of Leicester, it will be productive to compare 16th-century representations of courtly dance and the imagined dance of the monarch as it is displayed in Kapur's film. This comparison will show that the cultural perception of dance has undergone a thorough resemantization which is based on modernity's incapability of conceiving of the metaphysical on earth. While from antiquity through the Middle Ages to the early modern period, dance could be understood as a symbol for divine or even cosmic harmony on earth, more modern and materialistic times see in the dance of couples an articulation of (mostly heterosexual) desire and a decorous domestication (or downright displacement) of the sexual act. Kapur is by no means the originator of the image of queen Elizabeth dancing with Robert Dudley, whom she made Earl of Leicester in 1564, he just elaborates on a trope that is culturally available and used to downsize the queen from the 17th century on (cf. Scholz 2016). In our viewing experience of the film, the sexualization of the dancing couple is foregrounded, thus rendering impossible a metaphysical perspective of Elizabeth's royal potency. If Kapur makes an effort to represent her transcendental dimension, he does so exactly by making her give up dancing at the end of the film. In doing so, he brings out an aspect which is only just emerging in the discourse of early modern dance but will become its dominant feature in modern times, i.e. the use of dance to represent (hetero-)sexual desire.

Kapur's *Elizabeth* contains two scenes in which the young queen dances with Leicester in a courtly setting and both are eminently significant for the director's take on the question of the queen's power. The first of the two dances takes place immediately after the coronation; it shows the dancers in relaxed and harmonic movement, their bodies in tune, and the whole scene is highly erotically charged. It suggests that the newly made queen, after the tribulations of the previous years, enjoys her freedom and her agency and does not care for questions of decorum (it is obvious that the representatives of the establishment are not amused, neither by her choice of dance nor of her dancing partner). The spectators are fascinated, poised between scandal and scopic pleasure, and the dance scene takes up a lot of narrated space in the otherwise densely woven story of Elizabeth's first years. The dance itself, allegedly a volta, is enacted not exactly along the lines of dance manuals of the 16th century, but it makes use of the central (scandalous) features of this dance, the bodily closeness of the partners and the lift figures (*Elizabeth* 36:20-37:55).

Figure 2: Elizabeth dancing with Leicester

Source: *Elizabeth* (1998)

Apparently, this is what today's audiences want to see of Elizabeth I, maybe along the lines of "desire and adoration" sketched by Dobson and Watson (2002: 262). In *England's Elizabeth*, they elaborate on representations of Elizabeth from the 17th century to the present: While, e.g. the Victorians preferred Mary Queen of Scots as their 16th-century queen of choice and imagined Elizabeth as a man-like, empire-building virago, the advent of the second Elizabeth on the throne changed readers' and audience's perspectives on Elizabeth I. They claim that in the subsequent refashioning of the historical Elizabeth into "a woman, after all," the 'romance' with the Earl of Leicester became a marker of desired domesticity and the promise of nuptial bliss (Dobson/Watson 2002: 217 and 240-41, cf. also Moss 2006: 803).

This "normalization" (Dobson/Watson 2002: 241) of the historical queen continued despite massive changes in society ensuing between the 1960s and the 1980s, which changed the lives of contemporary (British) women. With the advent of the pill, equal opportunity action and a female prime minister, the option to 'have it all' replaced the 1950s wish for domesticity in representations and remediations of the queen, and Glenda Jackson's wonderfully self-confident impersonation in the 1971 BBC series *Elizabeth R* provides a perfect example for this (cf. Moss 2006: 799-800). However, Leicester still functioned as a signifier of 'what the queen wants,' while the queen, as a projection figure of our desires, gradually turned into a careful manager of sexual and career options.

The romance between Elizabeth and Robert Dudley, Earl of Leicester takes many forms in the biographies, films and bodice-ripper fictions of the 20th century (cf. e.g. Gregory 2004; Gristwood 2007; Jenkins 1961; Latham 2011). Looking at the host of literary and filmic representations, the question bears asking why romance is considered a suitable form or mode by which to remember Elizabeth, even if the historical evidence is scarce. What we are dealing with in this manner of emplotment is not 'romantic' merely in the everyday sense of a 'love story,' but makes use of romance as a mode which articulates specific cultural needs and anxieties. Romance in the latter sense constitutes a way of seeing or making sense which draws on cultural desires. Northrop Frye classically calls it a "wish-fulfilment dream" and a projection of society's ideals "in some form [...], where the virtuous heroes and beautiful heroines represent the ideals and the villains the threats to their ascendency" (Frye 1990 [1957]: 186). For him, the romance is also characterized by "its extraordinarily persistent nostalgia, its search for some kind of imaginative golden age in time or space" (ibid: 186). In both the colloquial and the academic uses of the concept, romance contains a promise of salvation or happiness or a better world. Speaking of a "wish-fulfilment dream" and the projection of desires, Frye's definition suggests that the fantasy in question acts out something that is important to its audiences. It thus seems legitimate to call this romance of 'Elizabeth-and-Leicester' a phantasmatic constellation, possibly along the lines of Lacan's claim that phantasms shield us from reality, or from our worst fears,[1] replacing them with a more palatable image. This obviously has an enormous impact on cultural memory. The entry for fantasy/*fantasme* of Dylan Evans' *Introductory Dictionary of Lacanian Psychoanalysis* states that "memories are continually being reshaped in accordance with unconscious desires, so much so that symptoms originate not in any supposed 'objective facts' but in a complex dialectic in which fantasy plays a vital role" (Evans 1996: 60). If this also holds true for collective memories, it suggests that contemporary imaginations of the queen are heavily inflected with cultural desires and anxieties, that they are essentially wish-fulfilling fantasies. Clearly, these representations are not arbitrary, so the question bears asking why a powerful woman of the 16th century – a time of personal rule, if not absolutism – is remembered today as a heroine in a romance? What are the unconscious desires or fears which fashion our cultural memory of Elizabeth in this way? And, more to the point, what do the cultural imaginations fail or refuse to represent? It is my contention that the *non-dit*, the thing that is hidden behind

---

1 The passage in Lacan reads as follows: "The place of the real, which stretches from the trauma to the phantasy – in so far as the phantasy is never anything more than the screen that conceals something quite primary, something determinant in the function of repetition – this is what we must now examine." (Lacan 1998: 60) Sarasin rephrases this as follows: "Das Phantasma ist ein 'Schirm', der vor einem Realen schützt" (Sarasin 2004: 17).

the screen of the phantasm, is in this case the independent, powerful female ruler. What it is replaced with is a vision of lost completeness, a heteronormative happiness that must, however, be given up in exchange for power, leaving behind a lack and a desire that cannot be fulfilled. So far, so (post)modern. This is what we see and (apparently) want to see, because it suits our frame of comprehension. Given the massive time gap between the 16th century and our time, it might be interesting to enquire why dance is the practice that brings out all these complex constellations and to investigate what Elizabethans would have seen when looking at the dancing queen.

MAKING THE MODERN SUBJECT: COURTLY DANCE

Courtly dance can be described as a disciplinary discourse. In the context of a process of civilization, it helps to form the courtiers' (and ladies') bodies into an instrument of courtly identity, as can be seen, e.g. in the following passage from Thoinot Arbeau's *Orchésography* (1588):

"You have executed your steps and movements nicely and kept the rhythm well, but when you dance in company never look down at your feet to see whether you are performing the steps correctly. Keep your head and body erect and appear self-possessed. Spit and blow your nose sparingly, or if needs must turn your head away and use a fair white handkerchief. Converse affably in a low, modest voice, your hands at your sides, neither hanging limp nor moving nervously. Be suitably and neatly dressed, your hose well secured and your shoes clean." (Arbeau 2011 [1588]: 118-19)

Like other courtly practices, dance thrives on a performance of body control which suggests natural grace, and on a discrepancy of the hidden inside of the subject and his/her outside, i.e. body surface. It is also a translation of social hierarchy into ordered movement or *kinesis*. A glance at the literature of the time, be it courtly poetry, plays such as Shakespeare's *A Midsummer Night's Dream*, or conduct books, shows that the discourse of dancing with its internal contradictions is frequently used to negotiate desires and anxieties about the status not only of the subject's bodies (in need of refinement) but also of the royal body. It can thus be seen as one of the practices which helps modulate the tensions of the ongoing modernization of the subject in the early modern period. In order to demonstrate the conflicting positions, I will focus on two diverging strands in the discourse of early modern dance, taking into account also the novelties implemented into the discourse and practice of courtly dance at the time.

One of these novelties concerns the increasing dominance of couple dance, as opposed to earlier forms such as circle dance or chain dances like hays and farandole. Skiles Howard has argued that the early modern period witnessed major changes in the cultural practices and social codes of dancing which in turn reflected and negotiated changes in the structure of early modern societies. She summarizes:

"As the Middle Ages waned, the dancing of the elite began a separate development, evolving into a means of courtly self-fashioning, an instrument for the acquisition and exercise of social power. [...] The dancing of the elite was a fully framed political discourse, an elaborate system of kinetic, spatial, and visual terms and interrelated ideas that organized a view of the world and the body that vindicated itself and excluded others." (Howard 1998: 3 and 23)

Howard shows how pictorial representations of dancers in the 15th and 16th centuries depict the bodies of noble and rustic dancers as belonging to different orders of society.

Figure 3: "Tanzende Bauern und Bäuerinnen und Tanz von Herren und Damen"

Source: Engraving by Thomas de Bry after an earlier woodcut by Hans Sebald Beham (1500-1550) (Howard 1998: 1)

While the aristocratic couples hold their bodies upright and vertical, there is much groping and fondling going on among the rustic dancers, and while the aristocrats pose as self-contained units, the rustics constantly invade each other's space. The differentiation addressed here casts the aristocratic couple, dancing in a stately and measured way, as the norm to be aspired to. Howard concludes that from the early modern period on, it is the aristocratic couple which comes to stand in for divine harmony (1998: 1-45 and 69-92).

Likewise, all humanists writing in favor of dancing emphasized the capacity of dance to civilize the untutored body and refine it into an instrument of courtly identity and maybe even an image of divine harmony. Sir Thomas Elyot's *Governor* (1531), for instance, makes much of the image of the gendered couple as a model for human concord and sees dance as a way of representing the perfection of creation and of human relationships:

"In every dance, of a most ancient custom, there danceth together a man and a woman, holding each other by the hand or the arm, which betokeneth concord. Now it behoveth the dancers and also the beholders of them to know all qualities incident to a man, and also all qualities to a woman likewise appertaining.
A man in his natural perfection is fierce, hardy, strong in opinion, covetous of glory, desirous of knowledge, appetiting by generation to bring forth his semblable. The good nature of a woman is to be mild, timorous, tractable, benign, of sure remembrance, and shamefast. [...]
Wherefore, when we behold a man and a woman dancing together, let us suppose there to be a concord of all the said qualities [...]. These qualities, in this wise being knit together and signified in the personages of man and woman dancing, do express or set out the figure of very nobility." (Elyot 1966 [1531]: I.xxi., 77-78)

Elyot's tract strongly insists on dance as a gendered performance; this in turn presupposes a compliance of both partners with gender hierarchies. In that respect his image of the aristocratic couple dance is also normative, providing behavior ideals on whose fulfilment the desired order depends. That this could also go wrong was not only a matter of concern for dance instructors, but also for Puritan dance-haters, who pertinaciously warned that dancing engenders lust and lasciviousness:

"Dancing is the vilest vice of all and truly it cannot be easily said what mischiefs the sight, and the hearing do receive hereby, which afterward be the cause of communication and embracing. They dance with disordinate gestures, and with monstrous thumping of the feet, to pleasant sounds, to wanton songs, to dishonest verses. Maidens and matrons are groped and handled with unchaste hands, and kissed, and dishonestly embraced: and the things which nature hath hidden, modestly covered, are then often-time by means of lasciviousness, made naked, and ribaldry, under the colour of pastime is dissembled." (Northbrooke 1843 [1577]: 136)

Both sides, however, by putting so much emphasis on the ordered movement of gendered bodies, highlight the sexualization of bodies that comes with the notion of gender complementarity. Arbeau points to the gendering of the dancing body when he suggestively asks "Does he not plead tacitly with his mistress, who marks the seemliness and the grace of his dancing, 'Love Me. Desire me.'?" (2011 [1588]: 16). He also sees dance as a practice by which to judge the bodily qualities of prospective marriage partners:

"[N]aturally the male and female seek one another, and nothing does more to stimulate a man to acts of courtesy, honour and generosity than love. And if you desire to marry you must realize that a mistress is won by the good temper and grace displayed while dancing [...].
And there is more to it than this, for dancing is practised to reveal whether lovers are in good health and sound of limb, after which they are permitted to kiss their mistresses in order that they may touch and savour one another, thus to ascertain if they are shapely or emit an unpleasant odour as of bad meat. Therefore, from this standpoint, quite apart from the many other advantages to be derived from dancing, it becomes an essential in a well-ordered society." (ibid: 12)

The dance in couples thus assumes a performative function in the early modern discourse of gender. It enacts, materially and kinetically, a hierarchy of men over women which is irreversible – any change in position will disturb the image of harmony visualized by a well-performed dance. It also, by focusing on the physical bodies of the dancers, their grace, their shapeliness and also their body odors, contributes to a sexualization of the partners and so turns into a means to articulate erotic desire. Arbeau also explicitly comments on the dance that is so prevalent in latter-day representations of Elizabeth dancing with Leicester, the Volta:

"[H]e who dances the lavolta must regard himself as the centre of a circle and draw the damsel as near to him as possible when he wishes to turn. [...] When you wish to turn, release the damsel's left hand and throw your left arm around her, grasping and holding her firmly by the waist above the right hip with your left hand. At the same moment place your right hand below her busk to help her to leap when you push her forward with your left thigh. She, for her part, will place her right hand on your back or collar and her left hand on her thigh to hold her petticoat and dress in place, lest the swirling air should catch them and reveal her chemise or bare thigh. This done, you will perform the turns of the lavolta described above. And after having spun round for as many cadences as you wish, return the damsel to her place, when however brave a face she shows, she will feel her brain reeling and her head full of dizzy whirlings; and you yourself will perhaps be no better off. I leave it to you to judge whether it is a becoming thing for a young girl to take long strides and separations of the legs, and whether in this lavolta both honour and health are not involved and at stake." (ibid: 120-21)

The erotic charge of the dancing couple, whether it is seen as a positive or a negative phenomenon, subjects both bodies to an economy of desire. In the gaze of the others, be they prospective dancers or spectators, it is the gender of the body that counts, that is articulated by dress, that is desired, that needs to be disciplined, subjected to specific notions of order etc. Sexualization, as it is articulated by these normative imperatives, also means individualization – which in turn implies a focus on the natural body. Contemporary representations of Elizabeth's dances with her favorites draw on this modern notion of sex, gender, desire and the individual body and project them back into a time when all these notions were only just emerging, and certainly not easily applicable to the body of a queen considered to be sacrosanct. If Elizabeth had really danced a volta with one of her courtiers, this would probably have been a disturbing sight to her contemporaries – but there is no evidence that she ever did. For us, however, this image of the dancing queen makes a lot of sense, as a representation of repressed desires, of sexual actions that must not be performed, of a wish for a 'normal' relationship with a beloved person.

VISUALIZING THE DIVINE:
THE QUEEN'S (REFUSAL TO) DANCE

For humanists, dancing had the capacity to embody cosmic harmony and thus a potential for transcendence. This transcendent moment, the capacity of dance to represent or even embody higher truths, is especially relevant in relation to the monarch's dance. That advocates of the dance increasingly fashioned gender complementarity into a sign of divine order can be seen as a modernization of a notion they had inherited from the classical tradition, which ultimately rendered the 'mystical' dance of the monarch impossible.

Generally, humanist culture had envisioned dancing as a way of understanding "the truth of the cosmos and therefore the nature of God" (Nevile 2004: 104). Unsurprisingly, then, the representative of God on earth, i.e. the sovereign, was thought capable of envisioning this harmony to beholders from less perfect ranks, to make them learn what perfection is and try to emulate it by disciplining their bodies in the same way (as enacted, e.g. in Gérard Corbiau's film *Le Roy Danse* 2001). Mark Franko and others have alerted us to the eminently symbolic function of the monarch's dance, which embodies (rather than represents) divine harmony and which makes it visible to his or her subjects (cf. Franko 1993 and Franko 2000: 35-51). This view of dance as a transcendent practice has its origin in Platonic notions of the cosmic dance of the spheres and planets at the beginning of the world as described in *Timaeus* 40a-d and *Laws* II, 653e-657b (cf. Miller 1986). Its Renaissance relaunch is especially suggestive when seen in the light of the political fiction of the two bodies of the sovereign. Many scholars have argued that the hyperbolic representations of Elizabeth as never-aging, ever beautiful virgin queen stage the fiction of the political body which is subject neither to age nor infirmity, thereby disseminating a concept which was originally revamped in order to deal with the pressing problem of the succession of an unmarried queen (cf. Strong 1977 and 1987; Scholz 2000). Ideally, the (imagined) spectacle of the dancing queen could be understood as another articulation of this 'political theology,' a dance of the body politic (cf. Kantorowicz 1997 [1957]; Axton 1977), by which the queen associates herself with the divine order of the cosmos. Again, this can be seen as a way of medializing power: If the monarch, in his or her political body, permanently performs a spectacle of divine and worldly power, then the royal body functions as an instrument of moral instruction and must be seen by its subjects, not only in order for them to learn their place in the 'microcosmic' constellation of the court, but also because the divine aura of the royal body recharges itself by being looked at (cf. Franko 2000: 44). And just as it is the subjects' duty to acknowledge the power of the sovereign (if by gazing and gawping), it is the monarch's duty to make divine order visible. It could be argued that, by way of a trickle-down effect, the aristocratic couple inherited the transcendental potential of the 'cosmic' dance, but with a significant difference: its metaphysical promise comes with a tacit subjection of the female partner of the couple. What, then, happens if the monarch is a woman?

The political body of the sovereign, as we know from Kantorowicz, is not only beyond the shortcomings and ailments of the natural body, it is also ungendered (cf. 1997 [1957]: 7). This is an important point which may help to clarify why the dance in gendered couples – and with it the queen dancing as the female partner of a couple – becomes such a precarious image. The confirmation, acceptance and reiteration of the social order through dancing is always celebrated for an audience of spectators. Yet, given the ambivalence of dancing in heterosexual couples, what happens if beholders see the queen, in courtly entertainment as well as in the context of marriage negotiations, as part of a gendered couple? While subjecting her to a kinetic code which tacitly acknowledges the superiority of the male partner, couple dance also implicitly sexualizes her body, directing the gaze away from her 'body politic' towards her 'body natural.' If this way of perceiving the queen becomes the dominant perspective, a notion of embodiment (in the quasi-sacramental sense of 'full presence') of the political body gradually becomes impossible.

It is this consideration, I contend, which is behind the conspicuous refusal of the queens to dance which I have investigated in some dance poems of the time (cf. Scholz 2013). At a crucial point in Book VI of *The Faerie Queene*, Calidore secretly watches a "hundred naked maydens" dance, together with the three graces, who dance around a forth figure who should have been Gloriana, the eponymous Fairy Queen, but is not (Spenser 1987 [1596]: 690-91; VI.x.10-17). In John Davies' dance poem *Orchestra*, Antinous, one of Penelope's most pressing suitors, tries to persuade her to dance with him, and in his rhetorically brilliant argumentation, he constantly makes use of the image of the cosmic dance that needs to be embodied by the queen in order to convey a sense of order to her subjects (cf. Davies 1596). Penelope, however, refuses to comply. Instead, she has a prospective vision of the Elizabethan court which directly transfers her ideas on dance onto the queen. Gloriana and Penelope can be identified as projection figures of Elizabeth and both conspicuously refuse to engage in an activity that kinetically subordinates them to their male partners. Instead of having their bodies gazed at, disciplined, and eroticized in dance, they stay outside of the visual field, "beholding all, yet of them unespyde," as Edmund Spenser puts it (1987 [1596]: 690; VI.x.11).

How do these historical contextualizations reflect back on the present? Shekhar Kapur's films, despite all the painstaking research that has gone into their making, have no investment in historical veracity. They play on our wishes and anxieties and present their version of Elizabeth in the light of current cultural concerns. They reshape, in the diction of Evans' Lacan dictionary quoted earlier, historical memories in accordance with our unconscious desires. What can be seen in the figure of the queen is certainly very different from what Elizabethans would have seen, but it speaks to contemporary audiences in significant ways.

My ideas about why we want to see Elizabeth dancing with Leicester – as enacted in Kapur's *Elizabeth* (1998) – bring together the two strands in the early modern discourse of dance that I have sketched before. The residual pre-modern notion foregrounds the privileged visibility of the monarch, endowing him or her with the power to visualize divine order through the harmonic movements of his or her body, thus fashioning dance into a spectacle of royal power. An inkling of this vision of harmony is present in Kapur's film, e.g. when Elizabeth dances with her ladies-in-waiting outside Hatfield House (1998: 7:31-7:42). It is, however, significant that this scene takes place in a pastoral setting, away from the center of the political world. The more modern idea concerns the increasing dominance of couple dance with its emphasis on gender duality, maybe even complementarity, bringing with it an eroticization of the gaze that falls on the two dancers and thus an emphasis on the gendered body. It is my contention that the historical Elizabeth refrained from using the image of the royal dance to visualize her power because the gaze of her courtly spectators (with humanist training) increasingly only 'saw' her natural body. That perception in turn interfered with the cosmic potential of the dance to visualize the body politic.

For a modern gaze, however, the frame of perception has changed dramatically: the notion of the embodied, sacramental mystical body politic is – at least since the late 17th century – no longer available as an interpretive frame, so modern audiences see nothing but the natural body. A cursory look at the afterlife of Elizabeth in the 19th and 20th centuries shows that different options of representing this body natural of the queen were available. Stories of a stillborn princess replaced by the baby son of one of her ladies abound in the 18th and 19th century, alternating with stories which claim that she was a hermaphrodite and incapable of bearing children or even of performing the act.[2] The 19th century concentrated on the empire-building man-woman, and generally had little sympathy for Elizabeth. The early 20th century focused on the relationship of the aging queen to the dashing but treacherous Essex and thus emphasized her decaying body. Lytton Strachey's *Elizabeth and Essex* (1928) sets the pace and provides the dominant ideology here, and Michael Curtiz's film versions with Bette Davis as the aging, frustrated and unhappy queen disseminated these ideas for generations to come (*The Private Lives of Elizabeth and Essex* 1939; *The Virgin Queen* 1955). Post World War II Elizabeth figurations, by contrast, have concentrated on the (at least potentially) sexually active young woman. As I have pointed out before, Leicester could serve here as a projection figure of prospective happiness in a heterosexual relationship. This Elizabeth was obviously fashioned in the image of the second Elizabeth of the 20th century, who was young, active, and almost middle-class in her ideological outlook and fed the harmony-hungry British public with home stories, which never failed to emphasize how much of a sacrifice the throne demanded of her.

---

2   See for example Hugh Campbell's claim that she suffered from "some obstructions from nature, which disabled her from the offices of a wife, precluded from her the pleasures of a prostitute, and, contending with her strong desires, raised such a ferment and fire within her, as she was ever endeavouring, and never able, to extinguish" (1825: 289 qtd. in Dobson/Watson 2002: 154).

NORMALIZING THE SOVEREIGN: KAPUR'S TAKE ON ELIZABETH'S SACRIFICE

In this frame of reference, the dance with Leicester as portrayed by Kapur can easily be read as a displacement or foreshadowing of the sexual act. In fact, it is followed almost immediately by a wedding night of sorts, the two scenes being separated only by Leicester's flirtatious encounter with the ladies-in-waiting, who clearly know what he is up to, and Sir William Cecil's somewhat helpless enquiry after the young queen's "proper functions." Cecil's imperious claim that "her Majesty's body and person [...] belong to the state" (*Elizabeth* 38:41-39:11) sounds like a desperate effort to position the notion of the body politic exactly against the sexual agency of the queen, but in the actual mise-en-scène, it rather seems like a (doomed) bid for control by a representative of the older generation. The act takes place on a bed whose curtains are embroidered with eyes and ears, suggesting the ubiquitous gaze of the courtiers on the queen, which is in turn enacted by the ladies-in-waiting witnessing the scene through the ornamental openings which separate the privy chamber from the queen's bedchamber. This scene seems to suggest that now, on the night of her coronation, Elizabeth has it all, her freedom, the crown, the power, and the man. Alas, as it turns out, this consummate fulfilment is impossible for a female ruler, and so, after various failed attempts to integrate desire and duty, a life as a wife and a life as reigning monarch, she has to give up one for the other. In any case, the romance with Leicester, which dominates the film, enacts the historical queen's sexual 'normalization' – thankfully, she is neither a man nor incapable of performing the act. So, as a 'woman, after all' she is safely brought into the fold of heterosexual domestic femininity. It might be interesting to pursue the idea of the wedding night with Leicester after a coronation ceremony which at least in Elizabeth's own imagination figured as a marriage with the land. In the logic of the sacrosanct body politic, Leicester here stands in for England, thus anticipating one option in the subsequent marriage negotiations, which centered around the question of marrying a (potentially Catholic) foreigner versus marrying an English aristocrat. Kapur's version, however, does not concede this plenitude of pleasures to the queen, and so in the conflict of desire and duty that characterizes representations of Elizabeth in the present, perspectives of domestic bliss must be sacrificed. Again, a dance of Elizabeth and Leicester is staged to convey the message.

Figure 5: Elizabeth's final dance with Leicester

Source: *Elizabeth* (1998)

The second dance is framed by the marriage negotiations with the French Duc d'Anjou and happens immediately after Elizabeth has discovered the Duc in drag, and after she has learned that Leicester is already married. Proclaiming that "there will be no more talk of marriage negotiations," she asks Leicester to dance a volta with her. In this second dance, the harmonious, erotic concord of the dancing bodies is disrupted by Leicester's 'will to power' ("you are still my Elizabeth") and the queen's unwillingness to submit to his lead. The scene ends with her furious assertion "I will have one mistress here, and no master,"[3] which signals not only the end of any possible plans to marry Leicester, but also of all further negotiations with France or Spain. This scene, by staging a volta gone wrong, marks the film's 'volta': It is the decisive moment which will lead to the almost violent makeover of the young Elizabeth into the iconic 'Virgin Queen.' Interestingly and maybe unsurprisingly, the memories going through her mind while her hair is cut end with her dance with Leicester outside Hatfield House which introduced the young princess to the film audience (ibid: 7:49-8:50). This is indeed the very last image before she dons her iconic masque of power. Prior to that, in one of the key scenes of the film, her councilor and 'spy master' Walsingham had brought up the notion of the body politic and the necessity to provide the queen's subjects with the possibility "to touch the divine here on earth" (ibid: 1:53:10-1:54:00). It is the subsequent auratic empowerment of the queen, the foregrounding of her political body, which in contemporary versions must go hand in hand with a sacrifice of 'private'

---

3 Reported in Robert Naunton, *Fragmenta Regalia* (1641), albeit in a different context.

pleasures. As Kapur's queen fashions herself into a projection space for our longings, and also our fears of the mystery of monarchy, she is safely banned into the formula of the iconic Ditchley portrait, pearls, ruff, wig, and all. This seems to be Elizabeth's 'pathos formula' for the 20th century, the emotionally charged visual trope figuring the inseparable link of power and sacrifice. David Grant Moss has shown how contemporary representations of Elizabeth are virtually trapped in the iconography of the queen's portraits (cf. 2006: 796-98), and how especially the Ditchley portrait turns into a visual shorthand for both Elizabeth and England. So in a very conventional, even reactionary move, what viewers get at the end of Kapur's film is a citation from the "dictionary of visual quotations that make up popular history" (Dobson/Watson 2002: 258), an example of what Elizabeth Bronfen and Barbara Straumann have called the "quotable Elizabeth" (Bronfen/Straumann 2016: 150). Unsurprisingly, given the semantic revolution of the discourse of dance, it is now virtually the opposite of dance that is used to visualize the sacrosanct aura of the queen: Stasis instead of *kinesis*, and a mask instead of a face. Here again, the queen's female body is dissociated from the body of power, and in Kapur's view of things, this power comes at a prize: what we get is the iconic virgin who does not dance, nor move, nor change, and who must leave the pleasures of the natural body behind.

Figure 6: Elizabeth as 'Virgin Queen'

Source: *Elizabeth* (1998)

In this frame of thought, dance cannot function as an image of divine power and the beginnings of this process of modernization can be found, precisely, in Elizabeth's own time. Her reticence when it comes to public couple dances, i.e. her 'invisibility' as a dancer and her unwillingness to use dance as a medium of political aesthetics can be seen as a reaction to incipient changes in the perception of the royal person that in the course of time relegated the sacrosanct body politic to the (no longer active) fundus of historical mythology, to be activated only in the transitional periods between monarchs and at coronations. The so-called 'cult of Elizabeth' may be so fascinating to us because it marks a moment of transition and contains, in an uneasy balance, both sacramental corporation and individualized body, both embodiment and representation of power. It is the auratic capacity of the body to incorporate cosmic order and make the divine visible on earth which attracts modern readers and audiences, but which is incomprehensible within a modern secular episteme. What we see when we see a human body is its individuality, its materiality, and its sex. The modern perspective thus privileges the natural body of the ruler, so that it is only plausible that 20th-century representations of the queen make use of the dance as an image of the desiring body, but also of gender order. Its cultural work is to domesticate the powerful woman by kinetically subordinating her to the male lead, and by reducing her to her (incomplete, lacking, ever desirous) body. Visualizing the queen as part of a dancing couple thus functions as a strategy of cultural stress relief vis-à-vis the threat of a powerful female ruler.

WORKS CITED

Arbeau, Thoinot (2011 [1588]): Orchésography, translated by Mary Stewart Evans, Mineola, New York: Dover.

Axton, Marie (1977): The Queen's Two Bodies, London: Royal Historical Society.

Bronfen, Elizabeth/Straumann, Barbara (2009): "Political Visions: The Two Bodies of Elizabeth I." In: Liz Oakley-Brown/Louise J. Wilkinson (eds.), The Rituals and Rhetoric of Queenship: Medieval to Early Modern, Portland: Four Courts Press, pp. 252-270.

Bronfen, Elisabeth/Straumann, Barbara (2016): "Elizabeth I: the Cinematic Afterlife of an Early Modern Political Diva." In: Mandy Merck (ed.), The British Monarchy on Screen, Manchester: Manchester University Press, pp. 132-154.

Burt, Richard (2001): "Doing the Queen: Gender, Sexuality and the Censorship of Elizabeth I.'s Royal Image from Renaissance Portraiture to Twentieth-Century Mass Media." In: Andrew Hadfield (ed.), Literature and Censorship in Renaissance England, Basingstoke: Palgrave Macmillan, pp. 207-228.

Campbell, Hugh (1825): The Case of Mary Queen of Scots and of Elizabeth Queen of England, London: Sherwood, Jones & Co.

Cannadine, David (1989): "The Context, Performance, and Meaning of Ritual. The British Monarchy and the 'Invention of Tradition', c. 1820 to 1977." In: Eric Hobsbawm/Terence Ranger (eds.), The Invention of Tradition, Cambridge: Cambridge University Press, pp. 101-164.

Davies, John (1596): Orchestra or a Poeme of Dauncing Iudicially Proouing the True Obseruation of Time and Measure, In the Authenticall and Laudable Vse of Dauncing STC 6360.

Dillon, Janette (2010): The Language of Space in Court Performance, 1400-1625, Cambridge: Cambridge University Press.

Dobson, Michael/Watson, Nicola J. (2002): England's Elizabeth. An Afterlife in Fame and Fantasy, Oxford: Oxford University Press.

Doran, Susan/Freeman, Thomas S., (eds.) (2003): The Myth of Elizabeth, Basingstoke: Palgrave Macmillan.

Elyot, Thomas (1966 [1531]): The Book Named the Governor, edited by S. E. Lehmberg, London: Everyman.

Evans, Dylan (1996): Introductory Dictionary of Lacanian Psychoanalysis, London: Routledge.

Franko, Mark (1993): Dance as Text. Ideologies of the Baroque Body, Oxford: Oxford University Press.

Franko, Mark (2000): "Figural Inversions of Louis XIV's Dancing Body." In: Mark Franko/Annette Richards (eds.), Acting on the Past. Historical Performance Across the Disciplines, Hanover and London, pp. 35-51.

Frye, Northrop (1990 [1957]): Anatomy of Criticism, Princeton: Princeton University Press.

Gregory, Philippa (2004): The Virgin's Lover, London: HarperCollins.

Gristwood, Sarah (2007): Elizabeth and Leicester, London et al: Bantam Books.

Howard, Skiles (1998): The Politics of Courtly Dancing in Early Modern England, Amherst: University of Massachusetts Press.

Jenkins, Elizabeth (1961): Elizabeth and Leicester, London: Phoenix Press.

Kantorowicz, Ernst (1997 [1957]): The King's Two Bodies, Princeton: Princeton University Press.

Lacan, Jacques (1998): The Four Fundamental Concepts of Psychoanalysis, translated by Alan Sheridan, London: Vintage.

Latham, Bethany (2011): Elizabeth I in Film and Television. A Study of the Major Portrayals, Jefferson: McFarland.

Miller, James (1986): Measures of Wisdom. The Cosmic Dance in Classical and Christian Antiquity, Toronto et al.: University of Toronto Press.

Moss, David Grant (2006): "A Queen for Whose Time? Elizabeth I as Icon for the Twentieth Century." In: The Journal of Popular Culture 39, pp. 796-816.

Naunton, Robert (1641): Fragmenta Regalia; or Observations on the Late Queen Elizabeth, Her Times and Favourites, London.

Nevile, Jennifer (2004): The Eloquent Body. Dance and Humanist Culture in Fifteenth-Century Italy, Bloomington and Indianapolis: Indiana University Press.

Northbrooke, John (1843 [1577]): A Treatise Against Dicing, Dancing, Plays and Interludes, London: Shakespeare Society.

Sarasin, Philipp (2004): Anthrax. Bioterror als Phantasma, Frankfurt: Suhrkamp.

Scholz, Susanne (2000): Body Narratives. Writing the Nation and Fashioning the Subject in Early Modern England, Basingstoke: Palgrave Macmillan.

Scholz, Susanne (2013): "'Dauncings True Nobilitie': Absent Queens in John Davies' *Orchestra* and Edmund Spenser's *The Faerie Queene* Book VI." In: Susanne Scholz/Daniel Dornhofer (eds.), Spectatorship at the Early Modern Court. Zeitsprünge. Forschungen zur Frühen Neuzeit 17, pp. 45-62.

Scholz, Susanne (2016): "Dancing Queen? Inszenierungen des königlichen Körpers am Hof von Elizabeth I. von England." In: Martin Doll/Oliver Kohns (eds.), Figurationen des Politischen 2: Die zwei Körper der Nation, München: Fink, pp. 555-582.

Spenser, Edmund (1987 [1596]): The Faerie Queene, edited by Albert Charles Hamilton, London: Longman.

Strachey, Lytton (1971 [1928]): Elizabeth and Essex. A Tragic History. Harmondsworth: Penguin.

Strong, Roy (1987): Gloriana. The Portraits of Queen Elizabeth I, London: Thames and Hudson.

Strong, Roy (1977): The Cult of Elizabeth. Elizabethan Portraiture and Pageantry, London: Thames and Hudson.

Walker, Julia M. (2004): The Elizabeth Icon, 1603-2003, Basingstoke: Palgrave Macmillan.

Films and Television

Blackadder. Season 2. Directed by Mandie Fletcher. 1986. BBC.

Elizabeth. Directed by Shekhar Kapur. 1998. Channel Four Films/Working Title Films/PolyGram.

Elizabeth R. Various directors. 1971. BBC.

Elizabeth. The Golden Age. Directed by Shekhar Kapur. 2007. Studio Canal/Working Title Films.

Le Roy Danse. Directed by Gérard Corbiau. 2000. K-Star/France 2 Cinéma/Canal +.

The Private Lives of Elizabeth and Essex. Directed by Michael Curtiz. 1939. Warner Bros.

The Virgin Queen. Directed by Coky Giedroyc. 2005. BBC/Power /Powercorp.

The Virgin Queen. Directed by Michael Curtiz. 1955. Twentieth Century Fox.

"Empires of all kinds collapse, but the fake tsars, they last forever."[1] Modern and Contemporary Memories of Tsar Šćepan Mali (1767-1773)

Stefan Trajković Filipović

In March 2017, during the presidential elections in the Republic of Serbia, an article was published in *Danas* (a popular Serbian daily newspaper) that commented on the appearance of one of the presidential candidates, Ljubiša Preletačević Beli.[2] The article, entitled *Tuga* ('Sorrow') (2017), reflected on Preletačević assuming the role of an exaggerated leader and presenting himself as a solution for the pressing political problems. The author of the article admitted that Preletačević aimed to produce a comic effect and that his performance was an expression of people's discontentment with the available political options. Nevertheless, he warned that Preletačević was not the first one who tried to assume a position of power by means of overstatements. Šćepan Mali, he argued, succeeded in that before him.

Who is this Šćepan Mali, that we, the article suggests, should be wary of? He made an appearance in the 18th century Montenegro as an impostor who claimed to be an exiled Russian tsar, after which he gained power over Montenegro for several years, as Tsar Šćepan Mali (1767-1773).[3] His appearance initiated diplo-

---

1 Kovač 2002: 51.
2 His name was imagined as a pun, where 'Preletačević' (derived from the word 'preletač,' meaning a 'defector') refers to politicians' practice of changing political parties for their personal benefit. 'Beli' translates as 'white.'
3 Translated as Stephen the Little (or 'the Humble'). The names 'Šćepan,' 'Stefan' or 'Stjepan,' which will appear in the text, are all variations of the name Stephen.

matic turmoil across contemporary Europe. Today, Šćepan Mali is part of the collective memory in Montenegro and the surrounding countries. He is occasionally invoked in newspaper and journal articles, researched and discussed among scholars, or serves as inspiration for works of literature and art.

In this article, I approach the character of Šćepan Mali from the perspective of memory studies and deal with his reception in the past two centuries. On the one hand, this article's aims are to research the process of the memory construction of Šćepan Mali and to understand the dynamics behind it. On the other hand, I discuss the functions of Šćepan Mali's remembrance that emerged from this long memory construction process. In order to address these concerns, I start from the notion of collective memory and the two sides it has according to Jan Assmann – communicative and cultural memory (cf. 2008: 109-118). Communicative memory relates to the level of everyday communication. It is disorganized, relies on personal recollections and deals with the recent past, spanning up to three generations (c. 80 years) (cf. Assmann 1995 [1988]: 126-127; cf. Assmann 2008: 111). Cultural memory, however, relies on institutions of learning or interpretation and is objectified and transmitted through the work of specialists (poets, teachers or scholars). Furthermore, it is stored in symbolical forms, ready to be transmitted across generations (cf. Assmann 1995 [1988]: 128-133). Finally, cultural memory relies on memory figures as a stable form of expression. These memory figures are then used for the retrospective construction of the past (cf. ibid: 129). One needs to have in mind, however, that these two aspects of collective memory – communicative and cultural – do not necessarily operate in chronological order. Communicative memory is not a stage to be completed before cultural memory develops. They often co-exist and even inform one another. This is apparent in the case of Šćepan Mali as the memories of him were, from the onset, often transmitted by specialists who were informed about him by people's living memory of the fake tsar.

In addition to this, I consider any research of memory as media research as well, since memory constructions cannot be observed separately from the media that transmits the memory (cf. Erll 2011: 114). When approaching the source material, I assume that media do not reflect a past 'reality,' but construct it by using different forms of expression, such as biographies, novels, historical overviews, plays, historical research, and films. These sources circulate, inform one another, disseminate, and shape collective memory (cf. ibid: 164). Furthermore, these interpretations, especially those providing fictional versions of the past, keep alive the dilemmas and even conflicts regarding the meaning of the memory figure, and point out the unrealized potential of the past and the memory in question (cf. Neumann 2008: 341).

The article begins with an overview of Šćepan Mali's rule and historical significance, before moving on to the chronological overview of his reception, starting from the late 18th century, until the second half of the 20th century. This overview allows us to observe the transition from the communicative to the cultural aspects of collective memory of Šćepan Mali, as well as their interactions. In the process, fictional and historiographical receptions informed one another and helped to shape Šćepan as an ambivalent figure in Montenegro's (and the surrounding countries') collective memory, due to variations in interpretations that accumulated through different media since the late 18th century. Finally, I will reflect on the memories of Šćepan Mali in recent times. His remembrance acts like a puzzle to be solved and triggers vivid discussions about both past and present, opens new research possibilities and inspires works of literature and art.

ŠĆEPAN MALI IN HIS OWN TIME

Šćepan Mali already attracted the attention of scholars in the 19th century. However, it was not until 1957 that the first comprehensive study of his historical character appeared, written by Gligor Stanojević. More recently, additional studies complemented the research of Šćepan Mali, focusing on addressing the 'riddle' of Šćepan's true identity. I will come back to these studies in the conclusion to this article, when considering the memory of Šćepan Mali in the recent past. Meanwhile, Stanojević's study from 1957 provides a concise and reliable overview of Šćepan Mali's life and rule.

After Tsar Peter III of Russia lost his throne in 1762 and was said to have been killed in a plot led by his wife Catherine II, the rumors circulated for years that the tsar was not really dead, which led to more than one person purporting to be Peter III in the following years, most notably Yemelyan Pugachev, who initiated the Pugachev's Rebellion in 1774.[4] Šćepan Mali was one of those people. At the time of his appearance, Montenegro was part of the Ottoman Empire. However, the weakness of the Empire's central government resulted in occasional conflicts between Montenegrins and Ottomans. On the Adriatic coast, Montenegro bordered with Venice, which also lost some of its influence in the region. Most importantly, Montenegro itself experienced internal struggles, vendettas and the ruling Prince-Bishop Sava's lack of authority. Šćepan's success partially resulted from such a

---

4   Pretenders appeared frequently in 18th century Russia. They often came from lower layers of society and offered more or less developed reformation programs. Peter III proved to be an especially popular identity for pretenders (Longworth 1975: 63, 70).

situation, building on a belief that an emperor savior would appear (cf. Stanojević 1957: 84).

In the autumn of 1766, Šćepan appeared as a medic in Maine near Budva, which was, at the time, a Venetian municipality bordering Montenegro. A group of monks and members of the Montenegrin elite supported him and started spreading a rumor of him being the Russian Tsar. About a year later, Šćepan was famous enough to pledge an official oath that he genuinely was the Russian Tsar. Consumed by the wave of excitement among Montenegrins, Prince-Bishop Sava himself believed this. Soon, however, he received assurance from the Russian official in Istanbul that Šćepan was a fraud. Sava tried to move against the impostor, but that led to Šćepan pillaging his property. In February 1768, Šćepan established himself as an absolute ruler, and in April 1768 finally moved his residence to Montenegro (cf. ibid: 18-25).

The news of Šćepan's appearance spread across the region and in some areas of the Ottoman Empire the population refused to pay tributes, which made the Ottomans fear an open revolt. The Russian court was soon informed about Šćepan, either from Istanbul or the Venetians inquiring about his identity. Officials and diplomats in Vienna also discussed the matter. Even though everyone agreed that Šćepan was an impostor, no one knew who benefited from his appearance and it was not easy to get rid of him. For example, as early as 1767, a Venetian attempt to poison him failed. Finally, in 1768, Venetian forces punished the municipalities bordering Montenegro and supporting Šćepan. Moreover, in late August 1768, Ottoman armies started advancing against Montenegro. Unable to stop them, Šćepan went into hiding. The solution to the problematic situation in which Montenegrins found themselves presented itself in the form of heavy rain that soaked Ottoman guns and powder, forcing them to cease fire, as well as in the Russian Empire's declaration of war on the Ottomans (cf. ibid: 45-62, 83).

Although the Ottoman army inflicted severe casualties on the Montenegrins, these 1768 campaigns had limited results. Šćepan reappeared, and even though the Montenegrin enthusiasm for him waned, the Ottoman pressure was not as intense anymore either: they were at war with the Russian Empire and wished to avoid further escalations in Montenegro. Russia, on the other hand, incited the Balkan peoples to rise against the Ottomans and sent Prince Dolgorukov to Montenegro. This mission failed despite initial success – Dolgorukov even managed to imprison Šćepan – when the prince realized that his authority among the Montenegrins was not sufficiently strong. He therefore set Šćepan free, reestablished his authority and then left Montenegro (cf. Petrovich 1955: 181-191). Even though Šćepan now had the official title of a Russian officer, his prestige was damaged, but was still widely recognized as an important figure by the Montenegrins. In

1773, the Ottomans finally managed to get rid of him by bribing one of his bodyguards to kill him (cf. Stanojević 1957: 63-74, 83).

In his research, Gligor Stanojević focused on evaluating Šćepan's historical significance, pointing out that earlier scholars often considered Šćepan as an adventurer who managed to introduce order and peace in Montenegro. According to Stanojević, these conclusions were not the results of comprehensive studies and were sometimes superficial. Šćepan's rule over Montenegro was not uninterrupted; indeed, a group of Montenegrin chiefs supported Šćepan and only with their support did he manage to become an absolute ruler. Furthermore, he was not a great reformer who fundamentally altered the social and political life, nor did he open a new chapter in Montenegrin history. He followed the practices already in place, except for his unusually severe punishments for disturbances of order and peace (especially vendettas). Šćepan did not question the rights of the chiefs who, when his authority waned, maintained order. He separated religious from secular power and introduced some small administrative changes, thus questioning the clergy's traditional claims to authority. Moreover, Montenegro gained more attention than ever before from abroad with the news of Šćepan's appearance spreading across Europe. It was considered both an interesting and inspiring curiosity and a concern for state officials and diplomats dealing with international relations. However, as Stanojević points out, this should not be overestimated. His impact was temporary, both on the national and international level (cf. ibid: 84-93).

"DUE TO THE IMPORTANCE OF THESE PAST EVENTS, AND BECAUSE OF ŠĆEPAN'S STRANGENESS, I WANTED TO WRITE SOMETHING ABOUT HIM..."[5] ŠĆEPAN MALI ON PAGE AND SCREEN

Šćepan's appearance puzzled the officials and diplomats of his time and continued to puzzle people after his death, inspiring a number of authors in the ensuing centuries. In the following section, I will provide an overview of selected interpretations from the late 18th to the second half of the 20th century that significantly influenced the development and changed the memory of Šćepan Mali. I will pay special attention to the form of the interpretations and the kind of sources the respective authors used. I will also focus on how the authors evaluated Šćepan's character and significance, as well as their potential interests and agendas behind their opinions.

---

5   Njegoš 1851: i.

Šćepan Mali on Page

The first edition dedicated solely to Šćepan appeared eleven years after his death, written by Stefan Zanović from Budva. Zanović grew up in Venice, but he spent his teenage years corresponding with Šćepan's appearance, in his hometown close to where Šćepan first appeared. Later, Zanović traveled across Europe, living an adventurous life and maintaining contact with relevant Montenegrin political figures of the time. He published poems and letters on the way, decorated himself with invented titles and even altered his identity, calling himself Šćepan Hanibal Zanović, Prince of Albania and Lord of Montenegro. After being imprisoned for fraudulent deeds, he committed suicide in 1786 (cf. Djurović 2010 [1978]: 168).

In 1784, Zanović published his book about Šćepan Mali (2010 [1784]). This publication was as mysterious as Šćepan's life. The place of publication was unclear, it was allegedly already the fifth edition of the book and, finally, he tried to remain anonymous by not signing himself as the author.[6] Zanović wrote his book in French and through a (pseudo) historical biographical narrative he described Šćepan as a bold, venturous, energetic but malicious character who was prepared to go to any lengths in order to gain power (cf. ibid: 23, 27). According to Zanović, Šćepan went to Montenegro believing that the people living there were naive. Once he was there, Zanović continues, he managed to impose himself as the leader despite the vanity of the local chiefs, and he harshly punished even the smallest offense. He won battles against the Ottomans and started planning conquest expeditions throughout the Balkans. Šćepan was undoubtedly an impostor, Zanović argues, who was prepared to manipulate the people in order to satisfy his desire to rule. Furthermore, according to Zanović, his economic endeavors remained modest, although he was extravagant in his promises. Zanović explains Šćepan's success by arguing that ordinary people tend to believe in miracles and the more miraculous or mysterious something is, the more likely it is to gain credulity.

In 1828, Karl Herloßsohn (1804-1849) published his version of the story. Herloßsohn was born in Prague, studied in Prague and Vienna and became a journalist, an editor of literary journals and an author. In 1825 he settled in Leipzig, where

---

6   The full title of Zanović's work is: *Stiepan-Mali c'est-a-dire Etienne-Petit ou Stefano-Piccolo le pseudo Pierre III. empereur de Russie, qui parut dans le grand-duché de Montenegro, situe entre la mer Egee, l'Albanie Turque & le golfe Adriatique: en 1767, 1768 & 1769.* Zanović claimed that the book was published in India, although London or Paris are more probable places of publication (Djurović 2010 [1978]: 149; Petrović 2010 [1992]: 248).

he published his novel, titled *Der Montenegrinerhäuptling*. The novel saw a second edition in 1853, and was translated into Czech the same year (cf. Djurović 1955: 654-655). For Herloßsohn (1828), Šćepan's identity was not an issue, as he imagined him as the Venetian officer Stefano Piccolo, who left for Montenegro in order to follow his ambition to become an emperor. After gaining the trust of the Montenegrins, he revealed himself as Peter III of Russia and claimed leadership. However, complications arose, and people appeared who could have revealed his true identity. Herloßsohn then introduced a twist in the plot. Realizing that he would never become an emperor in Russia, and not satisfied with his position among Montenegrins (he only felt like first among the chiefs), Šćepan decided to surrender Montenegro to the Ottomans and try to become a mighty ruler with Ottoman help. His scheme was revealed, and he was beheaded.

Both Zanović and Herloßsohn imagine Šćepan Mali as a romantic hero, motivated by his passion and will. In their works, Šćepan's story revolves around notions of ambition and genius, and he feels like an angel and devil at the same time, having an urge to face his destiny, whatever the consequences might be. Following Isaiah Berlin's (1999) interpretation of the romantic movement of the late 18th and first half of the 19th century, Šćepan's tragedy in these works derives from being true to himself, which is one of the main characteristics of a romantic hero in the literature of the time. In both of these works Šćepan is evaluated based on his boldness and not on his contributions (or lack of them) to Montenegrin society, nor is it based on the fact that he deceived his hosts.

Zanović provides a number of details in his biography of Šćepan, leaving an impression that he was well informed, although he also provides exaggerations and false information. It is possible that he met Šćepan in person at some point in Budva, or was informed by people who remembered Šćepan (cf. Petrović 2010 [1992]: 251-252; cf. Miljić 2010: 15; cf. Djurović 2010 [1978]: 155). Apart from that, Zanović could have learned about Šćepan from contemporary reports and writings as well, as Djurović pointed out (cf. ibid: 158-159). Zanović wanted his readers to believe him, and perhaps even to think that he himself was Šćepan Mali.[7] Herloßsohn, on the other hand, clearly aimed to produce a fictional novel narrative. He learned about Šćepan Mali from his friend and associate Sima Milutinović Sarajlija, who lived in Leipzig from 1825 to 1826. He probably read Zanović, as well as contemporary travel-logs which he used when describing

---

7 Zanović was inspired by Šćepan's appearance so much that, in 1776, he wrote a letter to Frederick II of Prussia in which he claimed to be Šćepan Mali, arguing that he was mistaken to be dead (Djurović 2010 [1978]: 157). The translation of the letter can be found in a 2014 publication *Paštrovski almanah* (Zanović 2014 [1776]: 222).

Montenegro (Djurović 1955: 654-657; Djurović 2010 [1978]: 162), all of which served as a starting point for his romantic novel to which he added newly invented characters and developments of the story.

Sima Milutinović Sarajlija, Herloßsohn's associate from Leipzig, was born in Sarajevo (Bosnia, Ottoman Empire) in 1791. Like Zanović, he led an adventurous life, traveling a lot and writing, mostly poems. In the early 19th century, he joined the First Serbian Uprising (1804-1813) against the Ottoman Empire, after which he spent some time in Bulgaria, Russia and in an Ottoman prison. In 1825, he moved to Leipzig where he enrolled at the university. However, during the next year he left for Montenegro, where he became the secretary to the ruling Prince-Bishop and tutor to his nephew and successor, Petar II Petrović Njegoš. Later, he continued traveling and worked with relevant political figures in Serbia and Montenegro of the time, until his death in 1847. In 1835 he published his *Istorija Crne Gore od iskona do novijeg vremena* ('History of Montenegro from the Beginning Until Recent Times') in which he dedicated a number of pages to Šćepan, delineating how he came to power using lies. Even though in Sarajlija's time, as he informs us, the people of Montenegro remembered Šćepan's period as the age of peace and stability, Sarajlija considered Šćepan as neither a strong nor capable leader, but rather a frivolous and childish character, adding that he was a liar and possessed no greatness of spirit or laudable personal qualities (cf. Sarajlija 2009 [1835]: 133, 136).

Sarajlija's contemporary, Vuk Stefanović Karadžić (1787-1864), also wrote a story of Šćepan. Karadžić was a philologist and linguist, who collected songs, fairy tales, and riddles across the Balkans, and introduced major reforms in Serbian language. He also published the first dictionary of the Serbian language and translated the New Testament into the reformed language. In 1834 and 1835 Karadžić visited Montenegro and collected material for his book entitled *Montenegro und die Montenegriner: ein Beitrag zur Kenntniss der europäischen Türkei und des serbischen Volkes*, published in Stuttgart in 1837. Giving an overview of Montenegrin history, Karadžić (1969 [1837]) dedicated several pages to the appearance of Šćepan Mali. According to Karadžić, once the rumor about the tsar being present started spreading, it was difficult to stop it because more and more people started believing in it. Montenegrins obeyed Šćepan in everything and, as Karadžić reports, people remembered his punishments for plunder and stealing. Nevertheless, Karadžić noticed that people had little to say about his role in the war against the Ottomans, although the war started because of him, which significantly damaged his reputation (cf. ibid: 29-30).

Sarajlija and Karadžić present us with similar narratives, embedding their versions of the story about Šćepan in broader historical overviews. Furthermore, the content of their versions is fairly similar. Both of their works are supported by living witnesses they met in Montenegro.[8] Nonetheless, it is also very likely that they draw on Zanović's work as well, as they reference some details from his work. They thus perpetuate common details and ideas of Šćepan's story (e.g. of his time as orderly), but they also put forward essentially negative evaluations of his character, designating him as weak, fraudulent and profiting from the naivety of his hosts (cf. ibid: 26).

A lot has been written about Petar II Petrović Njegoš (1813-1851), Montenegrin ruler and Prince-Bishop, Sarajlija's student and the most notable Montenegrin author of the 19th century. Continuing the work of his predecessor and uncle Petar I Petrović Njegoš, he worked towards further uniting Montenegro's tribes and establishing a centralized system of governance. His play, entitled *Lažni car Šćepan Mali* ('Fake Tsar Šćepan Mali', published in 1851) was, however, overshadowed by his other works, with literary criticism sometimes paying no attention to it at all (cf. Deretić 2007: 179). The play itself was first staged in 1969 in the Montenegrin national theater. Njegoš (1851) saw Šćepan as a negative character, liar, vagabond, populist, and coward. Furthermore, he did not give his character as much space as one would expect the main character of a play to have. Šćepan does not even appear in the largest part of the play, and when he does, he often plays a marginal role (cf. Deretić 2007: 174-175). In the introduction, Njegoš points to the comic aspect of the story by wondering how Šćepan managed to confuse the minds of his contemporaries. Nevertheless, in this play, Šćepan also managed to establish order among Montenegrins. The central moral of Njegoš's work revolves around the idea of the unity among Montenegrins, with political legitimacy coming from the people and serving the common good. This play can be approached as a political drama, dealing with topics such as heroism, obsession with power (which is the comic aspect of the play) and the relation between 'us' and the 'foreign world' as a broader context for the plot line. Šćepan's only contribution in this account was giving Montenegrins the opportunity to decide on their own, as a united political entity (cf. ibid: 175-177). Even though Njegoš presents his historical-dramaturgic work as the result of historical research, stating in the introduction that he wrote the play based on stories passed on by word of mouth and documents from the Venetian archives (cf. Njegoš 1851: i), his aim was not to

---

8 Even though Sarajlija informed Herloßsohn, his work's content is significantly different. This is to a large extent due to Herloßsohn's romantic imagination, but it also seems that Sarajlija got more versed about the past events after going to Montenegro (Djurović 1955: 656-657), which is complemented by him quoting historical documents in his work.

produce a historical narrative, but a poetic one. Šćepan, as presented in Njegoš's play, is the expression of the people's desire for unity, causing them to initiate social and political changes. (cf. Radojević, 1974: 44).

Unlike Njegoš, Stjepan Mitrov Ljubiša (1824-1878) produced a less poetic and more systematic narrative in the form of a biography, entitled *Šćepan Mali kako narod o njemu povijeda* ('Šćepan Mali according to folktales'), first published in 1868 and reprinted in 1875. Ljubiša was born in Budva, was politically active within the Austrian Empire, and assumed different offices in the Dalmatian and Montenegrin littoral. He started writing short stories relatively late in his lifetime, the story about Šćepan Mali being his first. Ljubiša (1924 [1868]) divides his story into four parts: 1. Šćepan the medic and healer, 2. Šćepan the Tsar, 3. War and battles, and 4. the Death of Šćepan. Ljubiša also writes based on stories he learned from older generations. He uses written material as well – for example, Šćepan's letters and Njegoš's work (cf. Ivanović, 2016: 287) – and distinguishes between reliable and unreliable stories (cf. Ivanović 2013: 216). His version of the story follows the previous interpretations, yet tends to be more balanced when it comes to evaluation. He carefully measures the good and the bad and avoids quick judgment. His Šćepan is a vagabond medic who takes advantage of the gullible Montenegrin people. He is also smart, kind-hearted, peaceful, humble, and fair. Šćepan brings unity to the people and is neither greedy nor a scrooge. Nevertheless, Ljubiša asks us to bear in mind that Šćepan manipulated the Montenegrin people despite this set of positive traits (cf. Ljubiša 1924 [1868]: 77).

Njegoš and Ljubiša expressed their visions of Šćepan through different formats and gave different perspectives. Nevertheless, they both agree that much can be learned from Šćepan's presence. They argue that he was not an ideal ruler, that he had numerous character flaws, that he did, in fact, lie to the people of Montenegro and took advantage of their naivety and need for a leader. Njegoš might even have had personal reasons to discredit Šćepan, as the tsar impersonator was an interruption in the line of prince-bishops, a line to which Njegoš himself belonged (cf. Nikčević 2011: 185). However, in his eyes, Šćepan's appearance proved that Montenegrin people (present in his play as a chorus) can unite, fight for freedom (from the Ottomans), and become the source of legitimacy for the ruler (cf. Nikčević 2014: 134-137). Ljubiša went even further and argued that Montenegro would have been a better place if only Šćepan had been able to invest more time and effort. It is true that Montenegro suffered a lot during his reign due to the conflicts with the Ottoman Empire and Venice, but, as Ljubiša concluded, suffering cannot be avoided on the path to progress (cf. Ljubiša 1924 [1868]: 110).

Šćepan Mali on Screen

Starting from the late 19th century, after the publication of Ljubiša's story, the memory of Šćepan Mali enters a "floating gap" – the point beyond which living memory no longer influences collective memory construction, thus ultimately separating the communicative from the cultural form of collective memory (Assmann 2008: 112-113). In the 20th century, the interpretations of the story no longer relied on oral traditions to any extent, but were exclusively based on written material and historical research. One of the most significant receptions of Šćepan is the above mentioned research by Gligor Stanojević dated 1957 that, despite being several decades old, still has great value and is indispensable when approaching the topic. Ten years later, Njegoš' play was staged for the first time (1969). Finally, after the Second World War, the story of Šćepan Mali was made into two films as well. Both films complement the 19th-century interpretations by borrowing from, combining, and adding to previous stories, but also relying on scholarly work, for example by Ratko Djurović (1914 -1998), Montenegrin and Yugoslav screenwriter.

The first film, *Lažni car* ('The Fake Tsar') was made in 1955. It was also the first feature film in Montenegro (cf. Kastratović 1999: 166) and Ratko Djurović and Velimir Stojanović worked on it as the scriptwriter and director. In the film, Šćepan appears as a new, kind-hearted medic in the region. Some members of the Montenegrin elite, who are convinced that he is the tsar in hiding, soon approach him. At first, he rejects their claim, but after some insistence, he exhorts them to end the internal struggles among Montenegrins and to unite against external enemies. If they manage to do that, he will reveal his true identity. Subsequently, Šćepan's supporters present the Montenegrin people with a choice between Šćepan as a ruler, or further chaos under the rule of the prince-bishop. Overwhelmed by these events, Šćepan tries to escape and admits his momentary enthusiasm about playing the role assigned to him to a Montenegrin duke. The duke admits that he is not taken in by the fake identity but also declares that the people need a ruler. Therefore, Šćepan decides to stay. He is popular among the people, he coordinates the building of roads, fortresses, bridges, introduces courts of justice, punishes crime and vendettas, and does not accept bribes. The Venetians hire a spy to poison him, while the Ottomans prepare for war. Šćepan is insecure about the coming war but, encouraged by other Montenegrins, he leads the army to battle and, eventually, victory. In the final scenes of the film, the Russian mission of Dolgorukov arrives in Montenegro, asking the Montenegrins to drive Šćepan Mali away as an impostor. Šćepan admits to the people that he is not a tsar, but an ordinary man and he surrenders to Dolgorukov in order to prevent further escalations. The Montenegrins wish to keep him as their leader nevertheless. Dolgorukov accedes to their claims and Šćepan is relieved as he no longer has to live a lie. At that point, an Ottoman spy ends Šćepan's life.

Ratko Djurović dealt with the same topic again in 1979, preparing the script for the *Čovjek koga treba ubiti* ('The Man to Destroy'), together with Bruno di Djeronimo and Veljko Bulajić.[9] The film offers a different take on the story, which is now set in a world divided between the forces of hell and church (interestingly enough, not heaven). Struggling for dominance, both sides manipulate people on earth by military force, plots, corruption, spies, and the police force. With the murder of the Russian Tsar Peter III (supported by hell) at the hand of Dolgorukov and Catherine II (both supported by the church), the power balance is disturbed. Consequently, the devil devises an action regarding a seemingly unimportant area of Montenegro, because Peter III was famous there. The devil will send a demon, Peter's double, whose mission is to establish himself as tsar in Montenegro, so the world would think that Peter is alive. Hell will then be able to return him to Russia and restore the balance. The devil then decides that Šćepan will be the demon's name.

Then Farfa is introduced, a low ranking demon and the tsar's double. He is a fearful demon, reluctant to go, but he has to follow the orders. As he leaves hell and enters Montenegro, he starts undermining the authority of the prince-bishop (who is an agent of the church). After settling a quarrel among Montenegrins, he publicly criticizes the church for causing internal conflicts and accumulating treasures. As the rumor that he is the tsar has already spread, the people welcome him. The church reacts quickly – Dolgorukov arrives in order to kill him. However, Farfa manages to beat him with his demonic powers.

Soon, Farfa is informed that his mission is suddenly over but he does not want to abandon the Montenegrins. He feels that he has changed and he cares about the local people. For that, he pays the price – he is stripped of his demonic powers and becomes mortal. Nevertheless, he is crowned as Šćepan Mali, Tsar in Montenegro. He calls himself a servant of the people, announces that the wealth of the church

---

9   Bulajić, also the director of the film, was the most exciting name behind this venture. His early films dealt with topics of challenges people met in the new socialist Yugoslav state. However, he later moved on to directing expensive and popular epic war films about the struggles of Yugoslav partisans during the Second World War (Goulding 2004: 59-60; 81). After establishing himself as a prominent director, usually designated as a contributor to the cult of Josip Broz Tito (Šakić 2009: 14), his *Čovjek koga treba ubiti* represented a strange episode in his career.

will be used for building schools and roads and that the people of Montenegro are free to act as an independent entity. He is offered a bribe from hell, which he refuses, as he wishes to live as a free man with his free will. At this point, the devil loses his patience and, afraid that other people in the world could follow his example, sends two demons to settle the issue. The two find Šćepan asleep in his bed with his earthly lover Elfa and successfully persuade her father to kill him.

Lažni car attempts to reconstruct the past events and tells a story about order, integrity, and sovereignty. These values were especially relevant in the time of tensions between Yugoslavia and the Soviet Union in the late 1940s and early 1950s (cf. Papović 2014: 229). *Čovjek koga treba ubiti*, however, takes an awkward turn, importing fantasy into the story. Nevertheless, its fantastic setting acts as a political allegory (cf. Ognjanović 2007: 70). The film alludes to the contemporary Cold War geopolitical situation in which Yugoslavia claims a non-aligned position between the two power blocks. Šćepan's Montenegro is a metaphor for the socialist Yugoslavia (and Šćepan becomes a representation of Josip Broz Tito, the leader of the socialist Yugoslavia) and offers a dark political message about the difficulties of being independent in a divided world – Šćepan cannot escape either from church or the demonic agents. He fails in his personal mission to be neutral and act according to his own free will (cf. Radak 2015: 50, 62-63), as both power blocks wish to present the world division as a necessity (cf. Šakić 2013: 209).

Both films develop the idea that Šćepan Mali is a positive character, despite him being a fraud. *Lažni car* is explicit with such characterization because Montenegrins become aware of his fraudulent character, while he never reveals his demonic origin in *Čovjek koga treba ubiti*. Both films grant Šćepan the role of a beloved ruler, misunderstood idealist, and initiator of progress and modernization (cf. ibid: 198). The films, for the first time, give an insight into Šćepan's inner struggle, his indecisiveness and his feeling of guilt (in *Lažni car*) or his identity crisis and transformation (in *Čovjek koga treba ubiti*). Basing the plotline on the 19th-century literature and repeating the common knowledge of the story (such as Šćepan uniting the people and installing order), these two films complement the memory of Šćepan by imagining his own perspective, turning him, and not the 'naïve' Montenegrin people, into a victim.

"I DIED, SO I COULD STAY..."[10]
THE MEMORY OF ŠĆEPAN MALI AND ITS FUNCTIONS

Until the 20th century, the reception of Šćepan Mali was based on a combination of oral and written sources. Furthermore, connections between the authors and how these interpretations informed one another can be established as well, both through personal contacts of the authors and by them using each other's works as source of (supposedly historic) facts or inspiration. This allowed the more recent (fictional) works to both share the same plotline and to introduce variations. Therefore, in the 20th century, when there were no more living witnesses (or people listening to their stories), a corpus of written literature establishing Šćepan as a relevant memory figure was rich and readily available. The overview of pertinent interpretations until the 20th century shows the progress of memory constructions about Šćepan from communicative to cultural within three generations, or about 80 to 100 years, as outlined by Jan Assmann (cf. 2008: 112-113; 117). With systematic historiographic research, two films, and the staging of Njegoš's play, Šćepan transforms fully into a figure of cultural memory, transmitted by specialists related to institutions of knowledge and culture (academy, film industry, theater). It should, however, be borne in mind that Šćepan was present in cultural memory even before the 20th century. Specialists participated in the shaping of his remembrance from the very onset of the memory construction about him. This co-existence of communicative and cultural memory, most evident in the coexistence of oral and written sources, does not come as a surprise. The same event can, in a given historical context, become an object of both aspects of collective memory, and it is more of a rule in modern societies, rather than an exception (cf. Erll 2011: 31).

The corpus shaping the collective memory of the fake tsar started with works written and published outside Montenegro (in French and German). Nevertheless, the cultural and political elites operating in Montenegro played a significant role in establishing Šćepan as a memory figure in Montenegrin history. Through the interplay of communicative and cultural aspects of memory, different receptions of his character and historical role, sometimes colored by personal interests, accumulated over time. He started as an ideal of a romantic hero in Zanović's and Herloßsohn's work – as a character whose virtues were derived from him being true to himself in his pursuit for power and satisfying his desire to rule. He was then incorporated in the historical overviews of two of the region's significant authors of the 19th century – Sarajlija and Karadžić. They considered him as an

---

10 Kovač 2002: 51.

intriguing episode of Montenegrin history and mediated the idea of his orderly reign, but did not fail to point out that he was (and is) not worthy of admiration due to his negative character traits. This is especially true for Sarajlija. It is possible that his negative evaluation of Šćepan was partially due to his close ties to the prince-bishops of Montenegro. Zanović, too, already had personal interest behind his version of Šćepan's story. Prince-Bishop Petar II Petrović Njegoš had even more reasons to emphasize Šćepan's fraudulent and cowardly character. Nevertheless, Njegoš gave a strong impulse to the further development of how Šćepan was remembered. In his work, the fake tsar was utilized beyond discussing an intriguing historical episode and became a point of reflection about the need for Montenegrin unity. This line of representation was further developed by Ljubiša, who used positive attributes when describing Šćepan and argued that he was crucial for the unity of Montenegrins in his time.

The use of Šćepan's remembrance for reflecting about the contemporary situation, as well as the shift towards positive framing of his character, both culminated in the two films, as they discussed the ideals and problems of Yugoslav sovereignty in the Cold War world. Šćepan was idealized on the screen and, more than ever before, served as a memory figure offering an alternative to internal chaos and corruption, to traditional types of legitimacy, or even to international divisions. In the films, there is no doubt whether Šćepan's rule was beneficial or not. He became the true protagonist of the story (perfect ruler and reformer), bringing a temporary golden age of modernization or a promised land in between the two worlds (blocks of power). This transformation towards an ideal ruler is the most apparent in Šćepan's relationship with the people. Previous receptions, before the films, regarded the naivety of the Montenegrin people as an important reason for Šćepan's success. In the films, however, the key for Šćepan's success is in his actions and good intentions (and supernatural powers). Unlike in the memory of Šćepan during the 19th century, his relation to the people is not problematic in the films, to the extent that he is greeted as an equal to the people (in *Čovjek koga treba ubiti*), who do not care whether he is a fraud or not (in *Lažni car*).

As the result of this long memory construction process, Šćepan Mali is present today in the collective memory of Montenegro (and surrounding countries) as a formative figure of an extraordinary historical episode, as an interruption, and even disturbance in the flow of Montenegrin history (even though, as Stanojević showed in his study, his reign did not have significant long-term effects). The multifaceted reception and representation of Šćepan Mali turned him into an ambivalent memory figure – both a fraud and an ideal ruler. Recently, however, one question that remained unresolved throughout the long memory construction process, came into the focus of new publications: what was Šćepan's true identity? In the early 2000s, two books were published, independently offering the same answer to this question. Both Dušan Martinović (2002) and Rastislav Petrović (2001) argued that the real name of Šćepan Mali was Jovan Stefanović Baljević. Baljević was the first Montenegrin to defend a doctoral dissertation, in 1752 in Halle, after which he spent some years working in Hungary (among other things, forging passports) and then as an officer in Russia. He died in 1769. These new studies, however, suggest that he actually disappeared some years earlier and traveled to Montenegro.[11]

Simultaneously, Šćepan continues to inspire literary production. Also in the early 2000s, another literary take on his memory appeared, in the form of a play by the acknowledged author Mirko Kovač, entitled *Lažni car Šćepan Mali koji je vladao Crnom Gorom od 1766-1773* ('The Fake Tsar Šćepan Mali who Ruled Over Montenegro from 1766 to 1773,' published in 2002). The first, and perhaps the most important character that we see in the play is not Šćepan, but a messenger who breaks the fourth wall and greets the audience. He announces the show, presents himself as an omniscient character that will linger on, for the purpose of providing guidance and necessary comments, in order to make sure that the show is carried out properly and any potential loose ends in the story are tied up (ibid: 3). In the play, Šćepan is found and supported by members of the elite who wish to use him as a puppet ruler so they would become rich. However, Šćepan does not comply. He starts introducing order, but is eventually disappointed, complaining that all his efforts have no real effect in that country. Meanwhile, the messenger carefully observes the development of the show and, by chance, gets involved as an active character and he delivers a gift to the tsar in the form of a golden chair. He explains to the tsar the context of relevant historical events. Finally, when no one knows how to proceed, he finds a witness to confirm that Šćepan is, in fact, Peter III, even though it is clear that he is not.[12]

Kovač's play acts as a social comment on the responsibility of people for the stories they tell and believe in. One can argue that the messenger represents us today, feeding the story of the fake emperor with acknowledgment and evidence.

---

11 Recently, another publication, written by Bogdan Sekulić (2016), emerged, offering further evidence to support this claim.

12 "What is my role here?" asks the witness. "You need to confirm," the messenger guides him, "in front of this honorable Council, or Senate, that Tsar Šćepan Mali is something like an incarnation of the dead Russian Tsar Peter III. Montenegrins believe that he resurrected here, if he died at all" (Kovač 2002: 20).

Informed by the accumulated functions over time, the memory of the fake tsar acts as a riddle, a mystery to be solved, meaning to be found, or truth to be revealed. The memory of Šćepan resides within the ambiguous space between fact and fiction, being approached by authors who either aim to deal with facts or to produce fiction. Only one thing is certain – the mystery is never fully resolved. Not even a detailed research of archival material and less well-known sources can clarify everything (cf. Ivanović, 2013: 196). Even if we fully agree with the suggestion that Šćepan Mali was the well-educated adventurer Jovan Stefanović Baljević, the story is still covered with a veil of confusion – for example, if he was Baljević, why did he choose Montenegro for his adventure? (cf. Lakić 2004: 135) All this enables Šćepan's memory to act as a field of possibilities for imaginative, social, and even political engagement, complementing the fact that, even today, we do not know for sure who he was or what his motives were. In Kovač's play, after Šćepan's character utters his last words "I died, so I could stay," the messenger reappears and makes sure he is dead. He then addresses the audience once again, saying that nothing changes as the centuries go by and the empires come and go. Fake emperors, however, last forever. Then, while leaving the stage, he notices that Šćepan's body is gone and wonders whether he was resurrected again (cf. Kovač 2002: 51).

WORKS CITED

Assmann, Jan (1995 [1988]): "Collective Memory and Cultural Identity." In: New German Critique 65, pp. 125-133.

Assmann, Jan (2008): "Communicative and Cultural Memory." In: Astrid Erll/Ansgar Nünning (eds.), Media and Cultural Memory, Berlin: de Gruyter, pp. 109-119.

Berlin, Isaiah (1999): The Roots of Romanticism, Princeton: Princeton University Press.

Deretić, Jovan (2007): "'Šćepan Mali' kao politička drama." In: Milo Lompar (ed.), Ogledalo o srpskoj književnosti, Beograd: Čigoja štampa, pp. 173-181.

Djurović, Ratko (1955): "Herloszonov roman o Šćepanu Malom." In: Stvaranje 9/11-12, pp. 653-676.

Djurović, Ratko (2010 [1978]): "Stjepan Zanović i njegov 'Šćepan Mali' (1784)." In: Dragan Kujović, Marijan Miljić (eds.), Šćepan Mali, Podgorica: Grafo Crna Gora, pp. 149-168.

Erll, Astrid (2011): Memory in Culture, Basingstoke: Palgrave Macmillan.

Goulding, Daniel (2004). Jugoslovensko filmsko iskustvo 1945-2001 – oslobodjeni film, Zagreb: V.B.Z.
Herloßsohn, Karl (1828): Der Montenegrinerhäuptling, Leipzig: Wienbrack.
Ivanović, Radomir (2013): "Književni mit o Šćepanu Malom u djelima Stjepana Zanovića, Petra Drugog Petrovića Njegoša i Stefana Mitrova Ljubiše." In: Riječ – časopis za nauku o jeziku i književnosti 10, pp. 191-219.
Ivanović, Radomir (2016): "Reprezentativna monografska istraživanja Njegoševog i Ljubišinog djela u XIX i XX vijeku." In: Godišnjak Fakulteta za kulturu i medije 8, pp. 279-297.
Karadžić, Vuk Stefanović (1969 [1837]): Crna Gora i Boka Kotorska, Beograd: Nolit.
Kastratović, Gojko (1999): Crnogorska kinematografija i filmovi o Crnoj Gori, Podgorica: Pobjeda.
Kovač, Mirko (2002): Lažni car Šćepan Mali koji je vladao Crnom Gorom od 1766-1773 godine – istoričesko zbitije osamnajestog vijeka, Podgorica: Crnogorski književni list.
Lakić (2004): "Ko je zapravo lažni car Šćepan Mali." In: Glasnik odjeljenja društvenih nauka CANU, 16, pp. 135-136.
Ljubiša, Stjepan Mitrov (1924 [1868]): Šćepan Mali – pripovijest crnogorska sredinom osamnaestoga vijeka. In: Stjepan Mitrov Ljubiša (ed.), Pripovijesti crnogorske i primorske, Beograd: Narodna misao, pp. 76-110.
Longworth, Philip (1975): "The Pretender Phenomenon in Eighteenth-Century Russia." In: Past & Present, 66, pp. 61-83.
Martinović, Dušan (2002): Dr. Jovan Stefanović Baljević (ili Šćepan Mali), Podgorica: Društvo za očuvanje crnogorske kulturne baštine.
Miljić, Marijan (2010): "Uvodno slovo." In: Dragan Kujović, Marijan Miljić (eds.), Šćepan Mali, Podgorica: Grafo Crna Gora, pp. 13-17.
Nikčević, Milorad (2011): Njegoš i Ljubiša – uticaji i paralele, Podgorica: Institut za crnogorski jezik i književnost.
Nikčević, Sanja (2014): "Lažni car Šćepan Mali kao afirmativni romantičarski spjev." In: Milorad Nikčević (ed.), Recepcija i novo čitanje Njegoševa djela, Zagreb and Cetinje: Društvo hrvatskih književnika, Fakultet za crnogorski jezik i književnost, pp. 129-151.
Njegoš, Petar Petrović (1851): Lažni car Šćepan Mali – istoričesko zbitije osamnajestoga vijeka, Trst: Andrija Stojković.
Neumann, Birgit (2008): "The Literary Representation of Memory." In: Astrid Erll/Ansgar Nünning (eds.), Cultural Memory Studies: An International and Interdisciplinary Handbook, Berlin: de Gruyter, pp. 333-345.

Ognjanović, Dejan (2007): U brdima, horori – srpski film strave, Niš: Niški kulturni centar.
Papović, Dragutin (2014): "Utjecaj politike na crnogorski igrani film u XX stoljeću." In: Časopis za suvremenu povijest, 46/2, pp. 223-242.
Petrovich, Michael Boro (1955): "Catherine II and a False Peter III in Montenegro." In: The American Slavic and East European Review, 14/2, pp. 169-194.
Petrović, Rastislav (2001): Šćepan Mali – zagonetka je rešena, Belgrade: Stručna kniga.
Petrović, Rastislav (2010 [1992]): "Prva knjiga o Šćepanu Malom." In: Dragan Kujović, Marijan Miljić (eds.), Šćepan Mali, Podgorica: Grafo Crna Gora, pp. 248-257.
Radak, Sanja Lazarević (2015): "Pokretne slike užasa: društveni aspekti jugoslovenskog horor žanra (1973-1990)." In: Antropologija, 15/3, pp. 47-68.
Radojević Danilo (1974): "Etički problemi u Njegoševom Lažnom caru Šćepanu Malom." In: Danilo Radojević (ed.), Studije o Njegošu, Belgrade: Petar Kočić, pp. 25-44.
Sekulić, Bogdan (2016): Identitet Šćepana Malog gospodara zemlje crnogorske, Podgorica: CID.
Sarajlija, Sima Milutinović (2009 [1835]): Istorija Crne Gore – Dika crnogorska, Bačka Palanka: Društvo za nauku i stvaralaštvo Logos.
Stanojević, Gligor (1957): Šćepan Mali, Belgrade: Serbian Academy of Science.
Šakić, Tomislav (2009): "Filmski svijet Veljka Balajića: poprište susreta kolektivnog i privatnog." In: Film i ideologija, 57 and 58, pp. 14-26.
Šakić, Tomislav (2013): "Dvije filmske interpretacije legende o Šćepanu Malom." In: Sava Anđelković, Paul-Louis Thomas (eds.), Njegoš u ogledalima vjekova: zbornik radova sa međunarodnog naučnog skupa 'Njegoš, prince-évêque et poète – de la montagne au cosmos.' Cetinje and Paris: Fakultet dramskih umjetnosti Cetinje, Université Paris-Sorbonne, GEST – časopis za pozorište, izvedbene umjetnosti i kulturu, pp. 197-212.
"Tuga", March 13, 2017, accessed September 20, 2019 (https://www.danas.rs/dijalog/licni-stavovi/tuga/).
Zanović, Stefan (2010 [1784]): "Šćepan Mali to jest Etienne Petit ili Stefano Piccolo lažni Petar III ruski car, koji se pojavi u Velikoj Knjaževini Crnoj Gori, smještenoj između Egejskog mora, Turske Albanije i Jadranskog mora 1767, 1768 i 1769." In: Dragan Kujović, Marijan Miljić (eds.), Šćepan Mali, Podgorica: Grafo Crna Gora, pp: 21-55.
Zanović, Stefan (2014): "Ja sam Šćepan Mali." In: Miroslav Luketić, Marko Kentera (eds.), Paštrovski almanah I, Sveti Stefan/Petrovac: Kentera, Luketić p. 222.

Films and Television

Lažni car (*The Fake Emperor*). Directed by Velimir Stojanović. 1955. Lovcen Film.
Čovjek koga treba ubiti (*The Man to Destroy*). Directed by Veljko Bulajić. 1979. Croatia Film/Filmski Studio Titograd/Jadran Film.

Long May He (Not) Reign? Literary Depictions of a 'Meddling' Future Monarch
Prince Charles in Mike Bartlett's Play *King Charles III* (2014) and in Catherine Mayer's Biography *Charles: The Heart of a King* (2015)

Marie-Theres Stickel

RAPPROCHEMENT TO THE CONTROVERSIAL CHARLES, PRINCE OF WALES

> "I won't be able to do the same things I've done as heir, so, of course, you operate within the constitutional parameters. […] I'm not that stupid. I do realise that it is a separate exercise being sovereign."
> *Prince, Son and Heir*: 56:48-57:17

With this statement Prince Charles, heir to the British throne, took a stand when asked about his future as a potential 'meddling king' in an interview for the BBC television documentary *Prince, Son and Heir: Charles at 70* (2018). The activist stance taken by the future monarch Prince Charles has spurred a general – and particularly controversial – debate about the British monarch's constitutional duties and the convention of his or her political neutrality. However, at the age of 70, Prince Charles continues to be outspoken about issues such as climate change, sustainability, and organic agriculture – despite his increasing involvement in monarchical duties. In 2018, Prince Charles assumed responsibility for some of the queen's overseas travel duties which revealed a certain transition within the British monarchy. Especially his trip to Australia including the opening of the Commonwealth Games seemed to aim at establishing Prince Charles more firmly in his role as future monarch. Moreover, his confirmation as the next Head of Commonwealth constituted a major milestone in determining the course of the British monarchy adumbrating a future kingship under Charles III.[1]

The year 2018 was, furthermore, marked by three major favorable reportages in magazines in which Charles underpinned his role as a long-time advocate for environmental concerns and philanthropic charities. In a written interview with the *Australian Financial Review*, the heir outlines his thoughts on sustainability in the fashion industry. He presents himself as someone who "couldn't be more delighted if, at last, there is a growing awareness of the urgent need to get away from the 'throwaway society' and to move towards a more 'circular' type of economy." (Prince Charles, qtd. in Hume 2018: n. pag.) In the article, the prince pursues his long time aim of emphasizing the importance of sustainability and states: "I happen to mind deeply about the poisoned legacy we are leaving our children and grandchildren and have been attempting to invest in their futures through reminding people of the urgent need to work in harmony with nature, rather than against her." (ibid)

In September 2018 Prince Charles featured in the cover story of the British men's lifestyle magazine *Gentlemen's Quarterly* (*GQ*) that presented his continuing engagement for charitable organizations – such as for his own 'Prince's Trust.' The article highlights the "fusillade of opinions" (Jones 2018: n. pag.) that Charles still expresses as heir and notes: "When he is king, he won't be able to do things in the same way. This is also one of the reasons he has recently aggregated his charities" (ibid) – a work the British *GQ* acknowledged by awarding Prince Charles the 'Editor's Lifetime Achievement Award For Services To Philanthropy' at the *GQ Men Of The Year Awards 2018*. Thirdly, in November 2018, Prince Charles guest edited the British magazine for rural lifestyle *Country Life*. In his lead article, the prince deals with threats to the British countryside such as the drive for efficiency and its concomitant environmental destruction and again formulates one of his central pleas:

---

1   It was Queen Elizabeth II herself who declared, during her opening speech of the Commonwealth Heads of Government Meeting in London in April 2018, that it was her "sincere wish" that the Prince of Wales would follow her in this non-hereditary position (Furness 2018: n. pag.).

"[We] may be the last generation fortunate enough to experience the wonderful people, skills and activities of our countryside. [...] I hope you might also reflect, as I do, on just how much the countryside and its people contribute to our national life, and what we can each do to help sustain them." (Prince Charles 2018: n. pag.)

These three magazine articles and contributions can be read as key examples of the heir apparent's activism. While they generally appear to regard the prince's 'meddling traits' favorably, some criticism was also to be found in 2018. Tom Bower's unauthorized biography *Rebel Prince* (2018) presents a highly negative portrait of the future king, which is immediately obvious in the preface: The heir is presented as a hypocritical activist longing for the social and medial recognition he once lost because of his marriage to Lady Diana Spencer and her death in 1997. It is stated that Charles's attempts to restore his reputation by leading debatable campaigns expired without success resulting in his growing unpopularity as heir apparent to the British throne:

"This book is the story of Prince Charles's battle for rehabilitation after Diana's death, and his refusal to obey the public expectations of a future king. [...] Few doubted the sincerity of his campaigns, but many feared that his provocative dissent made him unfit to be king. [...] The central question posed [...] is what kind of monarch will Charles make – given that he is the most unpopular heir for generations." (Bower 2018: xi-xiv)

These introductory examples reveal how controversially Prince Charles's personal involvement in public affairs is interpreted. As Queen Elizabeth II has reached an age which induces more and more speculation about the line of succession to the British throne, public debate frequently seems to revolve around possible future scenarios regarding the monarchy. Since Prince Charles is such a controversial figure, who does not always operate within the conventional and constitutional parameters pertaining to the sovereign, people have strong opinions about his possible succession to the throne. Therefore, it is not surprising that the topic is also picked up increasingly in literary and cultural productions. They often aim at demonstrating how Prince Charles's political and personal involvement may affect his kingship. In particular, the hypothetical questioning of how he will (not) handle his constitutional duties as monarch becomes a central approach in these works, as exemplified by Mike Bartlett's play *King Charles III* (2014; from here on cited as *KC*) or by Catherine Mayer's biography *Charles – The Heart of a King* (2015; from here on cited as *HK*). These two contemporary works are suitable to study possible future scenarios of the British monarchy, especially with regard to a possible future kingship of Prince Charles who takes center stage in both works.

By choosing two texts of different genres for the analysis, current tendencies of how Prince Charles is represented may be traced and compared. This article will examine how each of these works imagines the constantly overlapping dichotomy of 'the private' and 'the public' sphere in the future monarch's life. I argue that it is the long-established notion of the controversially 'meddling' Prince Charles, who tries to amalgamate his personal rights and views with his royal duties, which strongly influences current representations of the heir to the British throne.

Literary and cultural scholars are aware of the fact that "there is a 'real' Elizabeth Windsor and there has been a 'real' Henry Tudor" just as there is a 'real' Prince Charles, "but we can only approach them via texts, material practices, and discourses" (Pankratz 2017a: 17). Taking this idea further, and referring to Chaney who states that "media of mass communication [have] been essential for the dramatization and popularization of royal spectacle" (2001: 212), I argue that this also applies to literary and cultural productions. They become a force that makes it "impossible to maintain a façade of royalty as purely public figures […, thus overcoming] distinctions between public and private spheres for such figures" (ibid: 213). Therefore, the notion that a member of the royal family "is as a private person public and as a public person private"[2] (Peters/Jentz 1998: 25) is central to this article's argument. This configuration results from the hypothesis that 'being (a) royal' cannot be seen as an occupation, but that it is an ontological status in which there is no differentiation made between the private and the public sphere. Royal families do not only perform their representative duties, they are 'representations' in themselves, born into a structural position of public representation; to a certain extent, a prince's or sovereign's individuality is only expressed through his or her public persona (cf. ibid: 24). This duality pertains to members of the royal family like Prince Charles who is constantly exposed to public interest. Authors and playwrights are thus induced to fathom his 'private' personality and behavior in literary and cultural productions in print, on screen, and on stage.

In light of the presented framework, this article proceeds as follows: Taking a literary studies approach, I will examine *King Charles III* in a narrative- and text-based study of the play's dramatic text leaving aside aspects of performance, such as the stage directions, to ensure a comparative basis with regard to Mayer's biography. The analysis of the play will elaborate on the depiction of the monarchy's political functions and the constitutional position and duties required of a sovereign in connection with the imagined political involvement of a future monarch King Charles III. I will discuss how the play imagines Charles's public role to be

---

2   All translations from German are by the author. The original reads: "[…] ist als Privatperson öffentlich und als öffentliche Person privat."

influenced by his personal attitudes and values. The fictional Charles breaks with the traditional role of a constitutional monarch – a role that the 'real' Charles is expected to carry out in the near future. By staging how Charles exhausts the possibilities of actively taking advantage of the monarch's personal rights, I contend, this play depicts an almost dystopian vision for a future 'meddling' King Charles III.

The next section is devoted to an analysis of Prince Charles's portrayal in Catherine Mayer's biographic work entitled *Charles: The Heart of a King* (2015). I will investigate how Mayer depicts Prince Charles's controversial public role as an heir apparent and modernizer of the monarchy who openly expresses his personal views, thus redefining his royal role. The analysis will shed light on the question how Mayer's biography engages in a process of (positively) rebranding Prince Charles while focusing on his depiction as an heir who successfully applies strategies of soft power (cf. Nye 1990) to promote the monarchical cause in the 21st century. The conclusion will then consider the BBC production *Prince, Son and Heir: Charles at 70* (2018) and ask in what ways this television documentary – just as Bartlett's play and Mayer's biography – continues to negotiate in how far the heir tries to consolidate his personal rights with his royal duties.

CONSTITUTIONAL DUTIES AND PERSONAL RIGHTS OF A (FUTURE) MONARCH: PRINCE CHARLES IN MIKE BARTLETT'S PLAY *KING CHARLES III* (2014)

The British monarchy's official website describes the sovereign's duties as follows: "The British Monarchy is known as a constitutional monarchy. […] As Head of State, The Monarch undertakes constitutional and representational duties which have developed over one thousand years of history." ("The Role of the Monarchy" n. d.: n. pag.) This focus on the traditional aspect and historically developed structures of the British monarchy mirrors the very special form of the UK constitution with its absence of formal codification. It can be understood as "a product from history, in the sense that many crucial aspects relating to the monarch, Parliament, the protection of rights […] have evolved in response to significant events" (Leyland 2012: 23). That is why the understanding of the British monarchy's political functions, respectively of a sovereign's constitutional position and duties, is based on various conventions: "The pivotal convention which applies to the monarch is that he or she is bound to act on the advice of his or her ministers." (ibid: 93)

Today, the sovereign of the UK has only very little concrete political power since "[many] of the most far-reaching powers which formerly were exercised by the monarch, mainly prerogative powers, are now in the hands of the Prime Minister and the government" (ibid: 89). However, as part of the constitutional framework, the monarch is still of high importance because his or her – direct but rather symbolic – involvement is required in many constitutional matters. A triad of these prerogative powers can be described as the "three royal powers of state – (1) prime ministerial appointment, (2) Royal Assent to legislation, and (3) dissolution of Parliament" (Blackburn 2006: 80). Despite the (ceremonial) exercise of these prerogative powers, the sovereign has to hold back personal views on political matters. Therefore, "maintaining this political neutrality must be the golden rule for the continuity of the monarchy" (ibid: 107). The public role of a monarch has "to be carried out at the request of [the] elected government, even where the individual personalities or policies [...] may be at odds with the private view of the Queen or [...] future King" (ibid: 10). By analyzing Mike Bartlett's *King Charles III*, the following section will explore how the notion of a politically neutral monarch is presented in the play and what potential consequences arise from a breach with this conceptualization. A crucial point to examine will be why today's political realities require people to understand the 'royal prerogatives' as public constitutional duties and not as private 'direct legal prerogatives' of the monarch (cf. ibid: 79-107).

Mike Bartlett's 'future history play'[3] imagines the first actions of Charles as 'yet-to-be-crowned king' after the funeral of Queen Elizabeth II. Charles refuses to sign a new bill for statutory regulation of the press passed by parliament and thus disregards the constitutional convention of giving royal assent. As a virtuous and highly principled king, he aims at securing the freedom of the press as a basic democratic condition and rejects the convention of the monarch being bound to ministerial advice. By converting his constitutional duty to an instrument of personal political power, Charles provokes parliament into passing a second bill that restricts the monarch's ceremonial role of assenting laws. Before this legislative process can be terminated by the House of Commons, Charles makes use of a second royal prerogative and dissolves parliament to clear the path for new elections. The situation in Britain takes on threatening dimensions due to protests that arise throughout the country, jeopardizing the future of the British monarchy. Finally, Charles's son William is persuaded by his wife Kate and the Prime Minister Mr. Evans to replace his father as monarch and thus ensure stability for both the country and the monarchy. Charles feels betrayed and abdicates. In the last scene

---

3   This ascription of genre is given on the book cover of the of the play's printed edition: Bartlett, Mike (2014): *King Charles III*, London: Nick Hern Books.

of the play, William and Kate are crowned king and queen, thus restoring the (constitutional) power of the British monarchy.

Bartlett's play emphasizes the issue of the monarch's supposed political neutrality and negotiates his constitutional role. Throughout most of the five acts, Charles is presented as legally untouchable monarch. This is already prefigured during the first meeting of Charles and Prime Minister Evans when they disagree about the bill:

"CHARLES My views to you mean nothing then
MR EVANS [...] I disagree with what you think [...]
[...] The public vote
To choose the members of their Parliament
And that is where decisions will be made
Not in this room between the two of us."
(*KC*: 28)

Evans tries to keep the king in his place by referring to the traditional conventions of the weekly meetings between a constitutional monarch and the prime minister. The conventional purpose of these meetings is to inform the king about "significant domestic and international developments [and] not to have the opportunity to enter into intellectual discourse on the philosophical direction of the government" (Blackburn 2006: 22). In the play, Charles breaks with this convention twice: first, by arguing with the prime minister about the bill and secondly, by inviting the leader of the opposition for a meeting as well to demonstrate impartiality (cf. *KC*: 29). During his first meeting with the leader of the opposition, Mr. Stevens, Charles expresses his desire to be an activist king – "I always hoped as Crown I'd have some small | But crucial influence upon the State." (ibid: 31) However, he is still aware of the fact that his right not to sign the bill, which is fostered by Mr. Stevens, cannot be exercised because it is "a ceremonial right, not one to use" (ibid). The question of a constitutional monarch's personal royal activism is the central point of negotiation in *King Charles III*.

As Blackburn collates, the terminology of the monarch's constitutional duties and personal rights was a major contentious issue amongst authorities on constitutional law during the 20th century and provoked "uncertainties to exist over the parameters of the constitutional procedures to be followed by the future King" (2006: 82). Blackburn states that some influential scholars described the above-mentioned three royal powers "– inappropriately – as the 'personal prerogatives' of the monarch" (ibid). According to him, this approach to the prerogative powers of the monarch "claiming a non-circumscribed legitimacy for the monarch to act free from ministerial advice and instead rely on his or her own personal decision [...] is wrong, misconceived, and belongs to an earlier era" (ibid: 84). He specifies that it can be considered absurd and improbable within the political sphere of the 21st century that a hereditary monarch appears to be actively involved in political debates (cf. ibid: 85). By depicting Charles's persona in favor of the controversial concept of the monarch's 'personal' prerogatives, Bartlett toys with the constitutional speculations about royal activism. In the play, a core event is Charles's plea to the prime minister to redraft the bill with changes that preserve the freedom of the press. After parliament's refusal, Charles sees a violation of his position as the legally untouchable sovereign and explains in a speech broadcast on TV how he feels about his constitutional role in society and politics:

"CHARLES
[...]
So far, they [i.e. the parliament and ministers] have refused, so now do I,
As King, and servant to the populace,
Request your understanding, and your trust,
That this, a rare but necessary act
Is not me stepping too far from the throne,
But is my duty and fulfilling what
The King or Queen is sworn by oath to do."
(*KC*: 54)

He sees himself acting on behalf of the British people and above all in accordance with his constitutional duties as a monarch. Shortly before, Charles vehemently underlined his understanding of his personal prerogatives: "Without my voice, and spirit, I am dust, | This is not what I want, but what I must." (ibid: 52) Thus, he breaks with the traditional role of a constitutional monarch by autonomously refusing to give royal assent to the bill.

In contrast to the 'real' Queen Elizabeth II who "has been highly restrained in expressing her views on public affairs," (Blackburn 2006: 13-14) Bartlett's representation of King Charles III mirrors Blackburn's vision of the future king who has the urge "to take a stand on a wide range of public issues, some well within the field of political controversy" (ibid: 14). Moreover, Blackburn emphasizes that Prince Charles often requests personal meetings with ministers and writes a large number of letters to them in which he expresses his opinions on topics "close to his heart" (2006: 14).[4] In Bartlett's play, Charles's inclination is taken up and criticized by several characters, for example by the prime minister's chief political adviser, who states: "before he's e'en | Throned or got a crown to call his own | He's chosen to exert this power that | His wiser mother never thought to use." (*KC*: 35) In addition, Mr. Stevens, the scheming leader of opposition, criticizes Charles's behavior during a talk to the prime minister by declaring: "[…] We cannot have | The King approving laws depending on | His own opinion, or the way he feels. […] We may, […] | Explain to him the simple duty that | He must uphold, whatever his own mind." (ibid: 37)

These critics emphasize that Charles has to accept the fact that the rights he is legitimately invested with as a private person are not the same as those he possesses as a constitutional monarch (cf. Blackburn 2006: 3). As I argued before, the monarch embodies his public role at any time, which goes hand in hand with Blackburn's assumption that once Charles is crowned "he will be required to subordinate his private views to his public duties" (ibid: 186). However, in *King Charles III*, Charles's public role is heavily influenced by his personal attitudes and values, rendering him a stoical king who turns against both parliament and the prime minister:

"CHARLES
For if my name is given through routine
And not because it represents my view
Then soon I'll have no name, and nameless I
Have not myself, and having not myself,
Possess not mouth nor tongue nor brain, instead
I am an empty vessel, waiting for
Instruction, soulless and uncorporate,
[…]
The outer skin with nothing in the heart."
(*KC*: 50)

---

4   The most prominent examples of Prince Charles's written letters to ministers are the so-called 'black spider memos' (named after his unique handwriting) addressing amongst other issues the environment, food and rural affairs, health, and children. These letters were mainly sent in 2004 and 2005. Due to the very personal views and beliefs the prince utters in these controversial letters, it became possible to question whether Charles could be a politically neutral future king. This is why a ten-year legal dispute preceded their publication (cf. Eleftheriou-Smith 2015: n. pag.).

With this reflection about the functions of a monarch and the institution of the monarchy as a whole, Bartlett's play puts forth an "act of meaning-making, namely to think about what the monarchy means nowadays, what it is there for, and which functions it is to perform" (Polland 2017: 212). In the case of the play, Charles decides not to be a functionless monarch of no relevance: As a monarch, he is not willing to act differently from how he would as a private person, filling the monarchical "empty vessel" with a strong personal character. This melting together of Charles's private and public personae culminates in Charles's refusal to abdicate in favor of his son William and consequently in the breach with his family. Charles's sons are pressuring their father to resign by threatening him with a separation from his grandchildren. Charles finally admits that "[he] cannot live alone" and that "the King is at an end" (*KC*: 115-116) revealing his dependency on the family. Unlike the ambitious couple William and Kate, he is not willing to prioritize power and agrees to abdicate. Making way for his son, he intends to devote himself to his private life as a "[forgotten] gardener, who potters round | And talks to plants and chuckles to himself" (ibid: 116), which is, incidentally, a parodic element hinting at Prince Charles's engagement for environmental issues.

'The rise and fall' of King Charles III as staged in Mike Bartlett's play reveals the dramatic act of "passing on [...] royal power [that] has the potential for personal and political problems" (Pankratz 2017a: 8). I argue that the depiction of Charles's persona in this play is based on the long-established notion of him as a controversial 'meddling' prince. With the staging of possible disputable interventions by a politically opinionated future king, Bartlett depicts a destabilization of the British monarchy. Creating an almost dystopian vision of a future 'meddling' King Charles III, the play artistically participates in critical discourses addressing the monarchy's (future) influence on actual political and social questions.

UNDERSTANDING A FUTURE MONARCH? PRINCE CHARLES IN CATHERINE MAYER'S BIOGRAPHY *CHARLES: THE HEART OF A KING* (2015)

In her unauthorized biographic work[5] *Charles: The Heart of a King* (2015), Catherine Mayer puts a strong focus on Prince Charles's reputation and public image.

---

5   A biographic work is always strongly shaped by the writer who selects and creates an interplay of facts and fiction, of evidence and construction – "the novelist's art of arrangement, suggestion, [and] dramatic effect to expound the private life" (Woolf 1967 [1927]: 234). As a scholar with a tremendous impact on biography studies, Virginia

Furthermore, she examines the possible new, modernized model of kingship he promotes, especially with regard to his political activism. Extracts of this biography were published in the *TIME* Magazine's cover story "The Forgotten Prince" on November 4, 2013. Cele C. Otnes and Pauline Maclaran consider this article to play an important role in the process of Charles's "rebranding": "The substance of the sympathetic and somewhat laudatory cover story is that Charles is now understood as a man often ahead of his time, who has suffered ridicule for his once eccentric but now accepted opinions." (2015: 295-296) Mayer's rather positive approach to the prince can be regarded as conducive to Charles's reputational management. The central message that the article, and as I argue also the biography, communicate is that the heir "is the right persona for the right time within the royal narrative" (ibid: 296). Speaking of narrative: In the so-called information age of the 21st century, it is asserted that power is no longer a question of arms and warfare but of stories (cf. Nye 2013). This idea is underlined by the recent articles discussed in the first section, in which Charles fosters the narrative of his support for environmental concerns and sustainability and therefore presents himself as a caring and eco-conscious future king. The following analysis of *Charles – The Heart of a King* examines how Mayer's reflections on the prince's life and personality emphasize his compelling narratives that fashion him as a suitable and convincing future king.

In the introductory chapter Mayer herself states that with the biographic work on the Prince she intends "to bring clarity to both sides of the debate" about the future and purpose of the British monarchy (*HK*: 34) by "[revealing the heir] in all his complexity" (ibid: 42). She ends her introduction with the words: "Let daylight in." (ibid: 48) Here, Mayer alludes to Walter Bagehot's famous dictum: "We must not let in daylight upon magic" (2001 [1867]: 50) that illustrates the traditional reverent stance towards the monarchy as a sacral and mystic institution. However, Mayer counteracts this perspective highlighting a view on Prince Charles as a modernizer of the monarchy, who integrates his private persona into his public role. In this way, he can be conceived of as a philanthropic, caring future king.

Woolf deals with the handling of fact and fiction in biographies by differentiating biographic facts from facts of science. According to her, biographic facts are always subject to biographer's changes of opinion (cf. 1967 [1939]: 226). A biographer performs an imaginative task providing "creative facts" (ibid: 228) for the readers in which truth and fiction are equally combined (cf. 1967 [1927]: 234). Therefore, a biography can be considered as a semi-fictional literary work.

Mayer allows much space for presenting Prince Charles as a thoughtful future king who can be seen as "a knight on a quest [...] saving his adopted planet and the monarchy" (*HK*: 398). This touches upon a specific usage of authority and influence: While *King Charles III* particularly deals with questions of legal power, Mayer's biographic work holds another focus. She claims that: "This book will give new insight into Charles's [...] deployment of royal soft power" (ibid: 40), which is understood as "the ability to produce outcomes through attraction rather than coercion or payment" (Nye 2013: n. pag.). It can be argued that Prince Charles's persona functions as an important source of soft power, which is particularly connected to heirs to the throne.[6] Frank Lorenz Müller points out that "[a]s highly visible prominent figures [...] royal heirs were both expected and ideally placed to build consensus, popularize monarchical rule and generate renewed relevance for it" (ibid: 6). I argue that in *Charles: The Heart of a King,* the notion of Charles's royal soft power is strongly emphasized since the work focuses on his role as a "compulsive philanthropist" (*HK*: 26), or, as Rojek specifies, on his commitment "to be *for* the people by engaging in deserving causes and acting as a tribune for the public interest" (2002: 110).

A very prominent example of these 'deserving causes' is the Prince's commitment to environmental concerns. Mayer describes Charles as "the most thoughtful member of the royal family" (ibid: 54) who, for instance, established his own ecological brand Duchy Originals that sells organic products from his own farm (cf. ibid: 57). According to Mayer, the Prince – with his eco-friendly and philanthropic work – focuses on issues "on distant horizons [because his] activism is aimed at benefiting populations not yet born" (ibid: 397). Charles is depicted as an heir campaigning for change (cf. *HK*: 53) who "more than anything else [sees his] duty to worry about everybody and their lives in [that] country, to try to find a way of improving things if [he] possibly can" (ibid: 103). Throughout the biography, a strong focus is placed on Charles's commitments to various charities, especially his Prince's Trust, which intends to improve the situation of different groups and members of the British society, for example by ensuring education and employment for deprived young people (cf. ibid: 44). Mayer dedicates an entire chapter ("A Matter of Trust") to the portrayal of the success that Charles has as a "charitable entrepreneur" (*HK*: 383) with his Prince's Trust. This charity work can be regarded as a strong exertion of Charles's soft power because of the "moral force"

---

6 This is highlighted by Frank Lorenz Müller, when he describes the historical change of traditional forms of monarchical hard power (such as violent political strategies like war) to soft power strategies "achieved by co-opting, persuading, charming, seducing or attracting" (2016: 5) throughout the 19th century.

(Müller 2016: 3) his philanthropic work embodies. This also promotes the monarchical cause in the 21st century by renewing the monarchy's relevance as a caring and charitable institution. Therefore, the heir's work can be considered to function as a "means to win, rather than command, hearts and minds" (*HK*: 4).

It seems that Catherine Mayer is determined to present Charles in a positive light when she praises his charity work, choosing a daring allusion to his former wife Princess Diana[7]: "Charles is a king of hearts, compelled to reach out, to try to make a difference. [...] [This] stands not in opposition to his hereditary role – current and future – but offers a way to invest the monarchy with new relevance." (ibid: 33) This statement draws attention to the notion of a possible 21st-century-kingship under a King Charles III "unrolling a potential new model of kingship that melds the ceremonial aspects of the role with a much more active beneficence than the old formula of charitable patronage" (ibid: 381). By placing emphasis on Charles's modernizing view that "campaigning and kingship can be synthesised" (ibid: 114) and explaining that "Charles will never be neutral" (ibid: 398), Mayer establishes the conception of a modern monarchy in which public duty and the monarch's active personal commitment meet. At this point, the constantly overlapping dichotomy of the private and the public sphere in the heir's life unfolds its relevance for this biography. Mayer declares that it is not possible to draw a clear-cut boundary "where the sovereign's public duty ends and [the] private sphere begins" (ibid: 91).

This notion of the overlapping public and the private spheres in Prince Charles's life mirrors the conception of literary and cultural productions containing multiple truths when dealing with the lives of members of the royal family[8]: "To a certain extent, scholarship, journalism, and fiction use the same methods when writing about the monarchy, trying to fill the gaps between public image and private lives." (Pankratz 2017a: 14) With regard to biographies like *Charles – The*

---

7   Mayer transfers Princess Diana's self-chosen epithet "Queen of Hearts" to the heir and exhausts this laudatory expression when she uses the honoring capitalized spelling "King of Hearts" (*HK*: 400) for Charles on the last page of her biography.

8   Robert Lacey, lead historical consultant to the Netflix series *The Crown* (2016–) states that literary and cultural productions about the members of the royal family "reflect [their subjects'] lives but there are also multiple truths. You try to define what they are and assemble those different interpretations." (2019: n. pag.) *The Crown* presents itself as a drama series rather than a documentary since it ranges within the dimensions of fact and fiction narrating the life of Queen Elizabeth II. Lacey states: "You are watching a historical drama, [...] not a history documentary. *The Crown* is a work of creative fiction that has been inspired by the wisdom and spirit of real events" (2017: 6).

Heart of a King, this cannot be done without bias, as a biographer always depends on his or her sources. He or she can be considered a "slave of his [or her] documents" (Edel 1957: 5) who is never neutral because of the emotional relationship connecting the author and the subject (cf. Lee 2009: 12). In the conclusion of her biographic work on Prince Charles, Mayer also reveals her emotional relationship towards him. She feels sympathy for him as a child and admires him for his accomplishments, although she cannot agree with all his views. Mayer considers herself "not as a monarchist but as a pragmatist," (*HK*: 384) who would choose a republic over a monarchy. But she admits that she, as an American-born citizen, has been living in the UK almost all her life and is therefore convinced that a constitutional monarchy also includes benefits like the public service and that "the system still, mostly, works quite well" (ibid: 384). She states that she "like[s] the Prince" (ibid: 399) and makes obvious that she is kindly disposed towards Prince Charles.

This sympathetic approach of the biography towards the prince is already anticipated in the introduction of her work when Mayer claims with regard to the heir apparent that "[he's] easier to criticise than to comprehend" (ibid: 28) and when she formulates the book's intent: "As for the Prince, he deserves to be understood." (ibid: 34) I argue that *Charles: The Heart of a King* reveals strong characterization techniques that try to foster a better understanding of Prince Charles. The overall image of Charles that Mayer draws is the one of a misunderstood prince who suffers from intrigues in his royal household Clarence House and who trusts the wrong counsellors. She argues that he "hasn't always chosen his sages wisely" (ibid: 151) and that these dysfunctions interfere with his work (cf. ibid: 152). She picks up the idea of the misunderstood prince again in her conclusion and ends her work with a quote by Charles, which strengthens his own concern that his activism for environmental causes will not be conceived as his philanthropic commitment to secure the planet for future generations: "It's everybody else's grandchildren I've been bothering about [...] But the trouble is if you take that long a view, people don't always know what you're on about." (ibid: 400) At this crucial point of the text, Mayer refers to the central image of the misunderstood Prince Charles she created and concludes that his activism is not adequately appreciated.

This image of an underrated prince plays an important role in developing a positive understanding of the heir suggesting that "there is diminishing support for the idea of the crown passing straight to William [after the queen's death]" (ibid: 364) and rebranding Charles as a suitable, and convincing future monarch (cf. Otnes/Maclaran 2015). Thus, I argue that this (semi-)fictional literary depiction attributes to Prince Charles a central role for the stabilization of the British monarchy. Mayer's endeavor to underline Charles's activist performance supports the prince's compelling narrative of a caring and conscientious future monarch that was set up for him over the last decades with his commitment to various charitable and ecological causes. Therefore, by depicting a rather positive vision of a future 'meddling' King Charles III, the biography is able to influence public discourse in favor of Charles as future head of the British monarchy.

CHARLES AT 70 – THE FUTURE OF THE BRITISH MONARCHY?

This section aims at identifying representational tendencies in both of the examined works – *King Charles III* and *Charles: The Heart of a King* – that depict Prince Charles as an actively intervening and controversially outspoken 'king-to-be.' These works induce people to question their own perceptions and opinions on the monarchy and its political as well as constitutional functions in society. That his representations within these literary and cultural productions evoke controversies was demonstrated, for instance, by the media discussion that the BBC television adaption of Bartlett's play *King Charles III* (2017) provoked. Voices claiming that the drama disparages and discredits the royal family were echoed by politicians such as Tory MP Bridgen, who criticized that it was "unfortunate the BBC would seek to promote this flight of fantasy, which many licence-fee payers will find distasteful" (Davies 2017: n. pag.). The BBC then felt compelled to pour oil on troubled water and state that the drama is pure fiction: "The public know the difference between fact and fiction and King Charles III is a one-off BBC2 drama of the award-winning fictional play." (ibid)

However, since the play – as a contemporary creative cultural and literary production – fictionally renegotiates the future role of the British monarchy within the British constitution, I argue that it contributes to actual political discourse. The play underlines the demands for a reformation of the sovereign's constitutional duties within the political system of Great Britain and calls for a modernization of the monarchy to be "done to clarify, circumscribe and, where necessary, codify the role and duties of a British monarch operating in 21st-century conditions." (Blackburn 2006: 172) Thus, Bartlett's play creates room for speculations about future political realities that may change due to the potential royal activism of a 'meddling' King Charles III. By staging a thrilling political crisis, the play contributes to ongoing political discourse showing why the understanding of the 'royal prerogatives' as public constitutional duties and not as the monarch's private 'direct legal prerogatives' can be considered appropriate.

Mayer's biography also makes a significant contribution to current political discourse regarding the politically active and opinionated Prince Charles. As highlighted in the analysis, she expresses rather a positive opinion about the Prince's activism insisting that "Charles will never be neutral just as he will never be party political. For better or for worse […] the Prince is a man with a mission." (*HK*: 398) Her core issue of sympathetically depicting Charles as a misunderstood prince, whose activism is not sufficiently appreciated, reinforces the notion of his positive rebranding as a suitable and convincing future king (cf. Otnes/Maclaran 2015). I contend that the main representational tendency that can be deduced from the two works analyzed in this article is their focus on the blending of Charles's private and public personae with regard to his activism. This functions as the crux for the unfolding of events in *King Charles III* and in *Charles: The Heart of a King* as the central basic assumption of Charles's modernizing view. The thesis of a possible amalgamation of monarchical rule and activist campaigning is stressed in Bartlett's play by depicting a dystopian scenario for a future meddling King Charles III. His play can be read as an invitation to further negotiate questions concerning 21st-century-monarchy and its political, constitutional, and societal functions.

Referring back to the quotation by Prince Charles with which I began this article, I would like to take a final look at the BBC television documentary *Prince, Son and Heir: Charles at 70* (2018). Broadcast to mark the Prince's 70th birthday, the documentary provides much space for the heir to the British throne to find clear words regarding his future as a potential 'meddling king.' The highly orchestrated documentary suggests a strong and intimate cooperation with the royal family as Prince Charles, his wife Camilla as well as Charles's sons William and Harry give extensive interviews. Focusing on the heir celebrating his jubilee, his eco-enthusiasm and commitment to diverse charitable causes are presented and honored. During the last five minutes of the program, Prince Charles gives the interviewer detailed answers regarding his personal vision of his future as monarch. When the interviewer confronts the heir with the widespread criticism that people accuse him of meddling, Charles answers, with a wink: "Really? You don't say…" (*Prince, Son and Heir*: 55:34). This reaction gives a hint at how the future king might handle his actions with "creative tension" (Bent 2002: 62) since, as the interview continues, he describes his interfering actions as acts of motivation of which he is proud (cf. *Prince, Son and Heir*: 55:37-55:52). Furthermore, the prince reflects on his activist involvement as heir: He considers to have been non-party political and makes clear that "the idea somehow that [he's] going to go on exactly the same way if [he has] to succeed, is completely nonsense, because the two situations [being a monarch and being heir] are completely different" (cf. ibid: 56:06-56:31). The interview then continues by negotiating in how far the prince will try to consolidate his constitutional duties and personal rights and views as a monarch in comparison to his present activist role as heir apparent:

> "INTERVIEWER:
> Because, of course, people have expressed worries about whether this involvement will continue in the same way.
> CHARLES:
> No, it won't! (laughs) I'm not that stupid. I do realise that it is a separate exercise being sovereign. So, of course, you know, I understand entirely how that should operate.
> INTERVIEWER:
> But you could use the convening power you've spoken of for good.
> CHARLES:
> Well, you never know, but you could only do it with the agreement of ministers. That's how it works."
> (ibid: 57:04 – 57:37)

At this point, Prince Charles leaves no doubt that he will operate within the constitutional parameters when becoming head of the British monarchy. Nevertheless, he leaves room for interpretations adumbrating that he will be a more political monarch presenting his opinions and functioning as an intervening mediator. According to the prince, this will happen in accordance with political leaders and his constitutional boundaries. Thus, the bottom line of this interview remains the question of how, not whether Prince/King Charles's views will be expressed. Another interesting, nonetheless unanswerable, question is in how far literary and cultural productions like Bartlett's play and Mayer's biography have paved the way for representations of Prince Charles such as in the interview discussed above. It should be considered that the artistic, literary, and journalistic representations of the heir examined here constitute cultural productions that affect each other due to their embedding "in the medial feedback loop" (Pankratz 2017b: 55) that fosters their reciprocal influence. Despite – or perhaps precisely because of – the current (semi-)fictional literary works dealing with Charles as an activist future monarch, it is certain that the 'real' Prince Charles at 70 provides a compelling narrative that appeals to people. The future of the British monarchy under King Charles III is anticipated by the *Australian Financial Review* (Hume 2018: n. pag), which proclaims with great appreciation: "As for our King of Sustainability, for all our sakes, Long May He Reign".

WORKS CITED

Bagehot, Walter (2001 [1867]): The English Constitution, edited by Paul Smith, Cambridge: Cambridge University Press.
Bartlett, Mike (2014): King Charles III, London: Nick Hern Books.
Blackburn, Robert (2006): King and Country: Monarchy and the Future King Charles III, London: Politico's.
Bower, Tom (2018): Rebel Prince: The Power, Passion and Defiance of Prince Charles, London: William Collins.
Chaney, David (2001): "The Mediated Monarchy." In: David Morley/Kevin Robins (eds.), British Cultural Studies: Geography, Nationality, Identity, Oxford: Oxford University Press, pp. 207-219.
Davies, Caroline (2017): "'Distasteful'": BBC's King Charles III Sparks Anger Even Before It Is Aired." The Guardian May 1, accessed July 30, 2019 (https://www.theguardian.com/media/2017/may/02/bbc-king-charles-iii-anger-drama).
Davies, Caroline (2018): "Prince Charles: 'Me, Meddle as a King? I'm Not That Stupid.'" The Guardian November 8, accessed July 30, 2019 (https://www.theguardian.com/uk-news/2018/nov/08/prince-charles-me-meddle-as-a-king-im-not-that-stupid).
Edel, Leon (1957): Literary Biography: The Alexander Lectures 155-56, London: Rupert Hart Davis.
Eleftheriou-Smith, Loulla-Mae (2015): "Prince Charles' 'Black Spider' Memos: What Are They and What Impact Will Their Publication Have?" The Independent May 13, accessed July 30, 2019 (https://www.independent.co.uk/news/uk/home-news/prince-charles-black-spider-memos-what-are-they-and-what-impact-will-their-publication-have-10246815.html).
Furness, Hannah (2018): "Prince Charles 'Deeply Touched' to Be Confirmed as Queen's Head of Commonwealth Successor." The Telegraph April 20, accessed July 30, 2019 (https://www.telegraph.co.uk/news/2018/04/20/prince-charles-confirmed-successor-queen-next-head-commonwealth/).
Hume, Marion (2018): "Prince Charles: How Fashion Can Help Mend the Planet." The Australian Financial Review April 6, accessed July 30, 2019 (https://www.afr.com/business/media-and-marketing/prince-charles-how-fashion-can-be-sustainable-20180201-h0rv1l).
Jones, Dylan (2018): "Prince Charles Exclusive Interview: 'My Problem is I Find There are Too Many Things That Need Doing or Battling'." GQ Magazine UK September 6, accessed July 30, 2019 (https://www.gq-magazine.co.uk/article/prince-charles-gq-awards-interview-2018).

Lacey, Robert (2019): "How Advisor to The Crown Robert Lacey Gets Closer to the Truth." robertlacey.com January 19, accessed July 30, 2019 (http://www.robertlacey.com/2019/01/19/how-advisor-to-the-crown-robert-lacey-gets-closer-to-the-truth/).

Lacey, Robert (2017): The Crown: The Official Companion. New York: Crown Archetype.

Lee, Hermione (2009): Biography: A Very Short Introduction, Oxford: Oxford University Press.

Leyland, Peter (2012): The Constitution of the United Kingdom: A Contextual Analysis, Oxford: Hart.

Mayer, Catherine (2015): Charles: The Heart of a King, London: WH Allen.

Mayer, Catherine (2013): "The Forgotten Prince: Inside Prince Charles' World As He Quietly Takes Charge." TIME Magazine November 4, accessed July 30, 2019 (https://time.com/579/inside-prince-charles-world-as-he-quietly-takes-charge/)

Müller, Frank Lorenz (2016): "'Winning their Trust and Affection': Royal Heirs and the Uses of Soft Power in Nineteenth-Century Europe." In: Frank Lorenz Müller/Heidi Mehrkens (eds.), Royal Heirs and the Uses of Soft Power in Nineteenth-Century Europe, London: Palgrave Macmillan, pp. 1-19.

Nye, Joseph (1990): "Soft Power." In: Foreign Policy 80, pp. 153-171.

Nye, Joseph (2013): "The Infant Prince George is a Source of Real-World Power." The Financial Times July 24, accessed July 30, 2019 (https://www.ft.com/content/0bd55672-f482-11e2-a62e-00144feabdc0).

Otnes, Cele C./Maclaran, Pauline (2015): Royal Fever: The British Monarchy in Consumer Culture, Berkeley: University of California Press.

Pankratz, Anette (2017a): "Introducing the Monarchy." In: Anette Pankratz/Claus-Ulrich Viol (eds.), (Un)Making the Monarchy, Heidelberg: Winter, pp. 7-20.

Pankratz, Anette (2017b): "'That's Entertainment': Monarchy as Performance." In: Anette Pankratz/Claus-Ulrich Viol (eds.), (Un)Making the Monarchy, Heidelberg: Winter, pp. 41-64.

Peters, Sibylle/Jentz, Janina (1998): Diana oder die Perfekte Tragödie: Kulturwissenschaftliche Betrachtung eines Trauerfalls, Köln: Böhlau.

Polland, Imke (2017): "'A Golden Age of Monarchy?' Staging Hypothetical Crises in Mike Bartlett's King Charles III (2014)." In: Elizabeth Kovach/Ansgar Nünning/Imke Polland (eds.), Literature and Crises: Conceptual Explorations and Literary Negotiations, Trier: Wissenschaftlicher Verlag Trier, pp. 203-219.

Prince Charles (2018): "HRH The Prince of Wales: 'We May Be the Last Generation Fortunate Enough to Experience the Wonderful People, Skills and Activities of Our Countryside'." Country Life November 14, accessed July 30, 2019 (https://www.countrylife.co.uk/news/hrh-prince-wales-may-last-generation-fortunate-enough-experience-wonderful-people-skills-activities-countryside-188706).

Rojek, Chris (2002): "Courting Fame." In: Tom Bentley/James Wilsdon (eds.), Monarchies Demos Collection Issue 17, London: Demos, pp. 105-110.

"The Role of the Monarchy." The Royal Family. n. d., accessed July 30, 2019 (https://www.royal.uk/role-monarchy).

Woolf, Virginia (1967 [1927]): "The New Biography." In: Virginia Woolf, Collected Essays Volume Four. London: The Hogarth Press, pp. 229-235.

Woolf, Virginia (1967 [1939]): "The Art of Biography." In: Virginia Woolf, Collected Essays Volume Four. London: The Hogarth Press, pp. 221-228.

Films and Television

King Charles III. Directed by Rupert Goold. 2017. BBC/Drama Republic.
Prince, Son and Heir: Charles at 70. Directed by John Bridcut. 2018. BBC/Crux Productions.

Gendered Strategies of Power: Queen Elizabeth II as a Politician in the Plays *The Audience* (2015 [2013]) and *Handbagged* (2013)

Eva Kirbach

2017 marked the Sapphire Jubilee of Elizabeth II, Queen of the United Kingdom of Great Britain and Northern Ireland, making her the first British monarch to reign for 65 years. The occasion was widely commented upon by the media – both at home and abroad – and celebrated by the British public, the majority of which has only known her as their monarch. During the so-called New Elizabethan Age,[1] the queen has shaped British social and cultural life: For younger generations, she appears as an important link to the past, representing the memory of the British Empire and the Second World War, whereas elder generations are able to identify themselves with her. Yet in recent years, a more modern image of the queen has also been fashioned, for instance due to her participation in the James Bond clip in 2012. It was shot exclusively for the opening ceremony of the Olympic Games in London and features the monarch in a brief meeting with actor Daniel Craig before they fly to the stadium in a helicopter. Craig is dressed as James Bond, the well-known fictional secret agent acting on her Majesty's secret service, and thus links the queen to British popular culture. In this video clip, two British icons are combined in order to represent the United Kingdom to an international audience. Yet given the queen's age and her usually dignified composure, this performance is quite surprising and questions the traditionally rather conservative public image

---

[1] For a more in-depth discussion of the term "New Elizabethan Age," see Irene Morra and Rob Gossedge (2016).

of the monarch. Consequently, it can be argued that Elizabeth II represents both past and present, paving the way for a modern monarchy in the 21st century.

The British monarch occupies a quaint spot in British society: Although the king or queen once held a powerful political position and truly ruled the land, their "monarchical power" has been severely limited throughout the centuries (Berg 2017: 229). While "[r]oyal executive power has disappeared" (Oakland 2011 [1989]: 94) and been transferred to parliament and the prime minister, the monarch still fulfils "formal constitutional roles and is head of state" (ibid: 94), yet not, as Sebastian Berg notes, "head of government" (2017: 228). Despite her mainly symbolical role, the queen is still "informed of all aspects of national life" (Oakland 2011 [1989]: 95) and "spends much of her time reviewing important documents and state papers [...] to prepare herself for her typically weekly consultations with her PM" (Otnes/Maclaran 2015: 10-11). In this regard, she "acts as a political-constitutional counsellor" (Berg 2017: 229) to the prime minister and makes use of her constitutional rights, namely "the right to be consulted, the right to encourage, the right to warn" (Bagehot 2001 [1867]: 70). Furthermore, the British monarch is directly involved in political proceedings. For instance, by granting the royal assent to bills passed by both Houses of Parliament, the queen plays a significant part in transforming a bill into an Act of Parliament (cf. Oakland 2011 [1989]: 95). Additionally, she officially opens parliament by delivering a speech which "outlines the UK government's forthcoming legislative programme" (ibid: 97) yet is required to remain politically neutral. As monarch, Elizabeth II is not allowed to state her private political opinion in public. In this aspect, the queen stands in stark contrast to politicians, but also benefits from her unique position: According to Oakland, the monarch is thus regarded as a "permanent fixture" in British society, "unlike temporary politicians" (ibid: 94-95). Due to her lack of direct political engagement, she is therefore able to unite and "personif[y] the nation" (Berg 2017: 228).

Nonetheless, the media and the public both appear curious about the queen's private opinion, always speculating and attempting to solve this well-guarded secret. As a result, various newspapers frequently feature headlines and articles claiming to have received information from an anonymous source within the queen's inner circle. Prior to the Brexit referendum, for instance, *The Sun* claimed that the "Queen backs Brexit" (Newton Dunn 2016: n. pag.), probably hoping to give more weight and credit to their own pro-Brexit stance by linking it to the monarch. This indicates that the queen's political opinion may have an impact on the British public since she is regarded as an esteemed point of reference. Thus, it can be summarized that the queen "still play[s] a vital role in the historical and contemporary experience and projection of British national identity and ideas of nationhood" (Higson 2016: 339).

In recent years, the media's interest in the private opinions of Elizabeth II has been shared by playwrights who present their own fictional accounts to imaginatively fill the gaps of common knowledge. *The Audience* by Peter Morgan (2015 [2013]; from here on cited as *TA*) imagines and stages some of the weekly meetings between the queen and eight of her prime ministers.[2] The play hints at sympathies, common interests and secrets the monarch shares with the politicians against the backdrop of selected historical events taking place during the queen's reign. *Handbagged* by Moira Buffini (2013; from here on cited as *HB*) focuses solely on the relationship between Elizabeth II and Britain's first female prime minister, Margaret Thatcher, during the latter's premiership. Both protagonists, Queen Elizabeth II and Margaret Thatcher, are played by two actors respectively: Liz and Mags are the younger versions whereas Q and T appear as the older, more composed and experienced ones. Throughout most of the play, all four characters are on stage simultaneously, which results, for instance, in Q and T commenting on the behavior and actions of their younger selves. While this frequently allows for entertainment and irony, it is also a useful metatheatrical device to point out the constructed nature of history and identity. *Handbagged* imagines the two women's political and personal conversations and suggests potential disagreements while contemplating a new, rather sympathetic and humane portrayal of the Iron Lady.

Although, with Theresa May, a female prime minister has once again taken over 10 Downing Street, the majority of British politicians remain male, causing heated debates about the number of women in government. While the statistics are certainly improving, thus reflecting a modern Britain, the press regularly features conservative, almost backward articles about female politicians' taste in clothing, suggesting for example a link between Theresa May's leather trousers and her ability to chair a government (cf. Moseley 2016: n. pag.). Similarly, the queen's

---

2 The 2015 version of the play includes (ordered chronologically): Winston Churchill, Anthony Eden, Harold Wilson, Margaret Thatcher, John Major, Tony Blair, Gordon Brown and David Cameron. Harold Macmillan, Alec Douglas-Home, Edward Heath and James Callaghan are briefly mentioned yet do not appear in person. In the original 2013 version, Tony Blair did not feature whereas James Callaghan enjoyed a brief appearance on stage. It is noteworthy that *The Audience* is not Morgan's only work on Queen Elizabeth II and the royal family. He also wrote the film *The Queen* (2006) and the Netflix series *The Crown* (2016–), both of which focus on the private life of Elizabeth II.

clothing is frequently emphasized by the press rather than the duties she is performing for the British public. One might draw the conclusion that women's public appearances and their actions are still judged by different standards than men's. In addition to the British monarch's complex social and political position, the queen's gender therefore needs to be taken into account as well.

In the following, I will turn to a close reading of *The Audience* and *Handbagged* in order to discuss Morgan and Buffini's respective fictional presentations of the queen. I argue that in both plays, these fictional versions of Elizabeth II strategically combine characteristics that are stereotypically connoted as masculine and feminine. Thus, the fictional versions of the queen in *The Audience* and *Handbagged* make use of what I term gendered strategies of power in order to achieve political goals and to ensure their popularity; in short: the fictional Elizabeth behaves rather like a politician than a monarch. In order to define what is connoted as masculine and feminine in Western countries, such as the United Kingdom, I will critically reflect on gender stereotypes, defined as a "cultural system of binary oppositions of concepts with gendered connotations" (Chandler/Munday 2016: n. pag.). For instance, contrasting pairs include categories such as "active/passive, mind/body, reason/emotion, [...] public/private" (ibid), with the first term referring to masculine and the second referring to feminine behavior. In Western societies, the "male side of the equation is generally coded as the positive one" (Cranny-Francis et al. 2003: 2), elevating the masculine form to the general standard and simultaneously degrading attributes that are connoted as feminine. In the following analysis, I will take the implicit or explicit usages of these stereotypes in the plays into account and discuss their function. As will be seen, the fictional representations of the queen in *The Audience* and *Handbagged* unite notions of the state, commonly regarded as a masculine institution due to its political power (cf. Connell 2012: 163), and the nation, frequently imagined as a female figure, such as Britannia (cf. von Braun 2006: 22). Additionally, by cleverly juxtaposing stereotypically masculine and feminine traits in one and the same character, the plays encourage their respective audiences to look beyond the binary opposition of man and woman while making use of well-known stereotypes to provoke laughter, reflection and compassion.

My analysis is structured as follows: In a first step, I will look at behavior that is stereotypically connoted as feminine in selected scenes from *The Audience* and *Handbagged*. By emphasizing their emotional side and by offering a glimpse into their private lives, e.g.: through talks about their emotions and their family, Morgan and Buffini's fictional versions of the queen trick the prime ministers into underestimating their intelligence and grasp of political issues. Yet simultaneously, both representations of Elizabeth II show her as therapist and counsellor for her (mostly) male counterparts. Despite her gender, this behavior places her in a powerful position. Here, it already becomes apparent that a simple dichotomy of masculine/feminine cannot do justice to the rather complex reality of one's identity and would remain both one-sided and too simplistic. In a second step, I will turn towards strategies more commonly connoted as masculine that are employed by both fictional versions of the monarch. In order to be accepted among predominantly male politicians, Morgan and Buffini emphasize the queen's tough side, showing her to take action and highlighting her vast knowledge and experience, thus referring to the aforementioned rather masculine categories active, mind, reason and public.

THE RIGHT TO LISTEN AND TO ENCOURAGE: THE QUEEN AS THERAPIST AND COUNSELLOR FOR HER MALE PRIME MINISTERS IN *THE AUDIENCE*

In his article "From Political Power to the Power of the Image," Andrew Higson discusses contemporary films representing the constitutional monarchy, explaining that they "are much more focused on the private sphere: romance, family and the life of the royal household" whereas politics only serves "as a backdrop" (2016: 343). This has several implications, e.g. making it easier for the audience to relate to the monarchs or using the royal family "as a metaphor for the national family and a model for the nation" (ibid: 349). In accordance with Higson's claim that the monarch's "power is [...] restricted to the private sphere" (ibid: 350), I will argue that Morgan and Buffini employ a similar strategy for their versions of Queen Elizabeth II. Consequently, the queen's role as mother, sister and daughter is emphasized. This can be linked to a broader trend, equating "[t]raditional notions of women's sexuality [...] with [women's] reproductive function" (Cranny-Francis et al. 2003: 7). By reducing femininity, and women's sexuality in particular, to motherhood, women's confinement to one specific social sphere, namely the home, is highlighted. In contrast, masculinity and stereotypically masculine character traits are generally regarded as the norm in Western societies (ibid: 2), emphasizing the superiority of mind, reason and culture (cf. Chandler/Munday 2016: n. pag.). Women, on the other hand, are linked with emotions and orality (cf. von Braun 2006: 14). Yet the (usually negative) stereotype of women's allegedly inherent passion for gossip and chatting is interpreted differently in *The Audience* and *Handbagged*: Elizabeth's fondness for sharing secrets and stories is shown to be of great use and value to her when dealing with her (primarily male) prime ministers. Thus, the fictional monarch not only refuses to remain solely in the private sphere, but she also employs strategies and concepts usually connoted as feminine, such as a focus on emotions, to her advantage.

In *The Audience*, the queen frequently mixes the private and the political, sharing family secrets and gossip with her prime ministers to make them feel more at ease. Her strategy works so well that she appears almost like a counsellor or therapist (for instance to Brown and Major) which, in turn, places her in a powerful position despite her lack of political agency (cf. Jordan forthcoming). Here, a juxtaposition of traditional gender stereotypes can already be detected: While Elizabeth's feminine side is highlighted – her interest in gossip, an emphasis on emotions, the passive state of listening –, this is precisely what allows her to gain the upper hand in her conversations. Simultaneously, she exercises her constitutional rights, namely "the right to be consulted, the right to encourage, the right to warn" (Bagehot 2001 [1867]: 70). Brown acknowledges both, the Queen's right to listen, warn, and advise and her extensive knowledge of British politics, based on her long experience, when he reflects on lost chances and the current state of his premiership:

> "Brown: [… T]he candidate they fully expect to lose the next general election. I suppose it serves me right. I probably will lose, and only have myself to blame. After all, you told me to go for it.
> Elizabeth: For what?
> Brown: A snap election. In 2007. When I was still in my honeymoon. To establish a personal mandate."
> (*TA*: 39-40)

Similarly, Morgan presents the queen as the voice of reason when, in scenes that almost hauntingly mirror each other, she questions Anthony Eden prior to the Suez Crisis and Tony Blair prior to the invasion of Iraq about the actions of the British government, asking both of them: "Is it even legal?" (ibid: 42; 67). As will be seen, Morgan not only illustrates the monarch's right to warn and advise, but also slightly extends these duties to include comforting the politicians as well as giving them some much needed self-assurance. This way, Elizabeth's motherly side is highlighted as her prime ministers are turned into figures resembling helpless children who depend on guidance. While John Major "relives a private trauma" (ibid: 22) and confesses that his weak results at school must have disappointed his parents, the queen offers a handkerchief to her tearful prime minister. Major's emotional outburst makes him appear vulnerable and, to a certain extent, ridiculous since his behavior – crying over bad marks he achieved during his teenage years – does not fit the picture of a responsible prime minister, who is in control of an entire country. Consequently, Major is cast in the position of a small, helpless child whereas the queen acts like a surrogate mother. Responding to his confession, Elizabeth says: "Well, I have no O-levels at all. What fine hands the country is in" (ibid: 23), attempting to put Major's sorrow into perspective and to lighten the mood by making him laugh. Besides, she also makes light of her own education, presenting it as less valuable than Major's and thus enables him to feel at least equal if not superior to her.

She employs a similar technique with Gordon Brown: Their meeting starts somewhat wrong-footed discussing the UK's strained relationship with the US before turning to more personal matters, such as how Brown has spent his weekend (cf. ibid: 39-40). Yet their conversation only becomes more intimate after Elizabeth shares some gossip concerning Tony Blair, Brown's predecessor. Once they have found a topic they can agree on and both laugh at, a firm mutual trust and respect is established. This in turn allows the queen to direct her attention towards their respective illnesses and family histories, issues that are deeply personal. As she enquires after Brown's health, it becomes clear that common gender stereotypes are reversed: The male politician is presented with feminine traits since he allegedly suffers from depression (cf. ibid: 44). Hence, Brown's emotions and his bodily and mental reactions are highlighted, aspects that are usually connoted as feminine (cf. Chandler/Munday 2016: n. pag.). As several reviewers, such as J. Kelly Nestruck (2017: n. pag.), Michael Billington (2013: n. pag.) and Ben Brantley (2015: n. pag.) notice, the queen appears as his therapist and mother (confessor) alike, advising him to get enough sleep. Since Elizabeth has learned that Brown has OCD, she attempts – and eventually manages – to put him at ease. "I have it, too, you know," she admits, telling both Brown and the audience that her shoes and pens "need to be in a row" (*TA*: 45) in order to satisfy her. By sharing her own secret, the queen prompts Brown to reveal his compulsory nail-biting (cf. ibid), a characteristic that is frequently associated with nervous behavior. Elizabeth's strategy of opening up and turning the conversation towards more private aspects serves at least one important purpose: Brown realizes that they have something in common and actually appear as equals. Although his mental health issues have disturbed the usual power balance between prime minister and monarch by putting him in a weaker position, the queen cleverly resorts to the same topic to rectify the situation.

Furthermore, Elizabeth's confession of her own OCD contributes to a (re)presentation of her as a humane monarch, as someone who struggles with life just like everyone else. While Brown, in *The Audience*, is shown to sympathize with the queen, the same is potentially true for the actual theatre audience. This is in line with Otnes and Maclaran's analysis of contemporary filmic depictions of royal figures, stating that these portrayals "bring us closer to monarchy by making these people seem 'just like us,'" focusing on "a monarch shown as vulnerable and flawed" (2015: 142) with whom the audience can identify and empathize.[3] Consequently, the play may also promote a positive image of the queen. Apart from her own condition, Morgan's Elizabeth even acknowledges that Queen Victoria's mourning after her husband's death was in fact a depression and that two of her cousins were placed in "the Royal Earlswood Asylum for Mental Defectives" (*TA*: 45), thus again opening up to Brown and motivating him to reevaluate his current situation and health, in order to take care of himself while he simultaneously has to take care of the country. As Ben Brantley notes, the fictional queen "unbends with the politicians she likes just enough to allow them to intuit where her real interests lie" (2015: n. pag.). Consequently, she succeeds in creating an atmosphere of trust by remaining candid and honest which allows her to very gently push her prime minister into the direction she envisages for him. As Elizabeth thus cleverly behaves in a stereotypically feminine way, resorting to the private sphere and to emotional conversations, her performance reveals a degree of strategic agency that far exceeds these allegedly feminine ways. Simultaneously, her vast political knowledge and experience, for instance giving Brown advice on his speech (cf.*TA*: 47), make the queen a more than equal partner in the apparently unequal relationship between constitutional Head of State and actual Head of Government.

GOSSIP, FAMILY TALK, AND SECRETS: THE QUEEN'S FEMININE POLITICAL STRATEGY IN *HANDBAGGED*

A similar strategy can be detected in *Handbagged*, which plays with stereotypical assumptions and generalizations of feminine behavior. Buffini uses people's expectations to turn them around and make the audience both laugh and become aware of their own gendered perspectives. By frequently alluding to Liz and Q's close relationship with the female members of their own family, Buffini resorts to common knowledge about the queen, her mother, sister and daughter. When it

---

3   However, Otnes and Maclaran also note that "significantly and somewhat paradoxically, people also need to know that these figures differ from themselves, to allow the mystery that surrounds the idea of royalty to remain" (2015: 142). While Morgan indeed "emphasize[s] a theme of sacrifice to duty" (ibid), he also presents Elizabeth in all her regal glory, for instance by showing her "in full ballgown, tiara" (*TA*: 63) when meeting Anthony Eden.

becomes obvious that Mags and T, on the other hand, did not enjoy an intimate bond with their mother, Q exclaims: "Goodness," followed by Liz's confession: "I still can't get my mother off the phone" (*HB*: 24). In contrast, Mags' attitude towards her mother appears distanced and almost condescending. When Mags states: "[A]fter I turned fifteen, I had nothing to say to her" (ibid: 24), Buffini emphasizes the rather negative assumptions circulating in public opinion about Margaret Thatcher, for instance, arrogance and lack of empathy with common people. While both the queen and her prime minister enjoyed very close relationships with their fathers and express their adoration and admiration for them, their different viewpoints concerning their mothers appear striking. Buffini thus contrasts Liz/Q and Mags/T, attempting to turn the queen into a sympathetic, likeable character who shows love, gratitude and respect for both her parents.

Furthermore, the intimacy of Liz and Q and their closest family members is hinted at by T's accusation that Q used to call her "that bloody woman" (ibid: 31) behind her back. This way *Handbagged* presents a monarch who freely expresses her opinion in private, sharing her views with her family members. For instance, Liz remarks: "She [i.e. Margaret Thatcher] used to leave [Balmoral] at six in the morning | Really as soon as she could | One found it rude" (ibid: 95) while Q calls the prime minister's behavior towards her "patronising" (ibid: 99). Since the monarch's rather critical comments run contrary to her official, stiff and polite image, the play also hints at the queen's dry sense of humor and attests her a certain frankness and honesty that the audience can trust in. Additionally, Q's rather negative verdict on the prime minister is echoed by Prince Philip. As Mags insists on making herself useful at the royal family's picnic at Balmoral, Prince Philip demands: "Someone tell that bloody woman to sit down" (ibid: 94). Therefore, Buffini emphasizes the close bonds Liz and Q share with their husband and female family members, portraying Elizabeth as a family person. The depiction of the queen thus focuses on the private sphere and the home, linking her to stereotypically feminine attributes.

At the same time, it becomes obvious that Liz and Q love gossip and secrets. Q, in particular, "comes across as a rather fun-loving, gossipy old lady" (Barnett 2014: n. pag.) who can be imagined as a grandmotherly figure eager to share some of her stories; an image that runs contrary to that of the Iron Lady. When the Reagans arrive, T and Mags are therefore keen on illustrating their close political friendship with the American president, whereas Liz and Q resort to more mundane topics and declare that they and Ronald Reagan have a common hobby: "Horses" (*HB*: 47). Furthermore, Q and Liz embark on a lively discussion of Reagan's years in Hollywood, citing various films he appeared in and displaying their interest in popular culture (cf. ibid: 48-49). They also attempt to find some common ground with Mags and T, trying to connect and cooperate with their prime minister once the American guests have arrived. "Apparently," Liz says, "it's [Nancy Reagan's] hustling that's propelled [her husband] into the White House – and now that she's there, I've heard she's knocking down walls and throwing out all the china." (ibid: 50) Despite Liz's effort to initiate some good-natured chit-chat, she remains unsuccessful. "Why wouldn't you gossip?" Q asks, almost desperately, "[y]ou knew I wasn't going to tell anyone" – except, as she and Liz admit, she probably would have told Philip, her sister, "Mummy," and her daughter Anne (ibid: 50). Again, Buffini illustrates that *Handbagged*'s version of the queen shares everything with selected members of her family be it political issues or personal opinions. This again highlights the depiction of the queen as a family person who is very close to her relatives and who is able to be truly herself within this private circle. In the meantime, Mags and T continue to explain their own and Reagan's political ideas to the audience, emphasizing their similar outlook on the world. The monarch's chat about film trivia apparently lures the prime minister into a false sense of security, prompting T to claim "I was the first foreign leader to visit him in Washington after his inauguration." (ibid: 49) However, it becomes obvious that Liz and Q have been intently listening and immediately rush in to defy T's statement: "No you weren't," Liz says, "The Koreans were," (ibid: 49) thus contradicting T's claim. Once again, the queen's passion for gossip, a stereotypically feminine pastime, serves as a useful strategy in potentially misleading her prime minister and in conducting (difficult) conversations.

Throughout the play, Liz and Q talk a lot about their emotions, thoughts and family issues, usually to make a point, to illustrate their argument, or to (gently) manipulate their interlocutor. As mentioned earlier with regard to their respective mothers, Liz and Q's first meeting with Mags and T, after their election victory, turns out to be complicated. Apparently, they do not share the same understanding of families, politics, and the workings of the monarchy, setting them on a somewhat rocky path. In order to fix this problem, the queen decides to add a more personal note to their conversation: "Will you be bringing any pets to Number Ten?" Liz enquires, because "I thought," Q explains, "if she's got a dog we've got a subject." (ibid: 28) Here, Buffini shows the queen's effort to look for some common ground with Mags and T to improve their relationship with each other. Yet in this particular scene, the monarch's strategy fails: Mrs. Thatcher refuses to cooperate and solely discusses politics which is, after all, the purpose of their official meeting. Their different attitudes to and intentions for their meeting illustrate the contrast between Thatcher, the queen and, interestingly, the other male prime ministers in Morgan's *The Audience*. The men appear only too happy to unburden their sorrows to the queen who is shown as leaning towards a more emotional behavior, eager to improve the personal as well as professional relationship. Thatcher, however, is depicted as rational and solely focused on her work. Nonetheless, Liz and Q repeatedly employ the same tactic, namely shifting the conversation to more personal topics in order to make the other person feel at ease. Thus, the queen – sometimes effectively, sometimes not uses an allegedly feminine behavior that is frequently negatively connoted. Consequently, it becomes obvious that the success of her strategy is also highly dependent on the conversational partner and their respective state of mind.

Since *Handbagged* discusses to what extent both the queen (with the death of Lord Mountbatten) and Mrs. Thatcher (the bombing at the Conservative conference in Brighton) were personally affected by the IRA bombings, the two characters can bond over these events. Despite their various political and personal differences throughout the play, the queen acts warmly and concerned towards Mrs. Thatcher and enquires after her wellbeing, once again taking on the role of a therapist. As a consequence, Mags opens up and offers a rare glimpse into her mind: "The hatred in it | And the number of people | The number of people in this country who | Who wish they had got me." (ibid: 90) In this regard, the prime minister becomes vulnerable, almost like a patient seeking help and guidance, whereas the queen remains passive and listens. Apparently not quite knowing how to react, Liz turns to food in order to comfort Mags and T: She offers them a scone with homemade jam. The monarch's sympathetic attitude is unsurprising given that the play generally casts her in a positive light. Yet, Mags' reaction shows that, at least in this particular moment, she gives in to the queen's more mundane chit-chat. Almost sentimentally, Mags says, "I think one's always looking for the jam that tastes like home." (ibid: 91) Here, the close link between women and the private sphere, in particular the notion of home and homeliness, is highlighted. While Liz and Q, as has been shown, are frequently presented with more feminine attributes, Mags and T often appear in stark contrast. Yet by allowing them to bond and to share a rather intimate moment with each other, *Handbagged* illustrates the respect these women have for each other. While the scene once again highlights the queen's conversational and listening skills, proving her ability as a counsellor, the play also asks the audience to reconsider their opinion of Mrs. Thatcher by presenting her as a vulnerable human being.

Although being a good listener is frequently dismissed as a typically feminine characteristic, this behavior – listening to her counterparts, sharing little family stories and making her prime ministers feel at home – turns out to be a very successful political strategy for the queen in both *The Audience* and *Handbagged*. In her analysis of the film *The Queen*, Mandy Merck similarly notes that "the Queen must establish a parental relation with her *subjects*" (2016: 375) which can be compared to the role of counsellor Morgan's and Buffini's versions of Elizabeth frequently take on. Because she succeeds in creating a warm, friendly environment, the majority of her guests speak equally frankly with the queen and this consequently allows them to discuss the respective political situation as equal partners. Coincidentally, both plays create a similar effect with regard to the audience: They are supposed to become accomplices of Elizabeth and her prime ministers since they are given secret glimpses into their private lives. This prompts the viewers to regard the queen and prime ministers' actions and behavior in a new light as it becomes apparent that these political figures are human, too.[4] To a constitutional monarch, gaining their subjects' love and respect is the best (political) weapon they can possibly wield. Due to the British monarch's lack of actual political power, their popularity and their corresponding social impact act as a form of substitute. The queen, in particular, may thus serve not only as head of the royal family but equally as head of the national family.

WAR, DIPLOMACY AND POLITICAL SPEECHES: THE QUEEN IS IN COMMAND

Since nearly all prime ministers the queen encounters in *The Audience* are male and since it has often been claimed that Margaret Thatcher had to act "tougher than the toughest" (Connell 2002: 56) in order to be accepted as a serious politician, strategies of power more frequently linked to men's behavior feature in both plays and are adopted and adapted by the monarch. For instance, *The Audience* uses some of the queen's official titles to emphasize her central position in British society: She is also called "the Duke of Normandy," "the Lord of Mann," "the Duke of Lancaster," and "the Lord High Admiral of the Royal Navy" (*TA*: 23-24),

---

4   In her article "'That's Entertainment': Monarchy as Performance," Anette Pankratz discusses at length the "remedialisation" (2017: 56) of Queen Elizabeth II, referring, among others, to the video clip with Daniel Craig and to the film *The Queen*. According to Pankratz, "the public image of the monarch has shifted from a more or less passive, dull, and dutiful mouthpiece, to someone who does her job with a great deal of discipline, intentionally hides her dazzling personality, and is able to make important decisions herself" (ibid: 56). Pankratz argues that due to specific media examples, both fictional and documentary, the public perception of Elizabeth II has changed to the better over the years, creating a "21st-century queen [who] even brims with wit" (ibid: 56). *The Audience* and *Handbagged* similarly contribute to this image, as becomes apparent in my analysis.

a list which quite impresses John Major. He is forced to admit that he "do[es]n't know these people," (ibid: 24) illustrating his lack of knowledge which automatically renders the queen the more senior partner in their conversation. Furthermore, it can be argued that the queen uses her titles almost like an armor to dress herself in.[5] Similarly, Buffini emphasizes Liz and Q's refusal to be excluded from topics that are regarded as inherently masculine, "such as state-defined politics, war, foreign policy, international trade" (Waylen 2002 [1998]: 11). Instead, the queen highlights her role as "sovereign" (*HB*: 59) and as "head of armed forces" (ibid: 58) during the Falklands War. T and Mags, however, react differently than John Major in *The Audience* and are hardly impressed at all.[6] Consequently, T remarks offhandedly: "Yes, of course, but that's all titular isn't it?" when Liz emphasizes her official status (ibid: 59). On the other hand, T accepts the monarch's more personal involvement in the war as "mother of a combatant" (ibid: 59). Arguably, this illustrates T's refusal to recognize the queen's political power, which is connoted as masculine, and forces Liz and Q to adopt a more feminine position, namely that of a mother.

More importantly, both plays do not reduce the queen to her titles but also show her as an active character, ready to take decisions and to initiate action. While it may be argued that Elizabeth's detailed political knowledge and interest in her meeting with Major reflects her long experience, her conversation with Churchill proves that, even at a young age and when suffering from the loss of her

---

5   This may be related to other monarchs' self-representation, in particular to Queen Elizabeth I's famous Tilbury Speech in which she said about herself "I know I have the body but of a weak and feeble woman; but I have the heart and stomach of a king, and of a king of England too," telling her soldiers "I myself will take up arms, I myself will be your general, judge, and rewarder of every one of your virtues in the field" ("Elizabeth's Tilbury Speech": n. pag.). By acknowledging her (supposedly weaker) sex, yet reminding her subjects of her powerful position as monarch, Elizabeth I invalidated any doubts concerning her ability to rule. Similarly, Morgan's Elizabeth II refers to herself by explicitly using official, male titles which emphasize her important standing in British society.

6   *Handbagged* suggests that this is linked to Mrs. Thatcher's own involvement in the war: She became known as the Iron Lady, eager to fight, while Q bitterly remarks "Gloriana, the papers called her | Boadicea in pearls" (ibid: 63), linking Mags and T to strong women, independent of male support. For a more detailed analysis of Margaret Thatcher's self-presentation as Elizabeth I, see also Irene Morra's article "New Elizabethanism: Origins, Legacies and the Theatre of Nation" in which she discusses Thatcher's "image of untouchable female power" (2016: 35).

father, the queen is always well prepared and takes her duty as monarch very seriously. Initially, Elizabeth is linked to the more private, homely sphere usually connoted as feminine when she asks Churchill: "Can you give me a date for the end of rationing of sugar, butter and meat?" (ibid: 26). Though domestic issues are more generally associated with women, the queen is shown not to limit herself to these aspects. Instead, she rather emphasizes her intention to be informed about all political matters by further questioning: "What more can you tell me about our development of nuclear weapons? And do you envisage a military engagement, by UN forces, against China – in support of our allies in Korea?" (ibid). Although Churchill belittles her engagement with a "patronising laugh" (ibid) and avoids answering her questions, the queen has made it clear that she expects to be briefed both on domestic and foreign politics, the latter being more frequently connoted as masculine issues, since they are linked to the military and war.

Given Churchill's condescending behavior, it is not surprising that Elizabeth attempts to use her intimate knowledge of inner-party conflicts to stand up to him (cf. ibid: 28). Since party politics in the 1950s were still mainly restricted to men, the queen's comment clearly shows that she is nonetheless privy to this exclusive circle: "Your party wants you to resign and make way for a ... younger man. Mr Eden." (ibid: 28) Here, Elizabeth is seen to use her knowledge to gain an advantage over Churchill and is thus presented as a cunning politician, employing the same manipulation strategy Churchill had tried on her. Furthermore, it is striking that the queen unravels Churchill's clever plan to delay his own resignation thus reminding him that he is also dependent on her: "You know," she says, "no one would bring up your resignation while you were actively engaged in planning the Coronation." (ibid) Since Elizabeth has to agree to a specific date for her coronation, it is she who holds power over Churchill. This high status allows her to address issues more associated with femininity, namely the question of her family name. Although Churchill strictly rejects her proposition of taking her husband's name, he finally regards the queen as his equal and engages in a lively discussion with her. Arguably, this could not have been achieved without Elizabeth's prior revelation of her knowledge, which in turn granted her power over Churchill.

Handbagged employs similar strategies in order to represent the fictional queen as a tough monarch, emphasizing her oppositional stance against Margaret Thatcher. Both Liz and Q frequently speak their mind and stand up against the prime minister's political views and actions while also indicating that they are perfectly at ease when dealing with other male political figures. The scene "Dancing at Lusaka" presents Mrs. Thatcher's first Heads of Commonwealth meeting, contrasting her rather insecure behavior and weak position with the queen's experience and confidence. Although the monarch is not part of the elected British parliament, Liz and Q nonetheless insist on accompanying their prime minister to the conference. Q defends her decision by claiming that it was Thatcher "who needed protecting" (*HB*: 35) and thus presents herself as guardian and supporter. She further confronts T and Mags, stating "You were too green to see it | I knew I could be useful | To you and to Britain" (ibid: 35) and thereby referring to her own vast experience in international diplomacy. Consequently, Mags and T are shown as weaker since their position as 'newcomer,' who should not be left alone, is emphasized.

This aforementioned opposition of active (stereotypically masculine) and passive (stereotypically feminine) is further highlighted by the scene's set-up: While Mags and T are still on their way to Lusaka, "sick with dread" (ibid: 39) on the plane and busy preparing for their first international event, Liz and Q are already in Zambia, "determined to smooth [Mrs. Thatcher's] way" (ibid) and "asking [their] incisive questions" (ibid: 38) to keep up to date with current matters of the Commonwealth. Therefore, Mags and T are depicted as nervous and uncertain whereas the queen appears as one among equals when chatting with political leaders. Interestingly enough, though, both the monarch and her prime minister are shown by Buffini to regard themselves as responsible for the conference's positive outcome: "My work behind the scenes paid off," (ibid: 40) Liz proudly declares and describes how the other politicians welcomed and accepted Mags. Denis Thatcher, however, has a different opinion: According to him, his wife's dancing with Kenneth Kaunda, the President of Zambia, was "what turned the trick" (ibid: 41).[7] Consequently, it can be argued that *Handbagged* portrays two equally strong characters: While the queen actively turns to behavior patterns associated with masculinity, such as presenting herself as an active and public figure, Thatcher is initially forced to passive reaction but quickly adapts to the situation and uses her femininity to her advantage.

Additionally, the queen's passionate involvement in politics can be further illustrated in the context of her Christmas broadcast, "the only major speech of the year that is written without government intervention," (ibid: 54) and consequently one of the rare occasions the monarch may use to directly address her people with her own thoughts. In *Handbagged*, Liz uses this opportunity to become active and

---

[7] Interestingly, Denis appears to disregard the male lead usually expected in a dance between a man and a woman. Simultaneously, his comment may also point towards the representation of Margaret Thatcher as a strong woman who does not conform to stereotypical feminine behavior and thus refuses to be led by Kaunda. For more details on the intricacies of royal dance and power issues, see Susanne Scholz' article in this volume.

to criticize the press's treatment of Princess Diana as well as Thatcher's economy policies: She emphasizes the widening gap between the rich and the poor, citing rising child poverty and unemployment and thus directly contradicts the prime minister (cf. ibid: 81-82). Although Mags and T defend their view and emphasize the people's need to take care of themselves instead of simply relying on the government to fix their problems for them, Liz and Q resolutely disagree. "Prime Minister," Liz says, "we've travelled a great deal this year | As we do every year | And the problem is not just in Britain. | The poor are getting poorer | And we have seen first hand | The growing gap." (ibid: 83) She thus cites her own experience of the country's troubles as an important argument. Here, *Handbagged* establishes the queen as a compassionate and thus stereotypically feminine sovereign, who appears at the same time as an active and public figure (a rather masculine attribute), who frequently mingles with common people.

A similar attitude is expressed earlier when Liz speaks out about Mags' negative comments concerning the miners' strike. "Have you ever been down a mine, Mrs Thatcher?" Liz asks almost provocatively, "I have | I thought it was a dark and dangerous place to work | I was deeply impressed by the men who laboured there." (ibid: 70) Again, the play draws specific attention to the monarch's detailed knowledge of her people's hardships in order to cast Liz and Q in a positive light, particularly in contrast to Mags and T. By labelling mining as a dangerous occupation that deserves admiration, Liz also implicitly criticizes Thatcher's actions during the miners' strikes and presents her as someone who is quite detached from ordinary life whereas the monarch is shown seeking direct contact to the miners and their families. Furthermore, Liz openly contradicts Thatcher's negative assessment of the miners, stating: "And never, at any time | Have I found them to be | The enemy within." (ibid) *Handbagged* thus illustrates the monarch's willingness to oppose the prime minister both with words and actions. All in all, the queen's decisive stand against Mrs. Thatcher, against certain policies, and against injustice present her as an active, at times almost aggressive character, with a detailed, intimate knowledge of British and international politics. In particular, her long experience, her ability to move freely amongst male politicians and her willingness to put her people's well-being before her own are emphasized. Whilst these characteristics may not appear like explicitly masculine behavior, they can nonetheless be linked to rationality, reason, and being active. Thus, Liz and Q's recurring strong opinions and actions show that they are in command and in control of the respective situation and their country.

Both plays present a fictional version of the British monarch that refuses to let herself be reduced to stereotypically feminine topics and patterns of behavior. Instead, the queen is shown as a rather forceful character, who is eager to initiate action and who is not afraid of opposing her prime ministers. By making clever use of her official titles and of her position in society, Elizabeth II is presented as an intelligent political figure, who is very capable of holding her ground and engaging in (international) politics.

VULNERABLE AND ADAMANT: THE QUEEN AS A POLITICIAN IN *THE AUDIENCE* AND *HANDBAGGED*

Taking as its premise the British monarch's restricted political power in today's constitutional monarchy as well as common stereotypes regarding masculine and feminine behavior, this paper set out to explore strategies of power employed by two fictional versions of Elizabeth II. I argued that – to a certain extent – *The Audience* and *Handbagged* use the same character construction: They show the queen making use of an effective mixture of recognizably masculine and feminine traits. In order to enable theatre audiences to recognize these traits and patterns of behavior, the plays resort to well-known stereotypes: Feminine behavior is thus associated with the private and homely sphere, with passivity, and an emphasis on emotions. In particular, women's alleged passion for gossip and chit-chat is evoked, yet is shown to prove a valuable strategy for the fictional versions of the queen. On the other hand, typically masculine behavior is linked with the public sphere, with rationality, with being active, and with a focus on reason. Since the audience recognizes this exaggerated dichotomy, it can be regarded as an invitation to laugh at this representation of gender clichés. Through these comic elements and the plays' partially reversed expectations of allegedly masculine and feminine traits, the audience becomes aware of the stereotypical nature of these clichés and might reassess them in a critical way.

Both plays present fictional versions of the queen that are designed to win their audience's sympathy: Emotional aspects are foregrounded, such as the queen's close relationship with her mother and her grief for her father's early death. By showing the monarch as a vulnerable character, Morgan and Buffini prompt the respective prime ministers – and the audience – to feel compassion for her. Rather than solely focusing on the public persona, namely the queen's image as a dutiful, well-respected monarch, the plays foreground the private Elizabeth by providing an intimate insight into her life and thoughts. This feeling of compassion and sympathy is further accentuated when the fictional queen retells family stories, shares gossips and secrets, and expresses her love for dogs and horses. Consequently, some of the monarch's prime ministers become her accomplices, just like the audience. Since the viewers are allowed to witness the queen's more private thoughts and feelings, Morgan and Buffini attempt to create an emotional bond between their character and the audience, especially by contrasting the fictional version of Elizabeth with patronizing, mostly male politicians, who, it is suggested, frequently underestimate her intellect. By emphasizing the queen's fondness of gossip and seemingly trivial chit-chat, both playwrights lure the respective prime ministers into a trap where they imagine themselves as the stronger, more powerful partner compared to the queen. Thus, *The Audience* and *Handbagged* show the risk of underestimating someone based on their gender and focus on Elizabeth's ability to turn her apparent weaknesses into advantages.

At the same time, the monarch is presented as decisive, inquisitive and adamant. She refuses to limit herself to topics that are deemed appropriate for a woman, instead asking questions about traditionally masculine political spheres such as war and foreign policy. In several scenes Elizabeth is even shown to have the upper hand guiding her prime ministers through the dangerous labyrinth of international diplomacy and offering them counsel and support in their hours of need. Consequently, some of the male politicians appear weak and almost helpless, thus presenting a relationship in which the monarch generally succeeds. By resorting to her official titles and duties, the queen is able to demand respect and reverence powerfully reminding prime ministers and audience alike that her position is a traditional one that plays an integral role in British society. Her usage of these titles also reflects a world that is still mostly dominated by men who, in turn, are likely to be impressed by other (allegedly) male official figures – only to realize that the holder of these titles and powers is, in fact, a woman. However, *Handbagged* also shows that the fictional queen's usage of specifically masculine traits sometimes fails when dealing with another woman, in this case Mrs. Thatcher. This forces Liz and Q to emphasize their femininity instead in order to (re)gain popularity and power, e.g. by mentioning their family ties in order to evoke sympathy.

Consequently, it can be stated that *The Audience* and *Handbagged* use a variety of stereotypically masculine and feminine behavior in their character construction of Queen Elizabeth II. As has been argued, this strategy has a direct impact on viewers' reception of the fictional monarch – e.g. creating pity and evoking laughter – and toys with stereotypes that can easily be recognized and questioned. It also mirrors the notion of the queen being above politics. Since political institutions and the state are commonly connoted as masculine whereas the nation is frequently represented by a female figure, the fictional Elizabeth II combines these notions, enabling her to unite British society in a way that is not possible for and not open to her prime ministers. However, it is striking that both plays pay particular attention to presenting humane characters, both with regard to the queen and her prime ministers. While individual viewers are likely to have differing views on the various politicians, the playwrights encourage the audience to sympathize with the queen, highlighting her prominent position and role. Morgan and Buffini similarly emphasize the humane side of Britain's prime ministers. They are shown as suffering from depression and are inclined to doubt their own capability as politicians, therefore prompting the audience to question their previous understanding and reception of politicians. Yet the plays' focus lies first and foremost on the monarch, who appears both strong and vulnerable and who is able to counsel and support but also guide and manipulate the sometimes faltering politicians. By making use of the real queen's reticence, *The Audience* and *Handbagged* are able to attribute certain traits and abilities to her and thus create an ideal monarch. Consequently, the queen's continuous relevance as a national symbol and as an important political figure in today's Britain is accentuated.

WORKS CITED

Bagehot, Walter (2001 [1867]): The English Constitution, edited by Miley Taylor, Oxford: Oxford University Press.

Barnett, Laura (2014): "Handbagged." In: TimeOut, 10 April, accessed October 17, 2017. (https://www.timeout.com/london/theatre/handbagged).

Berg, Sebastian (2017): "Would Britain Be More Democratic If It Became a Republic?" In: Anette Pankratz/Claus-Ulrich Viol (eds.), (Un)Making the Monarchy, Heidelberg: Winter, pp. 227-243.

Billington, Michael (2013): "The Audience – Review." In: The Guardian March 5, accessed October 18, 2017 (https://www.theguardian.com/stage/2013/mar/05/the-audience-review-helen-mirren).

Brantley, Ben (2015): "Review: Helen Mirren Stars in 'The Audience' on Broadway." In: New York Times, March 8, 2015, accessed October 18, 2017 (https://www.nytimes.com/2015/03/09/theater/review-the-audience-with-helen-mirren-opens-on-broadway.html).

Buffini, Moira (2013): Handbagged, London: Faber and Faber.

Chandler, Daniel/Munday, Rod (2016): "Gender Stereotypes." In: A Dictionary of Media and Communication, Oxford: Oxford University Press, accessed December 1, 2017 (http://www.oxfordreference.com/view/10.1093/acref/9780191800986.001.0001/acref-9780191800986-e-1094).

Connell, Raewyn (2012): "Der gemachte Mann: Konstruktion und Krise von Männlichkeiten." In: Franziska Bergmann/Franziska Schößler/Bettina Schreck (eds.), Gender Studies, Bielefeld: transcript, pp. 157-174.

Connell, Raewyn (2002): Gender, Cambridge: Polity Press.

Cranny-Francis, Anne/Waring, Wendy/Stavropoulos, Pam/Kirkby, Joan (2003): Gender Studies: Terms and Debates, Houndmills: Palgrave Macmillan.

"Elizabeth's Tilbury Speech", In: British Library, n. d., accessed April 18, 2019 (http://www.bl.uk/learning/timeline/item102878.html).

Higson, Andrew (2016): "From Political Power to the Power of the Image: Contemporary 'British' Cinema and the Nation's Monarchs." In: Mandy Merck (ed.), The British Monarchy on Screen, Manchester: Manchester University Press, pp. 339-362.

Jordan, Christina (forthcoming): "Staging Britain's (A)Political Leader: Queen Elizabeth II in Peter Morgan's Play The Audience (2015)." In: Ansgar Nünning/Vera Nünning/Alexander Scherr (eds.), Literature and Literary Studies in the Twenty-First Century: Cultural Concerns – Concepts – Case Studies, Trier: WVT.

Morra, Irene (2016): "Origins, Legacies and the Theatre of Nation." In: Irene Morra/Rob Gossedge (eds.), The New Elizabethan Age. Culture, Society and National Identity after World War II, London and New York: I.B. Tauris, pp. 17-48.

Morra, Irena/Gossedge, Rob (eds.) (2016): The New Elizabethan Age. Culture, Society and National Identity after World War II. London and New York: Tauris.

Merck, Mandy (2016): "Melodrama, Celebrity, *The Queen*." In: Mandy Merck (ed.), The British Monarchy on Screen, Manchester: Manchester University Press, pp. 363-383.

Morgan, Peter (2015 [2013]): The Audience, London: Faber and Faber.

Moseley, Tom (2016): "Theresa May's Leather Trousers Prompt Political Row." In: BBC December 12, 2016, accessed November 8, 2017 (www.bbc.com/news/uk-politics-38287637).

Nestruck, J. Kelly (2017): "Peter Morgan's The Audience Feels Like a Rough Stage Outline of The Crown." In: The Globe and Mail January 20, updated March 24, accessed October 18, 2017 (https://beta.theglobeandmail.com/arts/theatre-and-performance/theatre-reviews/peter-morgans-the-audience-feels-like-a-rough-stage-outline-of-the-crown/article33683672/?ref=).

Newton Dunn, Tom (2016): "Revealed: Queen Backs Brexit as Alleged EU Bust-Up with Ex-Deputy PM Emerges." In: The Sun March 8, updated July 28, accessed November 8, 2017 (www.thesun.co.uk/news/1078504/revealed-queen-backs-brexit-as-alleged-eu-bust-up-with-ex-deputy-pm-emerges/).

Oakland, John (2011 [1989]). British Civilization: An Introduction, London: Routledge.

Otnes, Cele C./Maclaran, Pauline (2015): Royal Fever. The British Monarchy in Consumer Culture, Oakland: University of California Press.

Pankratz, Anette (2017): "'That's Entertainment': Monarchy as Performance." In: Anette Pankratz/Claus-Ulrich Viol (eds.), (Un)Making the Monarchy, Heidelberg: Winter, pp. 41-64.

von Braun, Christina (2006): "Gender, Geschlecht und Geschichte." In: Christina von Braun/Inge Stephan (eds.), Gender Studien: Eine Einführung, Stuttgart: Metzler, pp. 10-51.

Waylen, Georgia (2002 [1998]): "Gender, Feminism and the State: An Overview." In: Georgia Waylen/Vicky Randall (eds.), Gender, Politics, and the State, London and New York: Routledge, pp. 1-17.

Films and Television

The Crown. Created by Peter Morgan. 2016–. Netflix.
The Queen. Directed by Stephen Frears. 2006. Paris: Pathé.

**Royal Representations
in Contemporary
Popular Cultural Contexts**

The (In)Significance of Queen Victoria in Neo-Victorian Comics

Natalie Veith

(NEO-)VICTORIAN VALUES SINCE THE 1980S

During the last quarter-century, neo-Victorianism has established itself as an aesthetic and narrative mode in cultural production. Despite bearing historicist traces, its most notable characteristic is that it is at the same time anachronistic, intermedial, and metafictional: neo-Victorian works mash up historical events with elements from fiction and tend to emphasize their own constructedness. They are frequently double-voiced and, in addressing the past, also address the present and question our forms of historical engagement. Therefore, neo-Victorianism is not self-sufficient, it exists in relation and with reference to other, previous forms of addressing and depicting the past. The neo-Victorian has therefore often been used to oppose coherent and euphemizing narratives about the past and a corresponding ideological utilization thereof. Neo-Victorianism is an attempt to deal with the past without falling back on one-sided depictions, sentimental nostalgia, or complete rejection and without concealing processes of manipulation and mediatization. This critical perspective also extends to depictions of Queen Victoria, but despite the designation neo-*Victorian*, the queen herself plays a relatively small role in these works and is usually merely a side character. Moreover, she tends to lack agency, insight into the plots unfolding around her, and is easily deceived. But, as I will argue, her relevance lies just in this apparent insignificance, since it is used to deconstruct traditional notions of Britishness and imperial power that are often associated with her. Moreover, the nature of her appearance within the stories tends to echo the general anachronistic and intermedial logic of neo-Victorian narratives. To illustrate this, I will use examples from three neo-Victorian comic books: Alan Moore and Eddie Campbell's *From Hell* (2000 [1989-1996]; from here on cited as *FH*), Grant Morrison and Steve Yeowell's *Sebastian O* (2004

[1993]; from here on cited as *SO*), and Sydney Padua's *The Thrilling Adventures of Lovelace and Babbage* (2015; from here on cited as *TA*).

When the first neo-Victorian comic books emerged in the 1980s, the image of the Victorian era was undergoing a transformation in several areas of cultural production. The first half of the 20th century had still been characterized by a relative hostility towards all things Victorian, which decreased in the second half of the century and eventually turned into its opposite: the 1980s saw an increase in romanticizing narratives about the 19th century in fiction and in heritage culture (Mitchell 2010: 48-54). This revaluation also coincided with the Thatcher administration in the UK and provided fertile soil for Margaret Thatcher's conservative and traditionalist approaches, enabling a reciprocal discursive reinforcement of the upsurge of Victorian nostalgia and Thatcher's rhetoric.

Thatcher had from the start relied heavily on notions of Britishness and national pride and on evocations of past imperial glory. In an interview conducted by Michael Cockerell before her first election as Prime Minister, she claimed: "I can't *bear* Britain in decline. I just can't. We who either defeated or rescued half Europe, who kept half Europe free, when otherwise it would be in chains." (Thatcher 1979: n. pag.) A similar rhetoric can be found in her speech at the Conservative Rally in Cheltenham in 1982, less than three weeks after Britain's victory in the Falklands War. She fashioned the victory as a restoration of national pride and imperial power by proclaiming that with this, Britain had "ceased to be a nation in retreat," which would put an end to the

> "secret fears that it was true: that Britain was no longer the nation that had built an Empire and ruled a quarter of the world. […] The lesson of the Falklands is that Britain has not changed and that this nation still has those sterling qualities which shine through our history." (Thatcher 1982: n. pag.)

Thatcher's rhetoric of imperial greatness was reflected in the media and in popular discourse (e.g. newspaper caricatures), where she increasingly became associated with and depicted in the guise of female allegories of Britain's power: Britannia and Britain/England's queens, a phenomenon that Marina Warner has provided an elaborate analysis of in her monograph *Monuments and Maidens: The Allegory of the Female Form* (2000: 38-60). During Britain's 1983 pre-election campaigns, when Thatcher was running for her second term as prime minister, she intensified this rhetoric and launched what became known as the 'Victorian values' campaign. In a series of interviews and speeches, she created a narrative of Victorian England as a time and place of hard work, thrift, and national pride, based on the values she herself was raised with:

"I was brought up by a Victorian grandmother. You were taught to work jolly hard, you were taught to improve yourself, you were taught self-reliance, you were taught to live within your income, you were taught that cleanliness was next to godliness. You were taught self-respect, you were taught always to give a hand to your neighbour, you were taught tremendous pride in your country, you were taught to be a good member of your community. All of these things are Victorian values." (Thatcher 1983: n. pag.)

But even though some of Thatcher's concepts indeed echoed, for example, the Victorian concept of self-help or the canonization of the heteronormative nuclear family, in many ways her politics were all but traditional. Several long-established sectors and traditional industries, such as manufacturing, were in stark decline due to cuts in public expenditure and privatization, leading to a decomposition of the working class. Thatcher benefited less from an actual traditionalist approach than from a rhetoric that helped her legitimize her plans for the future by allegedly successful values from the past, which was "more a matter of style than of substance," as Raphael Samuel put it (1992: 10). It allowed her to fashion herself as someone "who was not afraid of sounding reactionary" (ibid: 17) and "it spoke to those who felt bewildered or alarmed by the shape of cultural change. It ministered to the belief, widely canvassed in the public press, that Britain was becoming ungovernable, in Mrs. Thatcher's words, 'a decadent, undisciplined society'" (ibid: 14-15).

This was, however, by many perceived as a rhetorical 'hijacking' of the past and hence prompted artistic and popular cultural reactions to both the Thatcher legislation in general and to her Victorian Values campaign in particular. *From Hell*, the first comic that I will discuss, can be read as an open attempt to write back against Thatcher's values and her utilization of the past, yet not so much in the form of a reappropriation than as a harsh counter discourse that makes use of both narrative as well as aesthetic techniques.

THE GHOSTLY QUEEN IN *FROM HELL*

Alan Moore and Eddie Campbell's *From Hell* was first published in single chapters between 1989 and 1996; a collected edition with additional material followed in 1999. The plot roughly adapts a popular conspiracy theory proposed by Stephen Knight in his 1976 book *Jack the Ripper: The Final Solution*, according to which the Ripper murders were a scheme to cover up the secret marriage between Queen Victoria's eldest grandson, Prince Albert Victor, and a catholic shop-girl named

Anne Crook upon whom he also allegedly fathered a child. In the comic, this conspiratorial plot is embellished by historical details and enriched with elements of the supernatural and horror fiction, and the murder case turns into an obscure media spectacle.

Victoria first appears in a two-page sequence consisting of one slightly larger, borderless introductory panel and twelve further panels that are smaller and equal in size and design (see fig. 1). In this sequence, set in 1871, she expresses her gratitude to doctor William Gull (who will in this story become the Ripper seventeen years later) for saving her eldest son and heir apparent from typhoid fever. As a reward, she appoints him Royal Physician in Extraordinary (*FH* ch. 2, 18-19). However, the honours she bestows upon him for rescuing her son are rather a sign of her appreciation of Gull's (masculine) strength and loyalty than of her concern for the prince. She asks Gull if he thought the prince's life was worth saving, adding: "If you mean 'No', Dr. Gull, you have our leave to say 'No'. Our son is a wastrel and a halfwit. We shudder to think of the throne in his hands." (ibid: ch. 2, 19) Victoria's *mise-en-scène* in *From Hell* is cold-hearted and bitter, emphasizing her tainted relationship to her son.[1]

Following the convention of most pictures of the elderly Victoria, she is depicted sitting in half profile, wearing her characteristic black mourning dress with white mourning cap and scarf. Her figure is depicted in front of a dark, cross-hatched background and the thickness and density of the lines increases towards the centre of the panels. This turns the mourning dress, which mostly lacks light reflections and details and thus appears as an almost solidly black mass, into the optical centre of the panel. It looks as if the surrounding darkness is emanating

---

1   Negative depictions of Victoria, emphasizing her bad relationship to her children and her controlling nature were still comparatively rare until the late 1980s. As David Cannadine has put it in a 1987 review of Stanley Weintraub's biography of Queen Victoria, "until very recently, the queen herself has effectively escaped this critical scrutiny. While the Victorian Age now seems so diverse and contradictory that the phrase itself has been virtually robbed of all meaning, the queen herself remains regina intacta" (1987: n. pag.). Her depiction in *From Hell* is therefore one of the earlier instances in which this shift is articulated. Over the last two decades, these depictions have become relatively common. The three-part BBC documentary *Queen Victoria's Children* (2013), for example, takes a rather psychologizing approach. It compiles excerpts from letters and personal diary entries that depict Victoria as a "Domestic Tyrant" (which is also the title of the second episode). But despite this, there is also an opposed tendency to return to more positive, 'likeable' depictions again, for example through Jenna Coleman's portrayal of the young queen in the television series *Victoria* (2016–).

from the queen, while she, in turn, fades ghostlike into it, rendering her visual outline unintelligible and her figure intangible. The imagery supports the impression created through the dialogues and suggests that Victoria is engrossed in thoughts about her deceased husband and that there is a mutual disinterest and detachment between her and the mortal world.

Figure 1: Victoria's first appearance in From Hell

Source: *FH* ch. 2, 18-19; copyright Alan Moore and Eddie Campbell

The first, larger panel of the sequence even lacks a panel border, making Victoria not only fade into the dark background but seep into the page itself. The sequence's last panel, by contrast, depicting Victoria in solitude after she said that she "would rather be alone" (ibid: ch. 2, 1), appears smudged and obscured by blotches of black ink that spread across the outline (ibid). Victoria's darkness sprawls across the confining borders of the diegetic reality and of orderly sequential storytelling, thereby also emphasizing both the materiality of the medium comic and the mediality of Victoria's depiction within it. This emphasis on mediality is enhanced by the significant lack of visual difference between the panels of this sequence: at best, there is a slight variation in the orientation of Victoria's head or her hands but nothing beyond that. The thirteen panels are practically identical, which echoes the mechanical reproduction of the historical Queen Victoria's image for the masses that her appearance in the comic is clearly modelled on, e.g. the historical jubilee photograph, which became a popular collectible in the late 19th century. The queen, conventionally mythologized as unique in being the single rightful sovereign, is here depicted as an iteration of mass-(re)produced photographs. Borrowing the words of Walter Benjamin, one could say that in this visual rhetoric "the technique of reproduction detaches the reproduced object from the domain of tradition. By making many reproductions it substitutes a plurality of copies for a unique existence." (2007 [1935]: 221) Just as Victoria will come to fear a scandal about her grandson's illegitimate child in 1888, which might obscure the singularity and linearity of the royal succession and "rock the throne" (*FH* ch. 2, 28), as she puts it in chapter two, her own singularity is already visually deconstructed during her very first appearance.

Moreover, it is notable that while the coexistence of this multitude of similar pictures on one page is enabled by the specific media properties of comics, it simultaneously subverts comics' visual and narrative conventions, thereby defying the expectations with which readers (be it consciously or unconsciously) approach comics. Even though in most cases a sequence of panels in a comic depicts a succession through time, they always coexist simultaneously on the page, effectively mapping out temporal fragments as a visual totality. So even when reading panels on a page in chronological order, the readers can usually not avoid catching at least a fleeting impression of the composition as a whole and may in some cases even choose to stray from a linear reading of the page. In this regard, as comic artist Will Eisner remarks, the general layout and grid of a page may have a disciplinary effect on the narrative by dictating the rhythm with which the action is structured and consequently perceived. Nevertheless, this rhythm remains only an offer to the readers, who are eventually left with a relative level of autonomy regarding reading order and rhythm (cf. Eisner 2006 [1985]: 40). Therefore, Eisner continues to point out, comic narratives require a certain level of cooperation on behalf of the readers that they invite by offering (both pictorial and verbal) cues on how to read and perceive a given sequence (cf. ibid).

This eventually enables 'closure,' which, in the specific context of comics, refers to the mental process taking place on behalf of the readers when they 'fill the gaps' between the individual panels of a sequence and construct a causal relationship between them (cf. McCloud 1994 [1993]: 63-67). Besides the simulation of linearity and time flow, other possible types of panel-to-panel transitions include indications of a change in location or the illumination of different aspects in a larger scene. A classification of these different panel transitions has been attempted, for example, by comic artist Scott McCloud in *Understanding Comics:*

The Invisible Art (1994 [1993]).[2] Comics researcher Thierry Groensteen, by contrast, has argued for the analytical importance of the rhythmicality of longer panel sequences and how single panels can be emphasized by narrative and stylistic effects such as repetition, alternation, and cinematic and optical progressivity.[3] What classificatory systems as these reveal is that in comics, there is a structural reliance on the concept of repetition-with-a-difference: while repetition and similarity or at least some common element is needed to establish a recognizable relation between single panels, difference is also necessary to perceive the temporal structure of the scene. But the lack of visual difference in Victoria's sequence eradicates all indications of time (cf. Groensteen 2013 [1999]: 145). Closure is "the agent of *change, time* and *motion*" (McCloud 1994 [1993]: 65), all of which is suspended in this sequence. Victoria transcends and obscures the readers' perception of and expectation towards narrated time and is the sole centre of attention. The overwhelming totality and visual homogeneity of this page disables the readers to determine how much time each panel takes up. Victoria's appearance is monolithic, motion- and lifeless.

The pages of *From Hell* – just like most of Moore's other works as well – are generally structured by a regular and minimalist three by three grid (what Groensteen also calls a "waffle-iron grid" 2013 [1999]: 138), thereby shifting the focus from the page layout to the contents of the narrative as well as supporting the autonomy of the readers by not formally privileging certain panels over others. However, through their similarity in this particular scene with Victoria, the panels

---

2 Examples for transitions that simulate the flow of time are what McCloud has termed "moment-to-moment" and "action-to-action" transitions (70), or "scene-to-scene" in case of transitions that "transport [the readers] across *significant distances* of *time* and *space*" (ibid: 71); richness in detail, by contrast, can be expressed through "subject-to-subject" and "aspect-to-aspect" transitions (ibid: 71-72). McCloud's categorization is, as he also remarks himself, not extensive and complete enough to describe all panel-to-panel transitions or to cover the range of the visual poetics of comics storytelling and therefore certainly not indisputable. However, it remains a well-known, extensive, and generally usable terminology.

3 The alternation of stylistic and narrative elements can indicate a marked shift in the story. Cinematic progressivity describes the temporal "decomposition of the action represented" over several panels and optical progressivity is "the equivalent of the zoom in or out, which gradually brings us closer to or further away from a given subject" (Groensteen 2013 [1999]: 146). The repetition of an earlier panel or framing can emphasize that this is a key moment and/or evoke the feeling in the readers that "time seems to stand still" (ibid: 145).

appear in the manner of geometrically ordered kaleidoscopic facets. Victoria's static appearance not only resists the rhythm dictated by the panels but also disturbs the readers' autonomy by presenting herself in totality and reproduced multitude: wherever the readers choose to look, the queen barely changes.

Her later appearances support this manner of depiction, both on the pictorial and the verbal level of the narrative: she appears as cold and lifeless, indeterminable and intangible, disturbing, embittered and resentful towards the world, which can be seen, for example, when she repeatedly voices her disdain for her living family members, such has her grandson, who "has apparently fathered a bastard child upon some filthy shop-girl" (*FH* ch. 2, 28). Gull is one of the few people in whom Victoria still trusts. In fear of the public scandal that the illegitimate child might cause, she asks him to handle the situation. It is significant that what exactly she asks of him is only vaguely indicated: she informs him that the prince's mistress has been brought to the hospital, where she is to "await your [Gull's] attentions" (ibid), as she puts it. Gull resolves the matter by removing Anne's thyroid gland with the intention to cause iodine to accumulate in her body, thereby mentally incapacitating and thus silencing her (ibid: ch. 2, 32). Similarly, in a later scene where Victoria 'commissions' the Ripper murders, the exact phrase with which she does it remains a gap, thereby hinting at her agency, but simultaneously keeping it invisible. After Victoria summons Gull, their dialogue opens *in medias res* with her saying: "We leave the means to you, Sir William. We would simply it were done, and done well..." upon which Gull inquires: "ALL of them, Your Majesty?" – "All of them" (ibid: ch. 4, 3). The readers are thus left in the dark, ignorant of what Victoria actually asks Gull to do, and can merely speculate on the degree to which she is knowingly involved in the murders. The order is given in a matter-of-fact way, implying both a disturbing indifference on her behalf about the lives of several women as well as about her own superior and privileged agency that she apathetically transfers to Gull, putting her into an oscillating position of (in)significance. This brief dialogue is again depicted in borderless panels, setting the sequence in a different relation to time and space, emphasizing its determining role for the entirety of the plot. It stands outside of the normal, orderly procession of events and at the same time conditions them.

As becomes clear over the course of the story, Victoria did at least not anticipate the exact scope the killings would take. In a later conversation with Gull, she questions "the necessity for such excessive ghastliness in these eliminations" (ibid: ch. 9, 11). Gull justifies his deeds by claiming that the exact manner in which he committed the murders was a warning sent out to enemies of Freemasonry and, as he puts it, in consequence also enemies of the crown. Lulled by his words, Victoria eventually gives in: "It appears that you know better than we. Go forth with our blessing." (ibid) She thereby gives up on reclaiming control over the situation and on regaining her agency.

And it is not only Gull who utilizes Victoria's helpless ignorance for his own means. During her last appearance in *From Hell*, the readers see her during a séance conducted by the alleged medium and spiritualist Robert James Lees (see fig. 2). He claims that he can see the ghost of Victoria's late husband hovering above her, which she readily believes (ibid: ch. 12, 1). Albert's appearance in this scene is modelled on a photographic negative with reversed dark and light shades, thereby once more introducing the issue of mediality and also bringing Victorian spirit photography to mind, where photographers like Frederick Hudson used techniques such as double exposure to fake the appearance of the ghosts of deceased friends and relatives in portrait photographs, just like Lees does with Albert, whose appearance in this scene thereby contains visual cues to his made-up nature. Moreover, as the readers know from the prologue of the story, which depicts an elderly Lees thirty-five years after the main storyline, "[he] made it up. All of them. All the visions. [He] made them up" (ibid: prologue, 3), just for the sake of fame and attention. Victoria, even though invested with a position of supreme power, lacks insight into the schemes and plots of the men she has gathered around herself as her presumably faithful servants. Her orders and requests end up becoming means of empowerment for them.

Figure 2: Victoria during a séance conducted by Mr. Lees

Source: *FH* ch. 12, 1, panel 1 and 6; copyright Alan Moore and Eddie Campbell

Over the course of the story, the queen's visual depiction gets increasingly sinister: The darkness steadily increases and her posture becomes weakened and bent. While Gull violates the bodies of his female victims, which he perceives as a symbolic act to reinstate male hegemony (cf. Miettinen 2012: 90), the queen is simultaneously withering away. In her last two appearances the background is almost completely black and she is barely distinguishable from it. She is but a cluster of white lines lurking in the shadows, bearing a stronger resemblance to Albert's make-believe ghost hanging under the ceiling in the previously mentioned scene than to an actual person. Ironically, on a visual level the queen achieves her desired reunion with her beloved husband through their common appearances as imprints of mortality and mediality.

Historically, Victoria was the ruler of the world's largest empire, encompassing more than a quarter of the world's total population, and it was this association that Thatcher was propagating and building on around the time *From Hell*'s serialization began. Within the story, the queen is initially powerful and privileged to decide over life or death of the Ripper victims. But on the other hand, she is a helpless victim of her grief caused by the loss of her husband. Furthermore, her own death is visually encoded in her spectral, ghostly appearance, which is in turn utilized by her male subordinates. The comic draws up Queen Victoria as a highly ambivalent character, oscillating between powerful ruler and subordinate woman, which is played out against Gull's violent assertions of masculinity and his obscure utilization of influence and power.

Sadly, the comic thereby reproduces the logic of Victorian gender roles of men being capable of rational planning and women, by contrast, being gullible and naïve (Victoria) and incapable of anticipating the outcome of their actions (the Ripper victims). But at the same time, this reductive juxtaposition allows for a critique of patriarchal structures that relates to the problems arising from conjunctions of femininity and power in the 19th century. Bernd Weisbrod has analysed how Victoria came to "embody the 'feminisation' of a once powerful male symbol," which, however, also coincided with the waning power invested in this structure (2006: 242). Part of Victoria's success and popularity as a constitutional monarch probably hinged on her attempts to impersonate the values of 19th-century middle-class femininity, such as female subordination and devotion to husband and family, which she combined with an image of political innocence in the public sphere (cf. Plunkett 2003: 20). Victoria thereby became the first British monarch who emphasized her female 'body natural' over her 'body politic' (cf. Schulte 2006: 8; Kantorowicz 1957: 4-13).[4] In *From Hell*, this transformation of royal representation escalates into a dramatization of the juxtaposition between the mortality of Victoria's 'body natural' and the mediality of her 'body politic.'

---

4   The body duality of the monarch, which has most famously been analysed by Ernst H. Kantorowicz, is a concept of corporation that established itself as a central element of

THE VIRTUAL QUEEN IN *SEBASTIAN O*

My second example, Grant Morrison and Steve Yeowell's three-issue miniseries *Sebastian O*, was published in 1993, shortly after the end of Thatcher's premiership. While it still bears traces of a deconstruction of 'Victorian values,' its main concern seems to be the general role of the mass media in British politics, which at this time was heavily influenced by media mogul Rupert Murdoch, from whose endorsement Thatcher had benefited and who would further the rise of Tony Blair's New Labour a few years later. In *Sebastion O*, the conceptual entanglement of mortality and mediality that can be detected in *From Hell* is taken to extremes by reducing Victoria's entire appearance to media manifestations and by weaving a plot in which those in control of the media are in control of the country and of people's perception of reality. The story is set in 19th-century London, the heart of the 'British Machine Empire,' under the rule of Queen Victoria. There is a high level of technological progress (video communication screens, horseless carriages, mechanical buildings, etc.) and the Empire seems to prosper under its monarch. However, as the story's eponymous protagonist Sebastian O'Leary soon finds out, her majesty has died a few months earlier and was secretly replaced by a computer simulation. While Lord Lavender, who controls this simulation, "rule[s] England," "command[s] the forces of [the] empire and guide[s] the destiny of nations," as he puts it (*SO* 68-69), the actual Victoria's disappearance remains unnoticed.

Once more, the queen occupies an ambivalent position of both presence and absence, of power and agency and a lack thereof. It is not the actual queen that the readers see, but a Baudrillardian simulacrum (1994 [1981]); a simulation that is not based so much on the 'real' queen as on a series of staged images, photographs, and kitschy jubilee collectibles that were produced for the masses and rendered the monarch consumable (cf. Schneider 2003: 58) and hence recognizable. Ironically it is the queen's very media plurality that popularized her among her subjects at the time of her reign and gave her a certain omnipresence through the everyday commodities adorned with her picture, which bereaves her of all individual agency

---

medieval and early modern juridical discourse, since it provided continuity and negotiated the tensions arising from tying the divine right to rule to a person who is subject to ordinary flaws and ailments by ensuring that the "the king is immortal because legally he can never die, or that he is legally never under age" (Kantorowicz 1957: 4). The body natural and the body politic formed a dogmatic unity, with the body politic being the worthier and the body natural being the lesser one, as Kantorowicz points out with reference to the *Reports* of Edmund Plowden (ibid: 9-13).

in the comic, since the original falls into oblivion. Lavender creates an artificial double, but the original had already been mediatized and mass reproduced in the first place in the form of material placeholders that mediate between monarch and public. Therefore, in *Sebastian O*, Victoria is "instantly recognisable [...] because her image had been mechanically mass-produced. [She] is always already a replica, a pictorial representation mass-produced by Victorian technology." (Good 2010: 212) So the antecedent omnipresence of Victoria's media persona in late 19th-century British culture enables Lavender to obscure the underlying reality and sustain the power structure by adapting a certain representational rhetoric.[5]

Similar to *From Hell*, Victoria's visual appearance is yet again modelled closely on historical photographs and paintings as mourning widow and proud ruler. Instead of appearing in person, Victoria remains physically absent from the very start. She is only shown on a communication screen with her voice being portrayed in jagged speech balloons (*SO* 14). Yet again her relation to death and absence is set in relation to mediality. Her iconicity emphasizes her artificiality and the plurality of her previous media manifestations. The screen contains and conditions the monarch's visual appearance and the uneasy, crackling sound indicated by the jagged speech balloons suggests noise interference and disturbance, an impurity in the depiction (or rather: transmission) of the divine ruler, caused by her mechanical reproduction. The uniqueness and authenticity of the monarch, which might be compared to the Benjaminian definition of the aura as a "unique phenomenon of a distance, however close it [the work of art] may be," (Benjamin 2007 [1935]: 222) is destroyed by mechanical reproduction even before the readers find out that she has been replaced. The natural, auratic distance is replaced by an actual physical removal and a flattened, superficial, and distorted reproduction. This results in a juxtaposition that is here taken to absurd extremes and illustrates Benjamin's depiction of the conceptual incompatibility of original and reproduction: "The presence of the original is the prerequisite to the concept of authenticity. [...] The whole sphere of authenticity is outside technical – and, of course, not only technical – reproducibility." (ibid: 220)

The encompassing system has outlived Victoria, but not in the sense of how the king's body (the 'body politic') is immortal and passes over to the next heir apparent. Rather, she has transcended the physical realm in a wholly different way: she has passed on into the medial realm where she exists as mere representation. While in the conventional body duality, the "[b]ody politic is a Body that cannot

---

5   For a more in-depth analysis of the relation between death and mediality in Queen Victoria's depiction in *Sebastian O*, please see my article on "The (Neo-)Victorian Rhetoric of Representation and the End of Referentiality in Sebastian O" (Veith 2017: 107-118).

be seen," (Plowden qtd. in Kantorowicz 1957: 7) Victoria's political power is tied to a media body constituted *entirely* by its own visibility in *Sebastian O*.

But it is not just the monarch, whose (corpo-)reality is questionable: towards the end, Lord Lavender claims that not only the queen, but the entire storyworld of *Sebastian O* is a virtual reality of his own making, that they are "*inside* a magic lantern simulation of *reality* itself" (*SO* 72; original emphasis). Following this train of thought, even the 'original' Victoria before her death would have been merely part of that "magic lantern simulation," just like everyone and everything else, again emphasizing the queen's artificiality and her existence as/in representation and questioning to which degree the royal power structure is actually just a representational act. After Sebastian kills Lavender, he chooses not to pursue the matter any further and the story closes on Sebastian's amused smile at the thought of the world's potential artificiality. Due to the lack of an omniscient narrative entity that might validate Lavender's potentially unreliable claims, the storyworld's ontology remains questionable until the end, just as that of Victoria. To Sebastian, the reality of queen and country is insignificant.

THE DISRUPTIVE QUEEN IN *THE THRILLING ADVENTURES OF LOVELACE AND BABBAGE*

My final example comes from *The Thrilling Adventures of Lovelace and Babbage* by Sydney Padua, originally a webcomic from 2009 that was partially reworked and published as a printed edition in 2015. It has a much lighter and comedic tone and is a less critical reaction to (socio-)political events than my previous examples. It is therefore a good example to illustrate how, despite the different approach, certain narrative and aesthetic techniques that were used as direct counter reactions to the political utilization of the 19th century in the 1980s and 90s have been absorbed into the general conventions of neo-Victorian storytelling. In episodic form, the comic tells the story of how the eponymous protagonists, Ada Lovelace and Charles Babbage, build and use the world's first functional computer, the difference engine, in the mid-19th century.[6] The story takes place in an alternative

---

6 Despite having drawn up elaborate plans and receiving extensive funding from the government, Babbage never managed to finish building his difference engine and eventually abandoned the project. The question in how far the course of history might have been a different one if Babbage had succeeded has repeatedly been explored in steampunk and neo-Victorian fiction, such as William Gibson and Bruce Sterling's novel *The Difference Engine* (1990).

reality (the so-called "pocket universe," which is governed by circular time loops and entertainment value, i.e. everything that is not entertaining enough is excluded [*TA* 41]) in which history takes a different course but is still permeated by our known reality: most dialogues consist of recontextualized quotes and many scenes are loosely based on well-documented historical facts. These relations are openly disclosed in a metafictional manner: every page has footnotes and endnotes, containing information on the characters, the origin of potential quotes and allusions made on this page, biographies, and anecdotes, all of them written in the same humorous, tongue-in-cheek tone as the rest of the story, thereby creating a continuum between fictionalized storyline, historical reality, and author's commentary. The readers find themselves jumping back and forth between the fictional(ized) storyline and historical sources; the comic thereby encourages a non-linear and non-immersive reading process.

Since the work on the difference engine is funded by the government, the young Queen Victoria comes for a visit to inspect it in one episode. Upon finding out that the machine does nothing but print out large algorithmic tables of numbers, she is quite disappointed. She rather expects the engine to "fight crime," (ibid: 75) to be of "social or economic benefit […] to [the] kingdom," (ibid: 76) and demands "improvements in the precognitive area" (ibid: 63). Only after Lovelace manipulates the engine with faulty punch cards to print out a table of numbers in the shape of a kitten, Victoria acknowledges that the engine is a "marvellous device" (ibid: 81) that will help her with her "little scheme to take over the world" (ibid: 85-86). She thereupon doubles the funding and presents Babbage with a knighthood. Victoria's oscillating status between lack and surplus of power and knowledge, her erratic behaviour and her megalomaniac ambitions paired with her utter cluelessness and absurd expectations of the engine make her the perfect monarch of the pocket universe in which historical accuracy and objectivity is compromised for the sake of entertaining anecdotes.

The subverted, circular time of the pocket universe is also manifest in her appearance: She is wearing her regalia (the small diamond crown, which was only made in 1870, and the sceptre with the cross) and a dress closely modelled on her historical wedding dress, even though she has remained single in the story, which is, in turn, an allusion to the 'Virgin Queen' Elizabeth I. This character-mashing of Victoria and Elizabeth I is visually elaborated in the previously mentioned scene in which Victoria proclaims her "little scheme to take over the world": she is depicted as standing on a globe, with her massive white dress falling over the British dominions, a clear reference to the Ditchley portrait of Elizabeth I. Victoria appears as an anachronistic composite character, just as the storyworld is an anachronistic composite. Ironically, Victoria is drawing on the imperial iconography associated with Elizabeth I just as she herself has been used, for example, in Thatcher's discourse. This shows the arbitrariness and easy displacement of modes of representation in media, also visible in other contemporary depictions of Britain's queens and their function as female allegories of Britain's wealth and power.

Moreover, Victoria disrupts the non-linear reading process even further and 'breaks the fourth wall,' by looking down at a footnote on a page and, apparently disliking either its extensive length that overshadows her own appearance, the fact that it discloses unfavourable information, or maybe just its lack of entertainment value, casts her sceptre over it and yells "Enough!" (ibid: 83-84). This scene has been added for the print version and did not exist in the original webcomic, thereby making it stand out all the more as a conscious play with the print medium and its publication conventions.[7] In contrast to the previous examples, Victoria is not associated with death and absence. Quite to the contrary, she is eccentric and quirky and has a heightened presence: her dress outsizes the other characters in the panels and even her speech balloons have the shape of banners and use an old-fashioned blackletter-inspired typeface with decorative initials. Her appearance is a comedic skit of the historical Victoria, some of whose attributes are overdramatized in this fictional queen, while others are reverted into their opposite.

---

7   Footnotes are a constitutive part of the webcomic version as well, but they are not located under the individual panels. They are located, like endnotes, at the very bottom of the webpage after each episode. However, instead of Victoria's metaleptic interaction with the footnote, the webcomic version of this chapter contains a scene yet again emphasizing her gullibility: Copenhagen, the horse of the Duke of Wellington (who is prime minister in the comic and accompanies Victoria during the visit), is visibly enthralled by the picture of the kitten the engine has printed. He whispers something into Victoria's ear whereupon she proclaims: "We are advised that the Engine, as well as producing kittens, may assist Us in Our little plan to… TAKE OVER THE WORLD!!!" (Padua 2009: part 3). It is significant that this humorous effect is achieved by depicting a queen who, despite her supreme position of power, is apparently naïve enough to be persuaded by a horse, yet again making her appear simultaneously powerful and powerless.

AMBIVALENCE AND INSIGNIFICANCE: NEO-VICTORIAN SUBVERSIONS OF ROYAL DIGNITY

Despite the short and few personal appearances that Queen Victoria makes in these comics as a character, her role in the narrative is a central one: she usually occupies an ambivalent position of power, in which she is shifting between the supreme position of a powerful monarch and utter impotence when she is deceived and utilized in other people's schemes. Her power lies in the structures surrounding her, in her royal rhetoric of representation and her iconicity rather than in her person. She dissolves into a mosaic of set pieces and clichés, or, as Elizabeth Ho has called it with reference to *From Hell*, the comics "un[do] the romance of Victoria by reducing her to an iconic figure: lacking in animation, shrouded in cross-hatching, she exists merely as clip art" (2013: 34). Values, such as those conjured by Thatcher, are subverted and history appears as chaotic and messy, resisting the straightforward integration into narratives.

While the monarch is conventionally mythologized as the personification of the state or the Empire, in neo-Victorian comics the queen also becomes the personification of the storyworld, of its specific manner of depiction, of the narrative's compositional logic and general message. By means of a poetics of disruption and artificiality, neo-Victorian comics hold the potential to become a counter move against the romanticization and political utilization of the past and of Queen Victoria. In *From Hell* she appears as an eerie spectre of death and as the nexus of an obscure, incontrollable network of conspiracy, based on her desire to keep her line of succession pure. In *Sebastian O* she is an ontologically questionable media fabrication. And in *The Thrilling Adventures of Lovelace and Babbage*, she oscillates between cluelessness and the desire to rule the world, is depicted as a montage of cliché set pieces, and threatens to disrupt both the scientific ambitions of the protagonists and the reading process of the audience at the same time. Victoria always has an ambivalent nature. She is irreconcilability impersonated, resists closure and coherent narratives of the past.

WORKS CITED

Baudrillard, Jean (1994 [1981]): Simulacra and Simulation, translated by Sheila Faria Glaser. Ann Arbor: University of Michigan Press.

Benjamin, Walter (2007 [1935]): "The Work of Art in the Age of Mechanical Reproduction." In: Hannah Arendt (ed.), Illuminations: Essays and Reflections, translated by Harry Zohn. New York: Schocken, pp. 217-251.

Cannadine, David (1987): "The Brass-Tacks Queen," Review of: Victoria: An Intimate Biography, by Stanley Weintraub. In: The New York Review of Books 34/7, accessed November 11, 2018 (https://www.nybooks.com/articles/1987/04/23/the-brass-tacks-queen/).

Eisner, Will (2006 [1985]): Comics and Sequential Art: Principles & Practice of the World's Most Popular Art Form, Paramus, NJ: Poorhouse Press.

Good, Joseph (2010): "'God Save the Queen, for Someone Must!': Sebastian O and the Steampunk Aesthetic." In: Neo-Victorian Studies 3/1, pp. 208-215.

Gibson, William/Sterling, Bruce (2011 [1990]): The Difference Engine, London: Orion.

Groensteen, Thierry (2013 [1999]): Comics and Narration, translated by Ann Miller. Jackson: University Press of Mississippi.

Ho, Elizabeth (2013): Neo-Victorianism and the Memory of Empire, London: Bloomsbury.

Kantorowicz, Ernst H. (1957): The King's Two Bodies: A Study in Medieval Political Theology, Princeton: Princeton University Press.

Knight, Stephen (1977): Jack the Ripper: The Final Solution, St Albans: Panther.

McCloud, Scott (1994 [1993]): Understanding Comics: The Invisible Art, New York: Harper Collins.

Miettinen, Mervi (2012): "'Do You Understand How I Have Loved You?': Terrible Loves and Divine Visions in From Hell." In: Todd A. Comer/Joseph Michael Sommers (eds.), Sexual Ideology in the Works of Alan Moore: Critical Essays on the Graphic Novels, Jefferson: McFarland, pp. 88-99.

Mitchell, Kate (2010): History and Cultural Memory in Neo-Victorian Fiction, Basingstoke: Palgrave.

Moore, Alan (2000 [1989-1996]): From Hell: Being a Melodrama in Sixteen Parts, illustrated by Eddie Campbell. London: Knockabout.

Morrison, Grant (2004 [1993]): Sebastian O, illustrated by Steve Yeowell. New York: DC Comics.

Padua, Sydney (2009): "Babbage and Lovelace Vs The Client." The Thrilling Adventures of Lovelace and Babbage, July 5, 2009, accessed October 12, 2018 (http://sydneypadua.com/2dgoggles/babbage-and-lovelace-vs-the-client/).

Padua, Sydney (2015): The Thrilling Adventures of Lovelace and Babbage: The (Mostly) True Story of the First Computer, London: Penguin.

Plowden, Edmund (1816): Commentaries or Reports, London.

Plunkett, John (2003): Queen Victoria: First Media Monarch, Oxford: Oxford University Press.

Samuel, Raphael (1992): "Mrs. Thatcher's Return to Victorian Values." Proceedings of the British Academy 78, pp. 9-29.

Schneider, Ralf (2003): "Consuming Monarchy: The Changing Public Images of Queen Victoria." In: Christa Jansohn (ed.), In the Footsteps of Queen Victoria: Wege zum viktorianischen Zeitalter, Münster: LIT, pp. 41-66.

Schulte, Regina (2006): "Introduction: Conceptual Approaches to the Queen's Body." In: Regina Schulte (ed.), The Body of the Queen: Gender and Rule in the Courtly World, 1500-2000, New York: Berghahn, pp. 1-15.

Thatcher, Margaret (1979): "TV Interview for BBC Campaign '79." Interview by Michael Cockerell, BBC, April 27, accessed November 20, 2017 (https://www.margaretthatcher.org/document/103864).

Thatcher, Margaret (1982): "Speech to Conservative Rally at Cheltenham." July 3, accessed November 16, 2017 (https://www.margaretthatcher.org/document/104989).

Thatcher, Margaret (1983): "Radio Interview for IRN programme The Decision Makers." Interview by Peter Allen, Independent Radio News, April 1, accessed March 27, 2017 (https://www.margaretthatcher.org/document/105291).

Veith, Natalie (2017): "The (Neo-)Victorian Rhetoric of Representation and the End of Referentiality in Sebastian O." In: Bernd Dolle-Weinkauff (ed.), Geschichte im Comic, Berlin: Ch. A. Bachman, pp. 107-118.

Warner, Marina (2000): Monuments and Maidens: The Allegory of the Female Form, Berkeley: University of California Press.

Weisbrod, Bernd (2006): "Theatrical Monarchy: The Making of Victoria, the Modern Family Queen." In: Regina Schulte (ed.), The Body of the Queen: Gender and Rule in the Courtly World, 1500-2000, New York: Berghahn, pp. 238-253.

Films and Television

Queen Victoria's Children. Directed by Rebecca Burrell/Lucy McDowell/Richard Sanders. 2013. BBC/Blakeway Productions.

Victoria. Created by Daisy Goodwin. 2016–. Mammoth Screen.

Monarchy and the Alien: Three Queens as Sites of Memory in *Doctor Who*

Marie Menzel

No matter how the continued existence of constitutional monarchy in the 21st century is to be evaluated politically, the members of the British royal family have become pop-culture icons (cf. Otnes/Maclaran 2015; Pankratz 2017b: 58). Constant remediation in all kinds of media and genres – be it sensationalist, nostalgic, satirical or dramatic – stabilizes the monarchy as a potent signifier of 'Britishness' at home and abroad.[1] In this signifying function, both the institution of monarchy and the individuals that have represented it, can be described as sites of memory, i.e. constructed memorial functions that "capture the maximum possible meaning with the fewest of signs." (Nora 1996: 15) Such highly potent signs are particularly relevant for the memory and identity of societies in which traditional forms of social and national memory have become fractured and multiple in an increasingly globalized world. In the term's broader definition, phenomena of varying material dimensions (locations, buildings, images, stories, events, persons etc.) can acquire the function of site of memory and operate in more than one mnemonic context as triggers of associations (cf. Erll 2011: 22-27). The employment of current and historical English and British monarchs as such sites of memory is effective, even as an element of fantastic storytelling on television. In fact, the remediation of prominent sites of memory in such an unexpected context may heighten their evocative potential. The BBC's (British Broadcasting Corporation) iconic and long-running science fiction television series *Doctor Who* (1963-1989 and the revived series since 2005) has always drawn generously and indiscriminately on all areas of British culture and cultural memory, creating absurd connections between the different elements, and "for those attuned to the spirit of the series, part of the

---

1 For an explication of the concept of remediation see Bolter/Grusin (2000).

pleasure comes from recognizing these sources." (Leach 2009: 50) The program's protagonist, known only as 'the Doctor,' is an extraterrestrial who takes ordinary humans on journeys through time and space, fighting injustice wherever he goes. As time travel narratives, his adventures have been mapped onto a broad spectrum of historiographic events.[2] This article analyzes how *Doctor Who* incorporates, represents and remediates historical and contemporary English and British sovereigns as sites of memory that invoke 'Britishness' and thus contribute to a persistent theme of national identity. It discusses the relationship the program entertains with each of the monarchical figures it has incorporated and with the notions they embody. The analysis is restricted to relevant instances from the official television series (in the following I will differentiate between the original and the revived series) because it has by far the highest accessibility and media penetration out of the franchise's many branches, even though stories that have been produced for other media (audio plays, novels, comics etc.) would provide a host of relevant and interesting further cases.

REMEDIATIONS OF ENGLISH AND BRITISH SOVEREIGNS IN *DOCTOR WHO*

Looking at the entirety of the episodes that constitute the official television program so far, three observations can be made regarding remediations of the English and British monarchy. Firstly, there is a very manageable number of noteworthy cases, meaning visual on-screen appearances of monarchs as characters, while keeping in mind that short casual references to these figures (which will not be discussed here) also contribute to their overall presence in the diegesis. Secondly, the majority of these cases occur in the revived series, meaning the episodes produced since 2005 following a fifteen-year hiatus, and this is true for the personages of historical sovereigns as well as for Elizabeth II. This quantitative distribution is representative of an increasing Anglocentrism that can be observed in the program's overall engagement with cultural intertexts and sites of memory – be they historiographic, literary, geographical etc. (cf. Menzel 2014)– and its growing interest in openly asserting its identity as a specifically British program.[3] And

---

2 Harmes (2014) provides a detailed analysis of the aspect of adaptation in *Doctor Who* scripts, including that of historiographic intertexts.

3 Knox (2013) for example discusses related aspects in regard to the program's transatlantic self-positioning as British, with special attention paid to the actor Matt Smith's

thirdly, those monarchs that have been paid the most attention regarding screen time and amount of involvement in the science fiction diegesis are the queens Elizabeth I, Victoria and Elizabeth II. In fact, with the exception of only two earlier cases, they have more recently monopolized royal screen time on *Doctor Who*.[4] Elizabeth I and Victoria represent historical eras of intense political and cultural relevance to English national identity and thus, British cultural memory. Elizabeth II holds a unique position at this moment in time as the current head of state in what constitutes another long and stable reign, qualifying her as an extremely potent signifier of contemporary 'Britishness.' Because of their prominence among monarchical characters on *Doctor Who* this analysis will focus on the remediations of these queens as sites of memory that evoke the British past and support a sense of national identity.

ELIZABETH I AND BRITAIN'S GOLDEN AGE HERITAGE

The continued cultural relevance of iconic historic personalities requires mythologized narratives. Although *Doctor Who* as a fantastic series tends to play with viewers' expectations through parody as well as pastiche and thus frequently questions or explicitly counters hegemonic historical narratives, we can find many examples of such mythologization in the representations of Elizabeth I that the program has offered so far. A self-contained scene in an early episode ("The Chase: The Executioners" 1965: 07:10) repeats a number of prevalent cultural myths. It imagines William Shakespeare being received in audience by the queen in the presence of another character that can reasonably be assumed to represent Francis Bacon. As Helen Hackett explores in depth, "the pairing of Shakespeare and Elizabeth is in fact one of England's, and Britain's, most entrenched and persistent cultural myths," (2009: 3) "a potent and irresistible image of the preeminence of the British nation" (ibid: 4) to which the figure of Francis Bacon also contributes. The scene repeats many more popular narratives about the present personages, for

---

embodiment of 'Britishness'. Furthermore, Nicol (2018) explores *Doctor Who*'s allegorical preoccupation with 'Britishness', particularly in relation to questions of nationhood, democracy and the law.

4 "The Crusade" (1965) and "The King's Demons" (1983) feature the medieval kings Richard the Lionheart and his brother and successor John in the context of their respective mythologies as heroic crusader and initiator of the *Magna Carta* and would merit their own analysis regarding their relationship with the British national narrative.

instance the queen's fondness for Shakespeare's plays and that she directly commissioned *The Merry Wives of Windsor* from him, and furthermore, Bacon's prominent role in the Shakespearean authorship debate.[5] The pairing of Elizabeth I with Shakespeare is reiterated in her next appearance on *Doctor Who*, four decades later. As the title suggests, "The Shakespeare Code" (2007) centers on the playwright and his plays as a cultural intertext and site of memory, but Elizabeth I has her cameo moment (43:18). In what may to some extent also be a direct citation of a similar scene in the successful feature film *Shakespeare in Love* (1998), it makes use of the non-factual trope that Elizabeth visited public theaters in person, a popular notion because it "presents in one neatly encapsulated scene the essential ingredients of the so-called Elizabethan golden age." (Hackett 2009: 10)

The third and so far, final appearance of Elizabeth I on the program is incorporated into no lesser episode than the franchise's much anticipated and promoted 50th anniversary special ("The Day of the Doctor" 2013). This version of her character differs from the previous cases in that it is much more rounded through significant screen time and actual narrative impact. The episode also references an abundance of mythical tropes. Elizabeth proclaims for example that she "may have the body of a weak and feeble woman" (47:03) but that she is nevertheless capable of defeating her enemies (in this case alien creatures instead of the Spanish Armada). This statement taken from Elizabeth's famous speech allegedly given to her troops at Tilbury (cf. Wagner 2010: 190) and which is crucial to the 'Elizabeth myth' (cf. Freeman/Doran 2003: 16-17) reflects the historical circumstances that prevented a female monarch from participating actively in battle. But *Doctor Who*'s version of her character is entirely willing and able (given the right circumstances) to make physical use of weapons herself (46:47). In that regard she represents the modern type of the 'strong female character' whose independence and equality with men is demonstrated through the display of physical aggression, and which is, in the manner of its employment on the narrative level, obviously anachronistic.[6] However, the character also proves to be clever and resourceful, planning and executing several ruses that lead to the defeat of the enemy (17:48, 46:48). This is very much in line with some of the qualities that the 'Elizabeth mythology' commonly attests her, such as her being "calculating," "shrewd," "indomitable," (Freeman/Doran 2003: 1) "resourceful," of "strong character" and

---

5   Hackett (2009) discusses these myths, e.g. 23-30; 152-154.
6   Innes (2004) and her contributors discuss the rising number of action heroines and the increasing popularity of female physical strength and aggression in all areas of popular culture from the 1990s onwards and what this means for notions of gender and equality.

"leadership qualities" (ibid: 9). Other aspects or versions of her in many respects contradictory character construct (cf. Dobson/Watson 2002: 4-6), such as her being "cold" and "unfeminine" (Freeman/Doran 2003: 16) or living a life confined to court (Betteridge 2003: 242), have not found their way into this representation. This Elizabeth conducts passionate and devoted courtships including picnic dates (19:47) and even marriage vows (47:25) with the Doctor, which are presented as in no way complicated by her monarchical duties.[7] In this regard, she is a thoroughly modern character, unencumbered by structural circumstance. Her representation in this episode falls somewhere between comedic or parodic – when it, for instance, explicitly undermines the "virgin queen" (21:52) narrative – and a simultaneous continuation and remediation of existing mythology. Her depiction in the episode has been criticized as "disappointingly sexist" (Nicol 2018: 46), due to her fawning devotion to a man. While this is a valid point, it disregards the amount of political and personal agency she is given. This Elizabeth's thoroughly modern behavior and her close association with a time travelling and immortal character may serve as a metaphor for her trans-historic existence as a stable symbol of British cultural heritage.

Related notions of historical immediacy, synchronicity and legacy are overall closely connected with Elizabeth I's character in all three of her appearances on *Doctor Who*. Her scene in "The Chase" is immediately followed by another 'important' moment, namely authentic footage of a studio performance by *The Beatles* (09:34) contemporary to the episode's production. The episode frames these events as historically crucial and particularly interesting and brings them into ahistorical proximity to each other as the time travelers 'channel surf' through history. This creates a sense of immediacy and synchronicity of history, and of cultural equality between modern British pop music and cultural heritage. Along the same lines, in the 2007 episode "The Shakespeare Code" the characters use spells from the *Harry Potter* book series alongside some faux-Shakespearean verse to defeat Macbethian witches (39:30), creating a 21st century version of the described effect of cultural equality.

Furthermore, all three remediations of Elizabeth I reference at least some of the most enduring elements of her iconography that originated in contemporary portraiture of the queen and are employed by most, if not all, representations of

---

[7] Dobson/Watson (2002: 216-246) discuss especially film's preoccupation with Elizabeth's sexuality and private self. Betteridge (2003: 244) mentions the conflict between duty and desire as a popular feature of filmic representations of Elizabeth I.

her in popular media (cf. Freeman/Doran 2003: 1).[8] Even though "The Shakespeare Code" approaches some of its visual historical referents in explicitly postmodern fashion – a character remarks that Shakespeare "is a bit different to his portraits" (6:11) – this is never applied to the iconography of Elizabeth, who is visually always clearly identifiable. Newer *Doctor Who* scripts are often self-consciously aware of the constructedness of the intertexts they employ and layer them anachronistically and parodically (if this Shakespeare resembles anyone, it is arguably Kenneth Branagh), but nevertheless rely on their effectivity when it comes to triggering pre-existing associations that contribute to the hegemonic national narrative.

VICTORIA AND THE BRITISH EMPIRE

The Victorian era has been a frequent and recurring setting for historical episodes on *Doctor Who* as well as a popular source of intertexts ready for adaptation into different Victoriana-inspired settings,[9] and this has only increased in frequency in the revived series. This may at least in part be a response to the emergence of neo-Victorianism as a genre in a host of different art forms evoking, re-creating and re-imagining the period, especially popular from the 1980s onwards (cf. Mitchell 2010: 1-3). At that time, engagement with the era was going through a qualitative change, from "communicative" to entirely "cultural" memory in Jan Assmann's terms (2010: 111). With the loss of living memory, remembrance of the 19th century began to rest necessarily entirely on externalized forms of memory that store knowledge, cue remembrance, and have to be remediated in order to remain properties of cultural memory. *Doctor Who,* especially in the revived series, exercises

---

8   E.g. Strong (1987) provides an in-depth analysis of the portraits and their iconography's historical political role in the 'virgin queen' narrative. Some visual markers (reddish hair, pale skin etc.) have translated into modern popular consciousness as Elizabeth's signature look.

9   Harmes (2014: 87-123) provides a detailed overview and analysis of the incorporation of different Victorian sources and intertexts into episodes (e.g. "The Evil of the Daleks" 1967, "The Talons of Weng-Chiang" 1977, "A Christmas Carol" 2010, "The Crimson Horror" 2013 etc.) and specifically of gothic literature, as well as of previous adaptations' aesthetics (e.g. Hammer films), into *Doctor Who*. Apart from anything else, *Doctor Who* owes to 19th century origin texts of science fiction and time travel such as H.G. Wells' *The Time Machine* (1895) and *The War of the Worlds* (1897) with their "narratives of dystopia and invasion" (Chapman 2013: 5).

this function for Victorianism with enthusiasm, and it often does so through a manner of storytelling characterized by a postmodern approach to history and historiography, which is also a frequent feature of many explicitly neo-Victorian works (cf. Mitchell 2010: 3-4).

Direct references to or appearances of the eponymous monarch Queen Victoria are much rarer on *Doctor Who* than the invocation of the period in general. The Victorian era seems to exist more independently from the associated monarchical figure as a cultural reference than the Elizabethan era. In many episodes Victorian settings are simply employed to invoke Christmas 'holiday spirit,' thus repeating a common aesthetic association.[10] So far only one episode ("Tooth and Claw" 2006) has featured an on-screen representation of Victoria, and it makes sure to construct the character from cultural myth. The iconography of her signature look, which has entered cultural consciousness mainly via frequent remediations of her portrait photographs, is retained for the character, and the episode comments self-reflexively on its fulfilment of visual expectations: "She was just sitting there," "like a stamp." (07:11)[11] In contrast to the marginalization of her character practiced by many neo-Victorian works that Natalie Veith observes and discusses in this volume, this Victoria is shown to be a cunning observer of the events taking place around her (22:05; 24:40) and an individual of great agency, physically defending herself against an enemy (22:28) just like *Doctor Who*'s version of Elizabeth I. Thus, Victoria is presented as another example of the self-sufficient and proactive woman, and additionally takes offence in gendered derogatory language (22:28). Significantly, she later denies the violent action and gives credit for it to one of her soldiers (25:00). This reflects the historical Victoria's respect for gender roles determined by Victorian values, even while at the same time fashioning her into a 'strong female character' for the 21st century that does not allow social mores to determine her fate. Along with a number of obvious markers associated with Victoria's person (the catchphrase of being "not amused," [e.g. 39:50] the location of Balmoral castle etc.) the script also incorporates the themes of the historical queen's grief for her late husband, her Christian faith, and her interest in

---

10 E.g. "The Unquiet Dead" (2005) is set at Christmas while "The Next Doctor" (2008), "A Christmas Carol" (2010), "The Snowmen" (2012) are Christmas specials.

11 The significance of the development of mass reproducible photography and moving images for Victoria's public image and iconography is well documented and explored, e.g. by Plunkett (2003). The remark refers to stamps like the iconic "Penny Black" that also featured Victoria's profile or portrait (ibid: 108-109).

the occult, which are all prominently associated with her in cultural myth.[12] She thus pronounces a penchant for "ghost stories," (11:15; 15:00) and unsurprisingly the plot involves the supernatural. However, Victoria aggressively rejects the experience and falls back on her faith (29:22; 36:55). Even while acknowledging an alien's (i.e. the Doctor's) assistance in averting a usurpation of her throne, she also condemns him for "consort[ing] with stars and magic," engaging with "terror," "blasphemy," and "death" (39:52) and strictly banishes all things supernatural from her empire, including the Doctor. This representation of Victoria very much embodies her status as "familiar and idealized icon of the British Empire" (Nünning/Nünning 2003: 108) that she responsibly, selflessly, and resolutely leads and protects: "I saw last night that Great Britain has enemies beyond imagination and we must defend our borders on all sides." (42:36) Not making a distinction between benevolent and malevolent forces from the realm of the supernatural, Victoria's ideology of defense and security is shown to be built on the principle of the 'other', creating the notion of a threat that is inherent in anything 'mysterious' and unfamiliar, even while she privately enjoys the thrills that stories about such things provide. This part of the plot invites a reading with Said's *Orientalism* (1978), but only in allegorical terms, since a critical stance towards historical imperialism (or its proponents in the shape of Victoria) is conspicuously absent from the episode. For example, the storyline incorporates the *Koh-i-Noor* diamond as the final puzzle piece needed to defeat the alien menace (36:05). The item is framed as a quasi-magical element that is fatefully predetermined to protect the queen and the British throne from usurpation, entirely ignoring the problematics of its colonial acquisition that enable it to fulfil this function in the first place.[13] The episode "Tooth and Claw" is not only reluctant to explicitly criticize imperial notions, but also the personage of Queen Victoria. In contrast to the rounded character version of Elizabeth I discussed above that contains at least some comedic or parodic elements, the overall presentation of Victoria arguably falls between fully individualized and iconic. Her introduction scene (05:03) illustrates this queen's status as icon: it builds suspense, revealing her person in several stages that culminate in a punctuating musical cue and the full list of her titles. Finally, the excitement and awe the

---

12 Specifically, Victoria's attendance of séances was reported by newspapers at the time, e.g. *The Washington Post* ("Queen Victoria a Spiritualist"), and has become popularized. Due to the period's general preoccupation with the topic, spiritualism and the occult are popular tropes in neo-Victorian works in general (cf. Mitchell 2010: 2).

13 The royal family's official website also simply defines the Crown Jewels as "ceremonial treasures which have been acquired by English kings and queens, mostly since 1660" ("The Crown Jewels" n. d.).

other characters display towards her (e.g. 07:05) frame Victoria as a historic marker of singular importance.

"Tooth and Claw" provides Victoria with all of the agency that her hegemonic cultural mythology demands, putting her center stage as a resolute leader and paying her "due deference" (05:15) as a fully individualized and iconic character. Not even the indirect reference to imperial discourse that results in the program's alien protagonist's banishment is explicitly condemned by the overall narrative.[14] In spite of what may also read as a modern vision of female agency, the episode uncritically remediates the existing narrative of Victoria, the opposite approach of the deconstruction that many recent neo-Victorian works are capable of providing by sidelining Victoria's person and agency and thus her mythology (cf. Veith in this volume).

ELIZABETH II AND POST-WAR BRITAIN

Remediating Queen Elizabeth II on *Doctor Who* presents a markedly different case than those royal representations previously discussed in this article. The representation of a current head of state involves additional aspects to that of a historical monarch, especially of one who predates the existence of modern mass media. The development of phenomena concerning the royal family into media events from the 19th century onwards, as well as the attendant opening up of their private spheres to public scrutiny in the form of news coverage and to representation in fictionalized forms is an ongoing gradual process (cf. Bastin 2009; cf. Pankratz 2017b: 51-55). Media representations of Elizabeth Windsor remain complicated, because they stand in direct opposition to one of the monarchy's central functions, that of "retain[ing] a sense of mystery and illusion." (Bastin 2009: 36)

---

14 Victoria's orders in that scene are later revisited by the diegesis of *Doctor Who* ("The Christmas Invasion" 2005, "Army of Ghosts" 2006) and its spin-off series (*Torchwood*, 2006-2011), where the scripts take an unambiguous moral stance against them (cf. Kydd 2010: 192-193). Vohlidka observes an anti-imperialist standpoint in science fiction allegories of empire and colonialism on *Doctor Who* from the 1970s onwards, when public discourse became "freer to confront [imperialism] directly as a critique," (2013: 125) although the episodes still often engaged in "benevolent racism" (ibid: 126) and the program's overall "position [...] was not consistent." (ibid: 135) It is questionable whether this has changed in the revived series despite its frequent assertion of ideals of equality and diversity.

Additionally, failure to fulfil existing expectations will automatically highlight the artificiality of fictional depictions in particular (ibid: 42). Nevertheless, the modern monarchy's success as institution and signifier depends on constant medial performance and remediation in what Pankratz calls a "medial and performative feedback loop." (2017b: 60, cf. ibid: 54)

Although representing Queen Elizabeth II on *Doctor Who* can hardly be compared to the 'serious' project undertaken by biopics or docudrama (that is already precluded by the program's fantastic approach), it does not deliver a clear parody or satire either. Apart from numerous acknowledgements of the queen's person as one of the many public figures with whom the program's protagonist is acquainted,[15] she has also been visually represented as part of the on-screen diegesis with varying degrees of involvement in the respective storylines and in tonally slightly different approaches. The first of these appearances can be found in *Doctor Who*'s 25th anniversary story "Silver Nemesis" (1988). That it comes rather late in the original run of the program is in line with the development of the possibilities of monarchical representation over the 20th century, as well as with newer *Doctor Who*'s increased interest in remediating intertexts, memory sites and symbols that are specifically British and in creating stories that center on a British setting.

Although this anniversary was not as spectacularly celebrated as the 50th in 2013, "Silver Nemesis" features several elements that speak of its status as a special, apart from the telling title (it is the program's 'silver jubilee'). This story remediates a number of specifically British sites of memory in a condensed manner. Windsor Castle of the present day (1988) serves as the linchpin location, attracting several hostile parties whose imageries are highly charged with cultural mnemonic power. Particularly a group of neo-Nazis literally on the queen's doorstep evoke (at the time of production still relatively recent) national identity defining imagery of the threat of invasion during World War II. Following some establishing shots of the castle (Part 1, 16:57), the character of the queen is briefly shown walking her Corgis in the grounds (Part 1, 18:14). The camera keeps a considerable distance to the actor, obscuring her features, while the overall image provides just enough reference points that in combination clearly identify her as Elizabeth Windsor (handbag, Corgis, general silhouette). But instead of exaggerating into parody, this scene creates the illusion of authenticity of the footage rather convincingly, and it is in line with what Bastin observes about the queen's appearances as a character in royal family biopics prior to *The Queen* (2006) as

---

15 E.g. "Robot: Part 4" (1975: 18:38), "Planet of the Dead" (2009: 53:20) refer to the Doctor's acquaintance with Queen Elizabeth II.

"either glimpsed fleetingly or sometimes not at all." (2009: 45) Since the character of Elizabeth II in this episode does not actively partake in the narrative and is cited alongside several other intertexts which are all relevant to the British national narrative in different ways, the significance of her representation in "Silver Nemesis" becomes clear: to signify 'Britishness,' to anchor the narrative in its particular contemporary cultural context that provides easy identification for the target audience, and to symbolically evoke a sense of what is at stake in this narrative of impending catastrophe. Her physical presence at Windsor Castle not only increases the symbolic power of the location, it also evokes a sense of security and guidance provided by a monarch. But Elizabeth II performing this function on screen is specifically evocative as her personal active involvement in the auxiliary armed forces as a young woman during World War II when she lived at Windsor Castle is a biographical fact that has already become part of her mythologized narrative (cf. Rothman 2018).

The episode thus continues long-standing and conservative associations about the monarch's role and function and practices a recourse to past achievements in warfare at a time when strong anti-monarchist sentiments that found expression in satire and ridicule of the royal family were also emerging in public discourse (cf. Olechnowicz 2017: 202-203). Thus, her appearance in this episode aligns Elizabeth II with the previous queens in their roles as successful protectors and defenders of Britain. Because as a character she displays no visible agency or involvement in the events, this effect is achieved only by triggering pre-existing associations in that regard.

Shortly following the anniversary special featuring Elizabeth II for the first time, *Doctor Who* was cancelled. All subsequent remediations of the queen can thus be found in the revived series after 2005. The episode "The Idiot's Lantern" (2006) incorporates original footage of Elizabeth II's coronation in 1953 (25:33; 40:34), the first televised royal media event (cf. Pankratz 2017b: 52), remediating from the BBC's own archives (cf. "The Coronation and the BBC" 2013) the iconic images of a moment that more than half a century ago marked the beginning of this monarch's reign. The episode frames the historic occasion as community-building for the nation as well as within local communities where families and neighbors are shown to gather around newly purchased television sets for the broadcast (25:21) and celebrating in the streets (41:46). These scenes recreate elements of the national communal experience of the event as they were recorded and interpreted at the time and have endured as a narrative (cf. Shils/Young 1953: 70-74; Merck 2016a: 4). As a follow up to the earlier appearance of Elizabeth II, the remediation of actual footage continues the project of avoiding an obvious fictionalization of the living person. Instead it creates a bond between the fictional story and the reality of its cultural context.[16] Similarly, "The Christmas Invasion" (2005) keeps the character off screen while repeatedly referring to the royal family being endangered by the episode's events, but provides an authentic visual reference via a portrait photograph of Elizabeth Windsor prominent in the foreground of an important shot (27:22).

Finally, "Voyage of the Damned" (2007) contains the most recent appearance of the queen on the program to date. This time she appears briefly even as a speaking character when she thanks the Doctor for his assistance (1:01:06). "In defiance of extraterrestrial attack" she "has remained in residence" (1:00:09) at Buckingham Palace in order to provide moral support for her subjects in London in a move reminiscent of the war-time spirit exhibited by her father George VI during World War II. This time, her role as a symbol of defiance and as provider of a sense of security in a moment of national crisis is not only evoked via association, but explicitly referred to in the narrative (13:52). In line with her appearance in "Silver Nemesis" her face is never shown, but in contrast her scene here is intentionally comedic in its portrayal of the queen as a private individual, creating an amusing disturbance of the aforementioned notion of 'royal mystery:' having to evacuate hurriedly from the palace with her Corgis, she is shown running along the corridors in hair curlers and matching pink bathrobe and slippers which reference the bright unicolored style she is currently known for (1:00:17).

Doctor Who employs Elizabeth II as a mnemonic intertext evoking national identity, community, and ultimately 'Britishness,' regularly remembering her stable presence as a representational figure in the protagonist's implied familiarity with the royal family. But it refrains from developing these references, glimpses and abstractions into either a rounded character or a critical parody. One possible reason could be that because Elizabeth II is so frequently mediated, this vagueness works in favor of her effectivity as a symbol because it creates a certain amount of 'authenticity.' Apart from that, although impersonations of the living monarch have not been prohibited by law since 1968 (cf. Pankratz 2017b: 51-52), *Doctor Who*'s continued hesitation in that regard is reminiscent of the longstanding historical notion that "only the queen had the licence to impersonate the queen on stage." (ibid: 51) Particularly since Elizabeth II was opposed to the abolition of this law at the time (ibid: 52), the program's approach can be read as indicative of the BBC being "concerned to maintain good relations with the royal family in order to uphold the institution's self-defined role as the primary national broadcaster, thus shaping and to some extent limiting the ways in which it depicts the

---

16 *The Queen* (2006) employs real footage of some personages alongside enacted scenes of others which creates interesting effects that e.g. Merck (2016b: 366-368) explores.

monarchy." (Bell/Gray 2016: 305) In light of this it might be more likely that Elizabeth Windsor (or future incumbents of the throne) will appear as herself on *Doctor Who* for which the (in)famous segment in the 2012 London Olympics Opening Ceremony that paired Queen Elizabeth with the character of James Bond is already a precedent (cf. "The Complete London 2012 Opening Ceremony": 34:10), rather than the program ever delivering a full fictionalization of a current head of state.

THE FUTURE OF THE BRITISH MONARCHY IN *DOCTOR WHO*'S IMAGINATION

By choosing these three prominent queens and their mythologized narratives as representative of British monarchy, *Doctor Who* perpetuates the notion that they occupy a singular position among their peers. The line of successful and famous queens that the program displays in their functions of British national sites of memory provides a streamlined narrative of female monarchs that *Doctor Who* as a time travel narrative cannot resist to continue when imagining the future. With Britain's monarchy being a central signifying element of national identity, it is unsurprising that a program that continuously sets out to create a sense of legacy, continuity, and immediacy by bringing together different temporalities and spaces imagines an unbroken line of future British sovereigns, even in a post-apocalyptic future, and particularly that the future of the British monarchy will be female. In a dystopian vision of the 29th century ("The Beast Below" 2010), Queen Elisabeth X – or as she introduces herself: "Liz X, […] I'm the bloody queen, mate. Basically, I rule." (24:11) – is another entry in the shows' portrayals of great long-reigning queens. Not only her gender and regnal name immediately imply the connection to her predecessors on the program (and in British cultural memory). Liz X also explicitly refers to all three of them, specifically to the "stories" about their encounters with the Doctor that she and her "family" were "brought up on" (23:42). In this self-referential storytelling (itself a frequent feature of *Doctor Who* stories) monarchical continuity appears unbroken and secure. As with *Doctor Who*'s versions of historical queens, Liz X's competencies are also demonstrated by her use of physical force against an enemy (22:46; 24:13), sharp minded curiosity and agency. Because her character arc is concerned with individual moral responsibility, her identity as Britain's sovereign serves the exclusive purpose of assuring a sense of stability and continuity: earth is destroyed, the remnants of humanity survive only on nationalistically segregated space ships, but there is still a strong British queen taking care of her subjects, guiding them responsibly through the crisis.

Most significantly, Liz X is portrayed by the black actor Sophie Okonedo. This casting decision is indicative of the efforts of the revived series to increase diversity among the cast and to construct a more inclusive vision of 'Britishness' on *Doctor Who*, which is of course a BBC policy in general (cf. "Diversity & Inclusion" n. d.).[17] The script itself makes no mention of the monarch's ethnicity, but the implications of 'color-conscious casting' of this particular role are clear.[18] Although the marriage of Prince Harry and Meghan Markle was not yet on the horizon when this episode aired in 2010, it seems to reflect that an openness to and yearning for larger progressive and inclusive steps by the real royal family already had cultural traction. After all, as Pankratz observes, when it comes to traditional notions of royal standards of propriety and morality, "by 2017, public opinion seems to be more relaxed […] and it seems plausible that the Windsors will continue to adapt to political, social and cultural trends." (2017a: 14)

CONCLUSION: A VERY BRITISH CULTURAL MEMORY

Considering how interested *Doctor Who* has become in remediating all types of British sites of memory, thus creating an undeniable British identity for this fantastic story and character, and how significant the monarchy is for the British national narrative, the instances in which the nation's monarchs are represented on screen are rare. Nevertheless, these figures' mythologies and enormous symbolic power are exploited by the program. In fact, in its employment of historical and contemporary monarchical personages it draws directly on the "less formal" ("The

---

17 Most currently, in the 2018 series a female actor was cast in the role of the Doctor for the first time and the new team of supporting characters represent a broad range of identities regarding race, gender and age (cf. "Meet the Cast …" 2017). Although the exact choices made in many scripts have invited absolutely justified criticism in the past – Dodson (2013) for instance shows how many narratives still tend to mistreat non-white characters – there is a pronounced interest in promoting values of diversity and equality on *Doctor Who*.

18 Different approaches to diversification, including 'color-blind', 'color-conscious' or 'race conscious' casting are a topic in public and artistic discourse, e.g. the opinion piece "The Guardian View on Colour-Conscious Casting" (2019) discusses some views and aspects on the basis of a very recent BBC series.

Role of the Monarchy" n. d.: n. pag.) functions that the British constitutional monarchy today claims for the sovereign: those of providing "a focus for national identity, unity and pride" and "a sense of stability and continuity." (ibid) It is certainly no coincidence either that monarchs in *Doctor Who* have a noticeable tendency to appear in episodes that have an extra-diegetic celebratory purpose (anniversary and Christmas specials), which make use of the ceremonial function of a representative monarch. Additionally, these representations are in line with "commemorative programming on the BBC [that] often seeks to represent a historical national identity and in doing so create a sense of community within a culturally disparate nation." (Bell/Gray 2016: 292)

With the three queens the program focusses its royal representations on a small group of culturally particularly relevant sovereigns. It remediates highly effective elements of their mythologized narratives and relies heavily on their abilities to trigger pre-existing associations and knowledge of these myths in the audience. These queens span culturally, politically and medially very different epochs of varying distance to the viewers' present. They thus represent different types of memory of the distant past, the Empire and the more recent past and present respectively. Yet despite these differences *Doctor Who* – at least in part due to its quality as a time travel narrative – recalls them all in structurally similar ways, as sites of memory with a common level of immediacy. It does so in the specific mnemonic context of cultural legacy and a hegemonic national narrative that excludes a critical stance towards any problematic aspects of either the institution of monarchy or the legacies of individual sovereigns. Danny Nicol perceives *Doctor Who*'s portrayal of Britain's monarchs in general as one of "gently ribbing support." (2018: 47) This accounts for the parodic elements and self-aware comments on historicity we can observe in some of these representations, but also for the fact that these never amount to a lasting effect of deconstruction of these narratives and myths. Nicol also notes that the concept of hereditary monarchy is not something that the series has ever actively critiqued, not even in a metaphoric way, which seems at odds with its general stance against class discrimination (cf. ibid: 42-48). Similarly, the uncritical remediation of historical and contemporary English and British monarchs as entirely positively connoted anchors of the program's origin culture contrasts with frequently employed techniques of storytelling on *Doctor Who* that provide multi-faceted and complex perspectives on political and ethical conundrums in the form of even provocative thought experiments (cf. Britton 2011: 28).[19] The discourses of both royalism and anti-monarchism in Britain

---

19 E.g. "Kill the Moon" (2014) can easily be read as a (somewhat tortured) allegory on the ethical problematics of abortion.

are complex, highly charged and divisive (cf. Olechnowicz 2017), and *Doctor Who* as an entertainment product of national public broadcasting carefully avoids partaking in them, even when it is not so reluctant in regard to other contentious topics. It simply acknowledges and makes use of the indisputable importance of the monarchy for Britain's hegemonic national identity and its mnemonic function as an "essential 'national' institution." (ibid: 207)

Not only are these monarchs treated as similar and immediate in their contributions to the current repertoire of cultural heritage but are imagined in their commonality as female, long-reigning, and successful protectors to represent the British monarchy as a trans-historical constant, an essential framework promising perpetuity into the far future. As Nickolas Haydock observes for the case of medieval film, postmodern popular culture's relationship with the past is not only based on the consciousness of the constructedness of history, but also on a "denial of difference" (2008: 8) between history and the present. It creates strong connections of "continuity," "analogy," and "synchronicity" (ibid: 17) that make the distant past relevant for a modern audience. In the case of the three famous queens on *Doctor Who,* this effect is perhaps most obvious in the way that all of them are reimagined as displaying modern markers of female agency and empowerment that are recognizable today. In this notion of denial of difference there also emerges an issue that would warrant further analysis and that opens up the discussion to broader issues in broadcasting and cultural politics: the apparent contradiction between the revived series' open agenda of proposing a British society based in cultural and ethnic diversity and equality (through casting and allegorical storytelling) and its apparent denial of crucial post-colonial (and class related) issues when it employs symbols of Britain's imperial past to evoke a sense of immediacy and continuity.

WORKS CITED

Assmann, Jan (2010): "Communicative and Cultural Memory." In: Astrid Erll/Ansgar Nünning (eds.), A Companion to Cultural Memory Studies, Berlin: de Gruyter, pp. 109-118.

Bastin, Giselle (2009): "Filming the Ineffable: Biopics of the British Royal Family." In: a/b: Auto/Biography Studies 24/1, pp. 34-52.

Bell, Erin/Gray, Ann (2016): "Television's Royal Family: Continuity and Change." In: Mandy Merck (ed.), The British Monarchy on Screen, Manchester: Manchester University Press, pp. 291-308.

Betteridge, Thomas (2003): "A Queen for All Seasons: Elizabeth I on Film." In: Susan Doran/Thomas S. Freeman (eds.), The Myth of Elizabeth, Basingstoke: Palgrave Macmillan, pp. 242-259.

Bolter, Jay David/Grusin, Richard (2000): Remediation: Understanding New Media, Cambridge, Mass.: MIT Press.

Britton, Piers D. (2011): TARDISbound: Navigating the Universes of Doctor Who, London: I.B. Tauris.

Chapman, James (2013): Inside the Tardis: The Worlds of Doctor Who, 2nd edition, London: I.B. Tauris.

"Diversity & Inclusion", n. d., accessed March 21, 2019 (https://www.bbc.co.uk/diversity/).

Dobson, Michael/Watson, Nicola J. (2002): England's Elizabeth: An Afterlife in Fame and Fantasy, Oxford: Oxford University Press.

Dodson, Linnea (2013): "Conscious Colour-Blindness, Unconscious Racism in Doctor Who Companions." In: Lindy Orthia (ed.), Doctor Who and Race, Bristol: Intellect, pp. 29-34.

Erll, Astrid (2011): Memory in Culture, translated by Sara B. Young, Basingstoke: Palgrave Macmillan.

Freeman, Thomas S./Doran, Susan (2003): "Introduction." In: Susan Doran/Thomas S. Freeman (eds.), The Myth of Elizabeth, Basingstoke: Palgrave Macmillan, pp. 1-23.

Hackett, Helen (2009): Shakespeare and Elizabeth: The Meeting of Two Myths, Princeton: Princeton University Press.

Harmes, Marcus K. (2014): Doctor Who and the Art of Adaptation: Fifty Years of Storytelling, Lanham: Rowman & Littlefield.

Haydock, Nickolas (2008): Movie Medievalism: The Imaginary Middle Ages, Jefferson: McFarland.

Innes, Sherrie A. (ed.) (2004): Action Chicks: New Images of Tough Women in Popular Culture, New York: Palgrave Macmillan.

Knox, Simone (2014): "The Transatlantic Dimensions of the Time Lord: Doctor Who and the Relationships between British and North American Television." In: Andrew O'Day (ed.), Doctor Who: The Eleventh Hour, London: I.B. Tauris, pp. 106-120.

Kydd, Elspeth (2010): "Cyberwomen and Sleepers: Rereading the Mulatta Cyborg and the Black Woman's Body." In: Andrew Ireland (ed.), Illuminating Torchwood: Essays on Narrative, Character and Sexuality in the BBC Series, Jefferson: McFarland, pp. 191-202.

Leach, Jim (2009): Doctor Who (= TV Milestones Series), Detroit: Wayne State University Press.

"Meet the Cast On the All New Series of Doctor Who!", October 22, 2017, accessed March 21, 2019 (http://www.bbc.co.uk/blogs/doctorwho/entries/ff2d1 30a-e278-4978-bf22-48cba0a5c9da).

Menzel, Marie (2014): Britain Travels in Time and Space: History, Memory and Doctor Who, unpublished manuscript (M.A. thesis), Goethe-Universität Frankfurt am Main.

Merck, Mandy (2016a): "Introduction." In: Mandy Merck (ed.), The British Monarchy on Screen, Manchester: Manchester University Press, pp. 1-19.

Merck, Mandy (2016b): "Melodrama, Celebrity, *The Queen*." In: Mandy Merck (ed.), The British Monarchy on Screen, Manchester: Manchester University Press, pp. 363-383.

Mitchell, Kate (2010): Victorian Afterimages: History and Cultural Memory in Neo-Victorian Fiction, London: Palgrave Macmillan.

Nicol, Danny (2018): Doctor Who: A British Alien?, Cham: Springer International Publishing: Imprint: Palgrave Macmillan.

Nora, Pierre (1996 [1984-1992]): Realms of Memory: Rethinking the French Past, Volume 1: Conflicts and Divisions, edited by Lawrence D. Kritzmann, translated by Arthur Goldhammer, New York: Columbia University Press.

Nünning, Vera/Nünning, Ansgar (2003): "The Invention of an Empress: Factions and Fictions of Queen Victoria's Jubilees of 1887 and 1897 as a Paradigm for the Study of Cultural Memories." In: Christa Jansohn (ed.), In the Footsteps of Queen Victoria: Wege zum viktorianischen Zeitalter (= Studien zur englischen Literatur, 15), Münster: Lit, pp. 83-112.

Olechnowicz, Andrzej (2017): "'For the Many May Be Better than the Few': Republicans and Anti-Monarchism in Contemporary Britain." In: Anette Pankratz/Claus-Ulrich Viol (eds.), (Un)Making the Monarchy, Heidelberg: Universitätsverlag Winter, pp. 201-225.

Otnes, Cele C./Mclaran, Pauline (2015): Royal Fever: The British Monarchy in Consumer Culture, Oakland: University of California Press.

Pankratz, Anette (2017a): "Introducing the Monarchy." In: Anette Pankratz/Claus-Ulrich Viol (eds.), (Un)Making the Monarchy, Heidelberg: Universitätsverlag Winter, pp. 7-20.

Pankratz, Anette (2017b): "'That's Entertainment': Monarchy as Performance." In: Anette Pankratz/Claus-Ulrich Viol (eds.), (Un)Making the Monarchy, Heidelberg: Universitätsverlag Winter, pp. 41-64.

Plunkett, John (2003): Queen Victoria: First Media Monarch, Oxford: Oxford University Press.

"Queen Victoria a Spiritualist." (1878): In: Washington Post October 31, p. 2.

Rothman, Lily. "The World War II Auto Mechanic in This Photo Is Queen Elizabeth II. Here's the Story Behind the Picture." In: Time USA, May 25, 2018, accessed March 21, 2019 (http://time.com/5287517/world-war-ii-queen-elizabeth-photo/).

Rowling, J.K. (2014 [1997-2007]): Harry Potter Children's Collection, London: Bloomsbury.

Said, Edward W. (1978): Orientalism, London: Routledge & Kegan Paul.

Shakespeare, William (2000 [1602]): The Merry Wives of Windsor, edited by Giorgio Melchiori (= The Arden Shakespeare, 3rd series), London: Bloomsbury Arden Shakespeare.

Shils, Edward/Young, Michael (1953): "The Meaning of the Coronation." In: The Sociological Review 1/2: pp. 63-81.

Strong, Roy (1987): Gloriana: The Portraits of Queen Elizabeth I, London: Thames & Hudson.

"The Complete London 2012 Opening Ceremony", Olympic Channel, YouTube, July 27, 2012, accessed September 18, 2019 (https://www.youtube.com/watch?v=4As0e4de-rI&t=2052s).

"The Coronation and the BBC", May 28, 2013, accessed March 21, 2019 (https://www.bbc.co.uk/blogs/aboutthebbc/entries/6e258b7f-3b29-399e-9356-c538706ff933).

"The Crown Jewels", n. d., accessed March 21, 2019 (https://www.royal.uk/crown-jewels).

"The Guardian View on Colour-Conscious Casting: Mixing It Up Can Be a Good Thing", January 30, 2019, accessed March 21, 2019 (https://www.theguardian.com/commentisfree/2019/jan/30/the-guardian-view-on-colour-conscious-casting-mixing-it-up-can-be-a-good-thing).

"The Role of the Monarchy", n. d., accessed March 21, 2019 (https://www.royal.uk/role-monarchy).

Vohlidka, John (2013): "Doctor Who and the Critique of Western Imperialism." In: Lindy Orthia (ed.), Doctor Who and Race, Bristol: Intellect, pp. 123-139.

Wagner, John A. (2010): Voices of Shakespeare's England: Contemporary Accounts of Elizabethan Daily Life, Santa Barbara: Greenwood.

Wells, H.G. (2005 [1895]): The Time Machine, London: Penguin.

Wells, H.G. (2017 [1898]: The War of the Worlds, London: Vintage Classics Penguin.

Films and Television

Shakespeare in Love. Directed by John Madden. 2011 [1998], Universal.
The Queen. Directed by Stephen Frears. 2006. Paris: Pathé.
Torchwood. Various directors. 2011 [2006-2011], BBC Worldwide Ltd./2entertain.

Doctor Who Episodes

"Army of Ghosts" (2006): Series 2, episode 12, In: *Doctor Who – Series 2*, BBC Worldwide Ltd./2entertain, 2014.
"The Beast Below" (2010): Series 5, episode 2, In: *Doctor Who – Series 5*, BBC Worldwide Ltd./2entertain, 2014.
"The Chase: The Executioners" (1965): Series 2, episode 30, In: *The Space Museum/The Chase*, BBC Worldwide Ltd./2entertain, 2010.
"A Christmas Carol" (2010): Series 6, episode 0, In: *Doctor Who – Series 6*, BBC Worldwide Ltd./2entertain, 2014.
"The Christmas Invasion" (2005): Series 2, episode 0, In: *Doctor Who – Series 2*, BBC Worldwide Ltd./2entertain, 2014.
"The Crimson Horror" (2013): Series 7, episode 11, In: *Doctor Who – Series 7*, BBC Worldwide Ltd./2entertain, 2014.
"The Crusade" (1965): Series 2, episodes 22-25, In: *Doctor Who – Lost in Time – Series 2*, BBC Worldwide Ltd./2entertain, 2004.
"The Day of the Doctor" (2013): In: *Doctor Who – 50th Anniversary Special*, BBC Worldwide Ltd./2entertain, 2013.
"The Evil of the Daleks" (1967): Series 4, episodes 29-35, BBC Worldwide Ltd./Radio Collection, 2005, Audio CD (video is almost entirely missing from the archives).
"The Idiot's Lantern" (2006): Series 2, episode 7, In: *Doctor Who – Series 2*, BBC Worldwide Ltd./2entertain, 2014.
"Kill the Moon" (2014): Series 8, episode 7, In: *Doctor Who – Series 8*, BBC Worldwide Ltd./2entertain, 2014.
"The King's Demons" (1983): Series 20, episodes 21-22, In: *Doctor Who – Kamelion Tales*, BBC Worldwide Ltd./2entertain, 2019.
"The Next Doctor" (2006): 2008-2010 specials, episode 1, In: *Doctor Who – The Complete Specials*, BBC Worldwide Ltd./2entertain, 2014.
"Planet of the Dead" (2009): 2008-2010 specials, episode 2, In: *Doctor Who – The Complete Specials*, BBC Worldwide Ltd./2entertain, 2014.

"Robot: Part 4" (1975): Series 12, episode 4, In: *Doctor Who – Robot*, BBC Worldwide Ltd./2entertain, 2007.

"The Shakespeare Code" (2007): Series 3, episode 2, In: *Doctor Who – Series 3*, BBC Worldwide Ltd./2entertain, 2014.

"Silver Nemesis: Part 1" (1988): Series 25, episode 8, In: *Doctor Who – Revenge of the Cybermen/Silver Nemesis*, BBC Worldwide Ltd./2entertain, 2019.

"The Snowmen" (2012): Series 7, episode 5.5, In: *Doctor Who – Series 7*, BBC Worldwide Ltd./2entertain, 2014.

"The Talons of Weng-Chiang" (1977): Series 14, episodes 21-26, In: *Doctor Who – Revisitations Vol 1*, BBC Worldwide Ltd./2entertain, 2010.

"Tooth and Claw" (2006): Series 2, episode 2, In: *Doctor Who – Series 2*, BBC Worldwide Ltd./2entertain, 2014.

"The Unquiet Dead" (2005): Series 1, episode 3, In: *Doctor Who – Series 1*, BBC Worldwide Ltd./2entertain, 2014.

"Voyage of the Damned" (2007): Series 4, episode 0, In: *Doctor Who – Series 4*, BBC Worldwide Ltd./2entertain, 2014.

'Party at the Palace': Popular Cultural Celebrations in the Context of Queen Elizabeth II's Golden and Diamond Jubilee

Christina Jordan

THE BRITISH MONARCHY AND ROYAL CELEBRATIONS IN THE 21ST CENTURY

Queen Elizabeth II is currently not only the world's oldest sovereign who is still in office, but also Britain's longest-reigning and longest-living monarch ever. In 2017, she became the first British monarch to celebrate a Sapphire Jubilee, i.e. 65 years on the throne. While the latter was not celebrated widely, her Silver (1977), Golden (2002), and Diamond Jubilee (2012) were celebrated extensively. For both her Golden and her Diamond Jubilee, there were festivities held in Britain and the Commonwealth, with London taking center-stage for the celebrations. Britain's capital became the setting for church services, festive and exclusive banquets, military parades, and flypasts as well as the by now traditional balcony appearance of the royal family.

While the monarchy epitomizes Britain's history and is generally associated with traditions, the calls for a modernization of the British monarchy became louder since the 1990s, when the royal household faced several crises like the divorces of the queen's children or the death of Lady Diana Spencer. This time saw a general demand for updated (family) values, a reformation of the Crown's finances, and, last but not least, a 'humanization' of the monarchy. The plea for a modernization of the monarchy on the whole is reflected by royal activities since the millennium and reflected in royal events such as jubilees or the latest royal weddings: traditional elements were complemented by modern ones, which offer an opportunity for audiences to simply enjoy themselves. The official celebrations for the Golden and Diamond Jubilee entailed not only traditional parades, but events which were labelled as "parties," e.g. – to name but a few – the 2002 "Carnival in the Mall" with parade floats of service organizations like the Red Cross, the Royal National Life Boat Association, or celebrity floats, the huge boat pageant of the River Thames in 2012, or the concerts given at Buckingham Palace in 2002 and 2012.

Most studies on royal events have focused on traditional aspects and analyzed e.g. their influence on the perception of the monarchy (cf. e.g. Laing/Frost 2018), while, as Anne Rowbottom claims, "popular royalism remains a largely neglected phenomenon" (2002: par. 1.2) in cultural studies. This article argues that popular cultural events are essential parts of celebrating a modern(ized) monarchy for several reasons: First, they are an easy way to 'update' the monarchy while at the same time sticking to (seemingly old, but often invented) traditions and rituals. The (seemingly) historical and traditional aspects' value for the success of royal events is not to be underestimated. Hugh O'Donnell argues that traditional elements like a "cast from bygone days" are necessary to create the magical appeal of the celebrations (2006: 167). Nevertheless, as David Cannadine points out, "no head of state is surrounded by more *popular* ritual than Queen Elizabeth II" (1983: 102; emphasis mine). According to him these rituals have the central function to act as markers of stability at times of change: "Old ceremonies have been adapted and new rituals invented, the combined effect of which has been, paradoxically, to give an impression of stability in periods of domestic change, and of continuity and comfort in times of international tension and decline." (ibid: 160) In consequence, royal rituals or celebrations which manage to amalgamate traditional aspects with popular innovations serve at the same time to anchor the monarchy in history and tradition and to update the Crown's public image. I contend that the implementation of popular cultural elements such as pop and rock concerts in the official celebrations extends this function by showing in an entertaining way that the monarchy is able to fuse past and present, adapt to new circumstances, challenges, and demands while at the same time serving as an anchor of stability and reliability. During the Golden and Diamond Jubilee festivities, popular and modern celebratory features were put next to the (seemingly) old-fashioned actions such as the queen touching the Pearl Sword, offered to her by the Mayor of London, when she entered the City of London for the Golden and Diamond Jubilee.[1]

---

1   There are five City of London swords, which are used for ceremonial actions. The Pearl Sword, used in the Diamond Jubilee, is believed to have been given to the City of London by Queen Elizabeth I in 1571, when the Royal Exchange opened. The tradition of

This is a prime example for how the orchestration of the celebrations is even able to enhance the monarchy's appeal of longevity by using the methods of 'comparison and contrast,' which underline their historical difference.

Second, the variety of the celebrations enhances their reach: The popular cultural elements like e.g. the pop and rock concerts might appeal to audiences who are no 'royalists' and therefore not necessarily in favor of the celebrations in general. The integration of performances by famous artists as varied as Robbie Williams, Shirley Bassey, Paul McCartney, and Ozzy Osbourne caters for the tastes of diverse audiences with regard to age, gender, or class and grabs the attention of people who might not have been interested in a royal event otherwise. As the article shows, these popular cultural celebrations thus entail the possibility of social integration and emotional involvement of the public and they therefore have the potential to strengthen the bond between monarchy and people.

The following section elaborates on theoretical considerations concerning (popular) royal events and their potential influence on public opinion about the contemporary British monarchy. In a second step, the article illustrates how such popular events, which are explicitly dedicated to people's enjoyment, function and complement traditional elements of the celebrations by drawing on the examples of the *Party at the Palace* in the context of Elizabeth II's Golden Jubilee in 2002 and the *Diamond Jubilee Concert* in 2012.

MONARCHY AND ITS CHANGING RELATION TO HIGH AND POPULAR CULTURE

While the younger members of the royal family further the project of modernizing the monarchy, the elder generations to which the sovereigns belong are often associated with traditional splendor, noblesse, pomp, and circumstance – and with what would usually be regarded as elitist and aristocratic 'high' culture. Matthew Arnold introduced the term "high culture" in his 1869 book *Culture and Anarchy* and defined it as "the best which has been thought and said in this world" (Arnold 1993 [1869]: 6). Part of this traditional corpus of high culture are art and intellectual works, which are considered to be of high quality and exquisite (aesthetic) value. This mindset implies that there is another sort of culture which does not fulfill these high standards: low, mass, folk, or popular culture – those forms of culture which appeal to less-educated social strata. The distinction between high

---

the monarch touching the sword possibly dates back to King Charles I, when he entered the City of London in 1641 (cf. Treasures of London 2013: n. pag.).

versus low culture implies an elitist stance and is of course highly questionable, first and foremost because it reproduces class distinctions and social prejudices. In the 1950s, Raymond Williams challenged this differentiation and the common assumption "that the ordinary people in fact resemble the normal description of the masses, low and trivial in taste and habit." (2008 [1958]: 88) Nevertheless, while the distinction between high and low – i.e. popular – culture has rightfully been attacked, it is in fact still pervasive nowadays. We still often tend to discriminate between the paintings of the 'great masters' and pop or even street art, between 'highbrow' literature such as Charles Dickens' *Great Expectations* and 'run-of-the-mill' pulp fiction, and between elaborate classical music and pop songs.

In 1977, the British punk rock band Sex Pistols released their song "God Save the Queen" during the Silver Jubilee celebrations. The song criticizes the monarchy, the establishment, and the queen herself so that the BBC as well as the Independent Broadcasting Authority refused to play it. Whereas this is certainly a prime example for how British monarchy and popular (sub-)culture diverge (popular culture did not play any official part in the Silver Jubilee celebrations) this changed with the new millennium and the Golden Jubilee in 2002, which featured the first (pop) concerts. However, a distinction between classical music – which might be viewed as part of 'high culture' – and pop music was made. The classical music concert *Prom at the Palace* (taking its name from *The Proms*, a series of classical orchestral concerts having taken place annually at the Royal Albert Hall since 1895) was held at Buckingham Palace Garden and officially opened the Jubilee Weekend. The pop cultural 'equivalent' *Party at the Palace* took place two days later, on June 3 and featured a range of the most popular pop and rock hits from all decades of the queen's reign, combining very diverse musical genres. The distinction between classical and popular music – and their audiences – is not only reflected, but reproduced in the set-up of these two concerts. However, as the following analysis will show, this changed once more with the *Diamond Jubilee Concert* in 2012, which featured a mixture of classical, pop, and rock music.

Music, especially popular music, is occasionally used as a powerful tool to create a modernized and popular image for a stately or political institution. David Cannadine elaborates on the role and importance of (classical) music in the context of royal ceremonial between the 1820s and the first 25 years of Elizabeth II's reign, referring e.g. to Edgar Elgar's compositions, which are still used in royal celebrations (cf. 1983: 130-131). As Rupa Huq shows, nowadays it is especially popular music which is instrumentalized in state affairs. She illustrates how Tony Blair used Britpop in the 1990s to publicly identify the New Labour Party with youth culture (cf. 2010: 95) and to "rebrand the UK as less stuffy, more forward-looking and culturally diverse" (ibid: 96) – or in other words, to benefit from the aesthetics and climate of 'Cool Britannia.' Cool Britannia is associated with a renewed optimism as well as pride in British culture.[2] At this time, especially the British pop and rock music scene flourished with globally successful bands like Oasis, Blur, or the Spice Girls, which contributed to updating Britain's image both at home and abroad.

In a similar vein, the monarchy might benefit from an association with popular music. However, the use of music and popular culture in both royal and other events would have no effects without being geared towards a spectacular and prominent media representation, which is in the case of the British monarchy facilitated first and foremost by the BBC. Douglas Kellner claims that contemporary media reporting itself takes on the form of a spectacle with excessiveness and entertainment becoming the dominant form of coverage (cf. 2003: 1). Media spectacles like huge royal celebrations, but also sports events, or other outstanding TV programs create ways to communicate not only obvious statements to the audience (e.g. through speeches), but also convey subtle messages concerning values and images. Partaking in the arena of media spectacles and thus in a modern version of 'bread and circuses' demonstrates that the monarchy not only opens up to what is considered as popular culture and entertainment, but that the institution acknowledges the achievements of these contemporary musical artists next to those of their traditional and classical counterparts. This should not only be interpreted as a step in the direction of a modernized monarchy, but also as a subtle way to communicate the monarchy's willingness to further adapt to contemporary social and medial circumstances.

PARTY AT THE PALACE AND THE DIAMOND JUBILEE CONCERT

Party at the Palace was the pop concert hosted at the gardens of Buckingham Palace on June 3, 2002, which was attended by 12.000 people who had won the tickets in a lottery. In addition, it is estimated that one million people watched the concert on big screens in The Mall as well as 200 million on television ("50 Facts

---

2   Funnily enough, the connection of old and new, popular and high culture is implied in the term itself as well: Cool Britannia is a pun on the patriotic song *Rule, Britannia!*, Britain's unofficial national anthem dating back to the 18th century, which is traditionally performed at *The Proms*.

on the Queen's Golden Jubilee Year" 2002: n. pag.). The *Diamond Jubilee Concert*, which followed on June 4, 2012, was organized by the former Take That singer Gary Barlow OBE, took place in front of Buckingham Palace and the Queen Victoria Memorial, and featured more than 50 artists from various musical genres. People could apply for 10.000 free tickets and it is estimated that between 250.000 and half a million people were on-site for the concert (cf. "Jubilee Concert" 2012: n. pag.), which was additionally broadcast worldwide by the BBC and its partners and attracted an audience of 17 million in the UK alone and 200 million worldwide ("60 Facts About the Diamond Jubilee Celebrations" 2012: n. pag.).

Andreas Widholm and Karin Becker, who conducted research on the Swedish and British royal weddings in 2010 and 2011, explain that "rituals consist of repetitions; they follow a recognizable and repeatable form, both the ritual itself and its components. Rituals that take place in public become collective events, and the place itself carries meanings that can give the observance additional power." (2015: 11) By now, the concerts have not only become popular collective events, but even acquired a quasi-ritualistic character (sensu Widholm and Becker) due to their similar forms and regular repetitions such as other royal invented traditions like the famous 'balcony kiss' after weddings. This article argues that the concerts – of which there are other examples such as the benefit concert for Lady Diana in 2007 – should be regarded as the newest generation of what David Cannadine (1983) scrutinized as "invented traditions"[3] in the context of royal ritual. In consequence, the question arises which ritual and cultural functions they fulfil both for the contemporary monarchy as protagonists and for their audiences.

The following analysis investigates the concerts against the background of this question and reveals, by scrutinizing the concerts' forms and functions, their underlying meanings. The analysis is based on the BBC live broadcasts of both Jubilee concerts and deals with three main sets of questions. First, the choice of artists and music is analyzed regarding their musical and historical context, appeal to diverse audiences, and their respective cultural functions. Second, the choice of place is discussed, with the royal family's home Buckingham Palace (one time inside the garden walls, one time outside) being the backdrop of the events. Third, the role of the queen and the members of the royal family as well as their status among other viewers and celebrities is examined.

---

3   The term "invented traditions" was made popular by Eric Hobsbawm and Terence Ranger in their 1983 edited volume *The Invention of Tradition*, in which Cannadine's extensive article on the intersection of invented traditions and royal ritual was published.

Catering for Everyone's Taste? The Choice of Music and Artists

The Golden Jubilee concert *Party at the Palace* featured almost 30 famous (mostly British) pop and rock acts including the band Queen, Phil Collins, Tom Jones, Elton John, Brian Wilson, Eric Clapton, Joe Cocker, Ozzy Osbourne, and Paul McCartney. Classical music performances had taken place two days prior to the pop and rock concert during the *Prom at the Palace*. As mentioned above, the *Diamond Jubilee Concert* followed this newly invented tradition, but integrated both musical genres, classical music and popular music, thus covering not only a broad range of musical styles, but also national and international artists who have been successful during the queen's reign, such as the British singers Robbie Williams, Ed Sheeran, and Shirley Bassey, the Chinese pianist Lang Lang, the Australian Kylie Minogue, but also the British tenor Alfie Boe and the American soprano Renée Flemming.

This comprehensive selection caters for very diverse musical tastes and, in consequence, has the ability to attract people with different backgrounds, e.g. regarding their musical and stylistic preferences, but also their age group. Stevenson and Abell explain for the whole of the Golden Jubilee that "[n]otably when the Jubilee was conceptualized as representing the entire population, this was done in terms of spanning their diversity, as facilitating the coming together of many diverse national elements under the umbrella of the celebration." (2011: 135) Even different gender identities were wittily represented during the 2002 concert with Dame Edna Everage, a drag queen impersonated by the Australian comedian Barry Humphries, who mocked class snobbery and actually introduced Queen Elizabeth and Prince Philip's arrival.

One might thus argue that these popular cultural celebrations (which in the case of the Diamond Jubilee even incorporated 'high' culture as well) have an integrative function for society. Furthermore, the events are an occasion to celebrate the queen, the monarchy, and the British nation – or simply to party. The queen herself declared in a speech for her Golden Jubilee: "I am very glad the 50th anniversary of my accession is giving so many people all over this country an excuse to celebrate and enjoy themselves." ("Golden Jubilee Speech at London's Guildhall" 2002: n. pag.) Ben Pimlott argues that it is exactly the entertainment value that keeps the monarchy popular, stating that "in key ways, contemporary demands of the monarchy are mundane: people look not for mystery or magic, but for value for money" (Pimlott 2002: 31) – something offered to people with the broad variety of famous artists partaking in the concerts.

My analysis of the entirety of the popular cultural aspects of the Jubilee celebrations (i.e. concerts, parades, street parties) indicates that they evoked stronger associations with pride in (British) achievements, the British nation, and history, as well as a diverse but integrated British nation and Commonwealth of Nations, than with the institution of the monarchy or the queen herself.[4] Especially the representation of the musical achievements during the queen's reign further pride in British (high and popular) culture. Prince Charles, too, mentioned in his speech after the 2002 concert that the event has made him "feel extraordinarily proud of this country" (*Party at the Palace*[5] 01:26). However, he instantaneously linked this observation with the community's pride in the queen: "And we, Your Majesty, are here tonight because above all, we feel proud of you" – followed by at least 30 seconds of applause (ibid).

His speech was visually underlined by a giant projection of the Union flag onto the facade of Buckingham Palace and followed by the national anthem "God Save the Queen" – not just being played with the audience listening passively, but the public was supposed to join in singing. Singing together creates collectively shared emotions and a feeling of unity (cf. Brauer 2012). The concert thus culminates in an enactment of unity and national pride with the queen – the textual subject of the national anthem – as focal point.

Participating in royal events, especially on site, can be a rousing experience and strengthen social bonds both amongst family and friends attending together and even amongst strangers, as Ruth Adams has found in her research on outdoor screens and public congregations on the occasion of royal events (cf. 2016: 272-273). She explains that "[a]udiences who are present at live events get to enjoy the atmosphere and excitement from being part of a like-minded crowd, and the sense that they are part of history in the making" (ibid: 273). Furthermore, she claims

---

4 Rosalind Brunt explains that the British royal family serves the end of celebrating national pride particularly well: "So thank goodness for the big state occasions, which no other country can do like the British, for nowhere else boasts the Royal Family and such pageantry and tradition. Moreover, the Royal Family is better equipped to carry British pride because they rely, not on transitory merit, but on heredity." (Brunt 1992: 288) Her argument ties in nicely with Couldry's and Rojek's observations on royal celebrity, which are discussed in the part on the royal family members' role in the celebrations. That pride in the nation during royal celebrations sometimes even reaches nationalist levels is addressed by Ruth Adams. One attendant of the *Diamond Jubilee Concert*, whom she interviewed for her study, reported he perceived a "'fervent nationalist tone [which] undermined the positive aspects of the occasion'" (Adams 2016: 277).

5 The TV programs *Party at the Palace* and *Diamond Jubilee Concert* were viewed and transcribed at the British Film Institute (BFI) National Archive, London.

that the experience of communal viewing can enhance the "emotional engagement" with the event (ibid: 275). One might thus argue that next to their socially integrative function of fostering a collective identity, another of these events' central functions might be to strengthen the emotional bonds between the audience and the monarchy embodied by the queen, i.e. the official protagonist of the "history in the making." However, a study by the social psychologists Stevenson and Abell, who conducted interviews at the Golden Jubilee celebrations, showed that most interviewees were indifferent or even distanced themselves from the events (cf. 2011: 18). Nevertheless, some interviewees stated that "people's negative beliefs about the monarchy do not square with their celebrations" and thus did not hinder their participation in the events (ibid: 130). Completely in line with their observation, some public voices during the two Jubilee celebrations expressed irritation on how exactly to unite their love for music on the one hand and their dislike of the monarchy on the other. An example is *The Guardian*'s music blog, where a journalist commented live during the concert:

"8.31pm: Ed Sheeran doing his one about the smack addicted prostitute. Sheeran's dead young ... what is he doing? There are lots of perfectly valid reasons for hating the monarchy of which I won't go into now, but chief among my own personal reasons is it's just so bloody square. Surely the point of getting into pop music in the first place is that it's quite a cool place to be: Sex! Drugs! Hurling coffee makers from the window of the Alfreton Travelodge! Why go and blow it all by playing a concert in honour of the monarchy? Britain really is in a bit of a state right now isn't it?" ("The Queen's Diamond Jubilee Concert" 2012: n. pag.)

The representation of such views that deviate from the message of the program is of course non-desirable for the monarchy, the organizers, and for the broadcasting institutions. Hugh O'Donnell explains with respect to the case of Lady Diana's funeral that the images broadcast on BBC and ITV were highly selective with the purpose to demonstrate "that the behaviour of the public chimes in *ideologically* with the aims of the organisers" (2006: 173; original emphasis), while in fact other programs showed that not all people who gathered for the funeral were mourning, but that some were also celebrating (cf. ibid: 173-174). It is fair to assume that this is also true for other large-scale royal events. Widholm and Becker's on-site observations support this hypothesis. They describe that they "saw media professionals 'directing' audience behaviours on several occasions, and most people accepted their advice by performing in a media-friendly manner" (Widholm/Becker

2015: 14) and that they perceived transgressive behavior, which revealed "alternative interpretations of the event" especially in public settings such as parks (ibid: 18).

It can be concluded that such events with their huge variety of artists and musical styles, their spectacular size, and the vast media attention they receive, have the potential to reach the majority of people. People who are already in favor of the monarchy experience the events in a positive way and might even renew their (emotional) ties to the monarchy. Nevertheless, it is very unlikely that they succeed to change people's attitude towards the monarchy or even their convictions regarding appropriate state forms. Although the representation of deprecating attitudes is avoided in the official TV broadcasts, one can assume that they still exist not only in quiet, but that deviant behavior is also acted out at the official sites of the celebrations.

Letting People in? The Choice of Place

For a long time, Buckingham Palace has been a fortress of the monarchy's seclusion. Terry Farrell comments:

"Yet while the royal family barricade their gardens behind high walls, the experience for all is hesitatingly and incompletely revealed – the opposite intention of the original designs. The walls around Buckingham Palace's gardens depress the urban scene for over a mile of central London. They are the epitome of bad neighbourliness and characterise the palace as a series of signs that say 'Keep Out'." (2002: 93)

Having been the London home of the sovereign and their spouse since 1837, it has been the location for state ceremonies such as investitures and the conferring of knighthoods, the reception of foreign heads of state, or state banquets, while 'normal' people rarely had a chance to see the palace's interior.

However, this image of seclusion as well as the accessibility of Buckingham Palace have changed over the last two or three decades, especially in the realm of popular cultural events.[6] The opening of the palace to the people goes hand in hand with processes of modernizing the monarchy. Nowadays, summer garden parties take place in Buckingham Palace's gardens and since 1993, the State Rooms can

---

6   Recent fictional depictions (e.g. Peter Morgan's *The Queen* from 2006 or the Netflix series *The Crown* [2016–]) also play a major role in the process of 'opening up the palace doors,' as they imaginatively stage the royal family's life behind the palace walls.

be visited by the public in August and September while the queen is not in residence ("40 Facts about Buckingham Palace" n. d.: n. pag.).

One of the high points in Buckingham Palace's public history is the role it occupied during both Jubilee concerts. In 2002, the concert took place at Buckingham Palace Garden, i.e. inside the palace's walls. This was the first time during the queen's reign that people were invited into the garden for mere entertainment. All 12.000 guests of the *Party at the Palace* concert were also invited to dwell in the gardens in the afternoon before the concert took place during a picnic hosted by the queen. Farrell argues that opening up the palace and thus rendering it "permeable to the people" is a symbolic gesture of the monarchy (2002: 90), which not only creates a new physical, but also a new emotional relationship between monarchy and people (cf. ibid: 94). Not only allowing people in to visit Buckingham Palace like a museum, but inviting them to participate in activities such as feasting in the afternoon picnic and partying in the evening concert can be regarded as a progressive and extraordinary step in the process of rendering the place "permeable" and the monarchy accessible.

In both concerts analyzed in this article, Buckingham Palace played a central role in the staging of some songs, becoming a protagonist itself. The 2002 concert began with Brian May, lead guitarist of the band Queen, standing on the roof of Buckingham Palace and playing "God Save the Queen" (*Party at the Palace* 00:01:00-00:02:45). This performance became one of the most iconic moments of the whole Jubilee Weekend and is even featured as a video on the monarchy's official website of Buckingham Palace (cf. "Royal Residences: Buckingham Palace" n. d.: n. pag.). However, it is not a traditional version of the national anthem, but May's interpretation as an electric guitar solo, without the lyrics being sung. This striking beginning of the concert set the stage for what was to follow: the admission of popular culture to this time-honored building and, in consequence, to the celebration of the queen's Jubilee.

In 2012, the gates of Buckingham Palace remained closed and the building was 'merely' used as the impressive backdrop of the stage set up around the Victoria Memorial in front of it. After Robbie Williams opened the concert with his song "Let Me Entertain You," the Welsh actor and comedian Rob Brydon welcomed the audience with the following, rather mocking, introduction: "Well, good evening loyal subjects and welcome to the noisiest party the queen has ever seen. Oh, she won't like this. She won't like this. This will be too noisy for her. This is the equivalent of a well-meaning parent handing over their home to their sixteen-year-olds for a Saturday night. And it ends up on Facebook." (*The Diamond Jubilee Concert* 00:07:00-00:07:40) Apart from making fun of the queen, Brydon also highlighted how exceptional it is to have this noisy party at this venue, the queen's home. Although he compared the queen to a sweet-tempered mother, this image cheekily teased her as being rather naïve. In this exuberant and celebratory mood, both for Brydon and for the audience it did not even seem to matter that this time, the celebrations took place outside the walls.

Nevertheless, one remarkable 'conquest' of Buckingham Palace took place. The band Madness performed their song "Our House" on the roof of the palace with a giant projection on the palace's front, which showed typical British terraced houses. In the course of the song, the projected houses partly swung open to reveal people dancing in their living rooms to Madness' song. The performance can be seen as an appropriation of the palace in several ways: First, the band played on the roof – just like Brian May ten years earlier. Together with the band, popular culture thus figuratively entered the palace and used it for its own ends. Second, the palace was visually seized through the projection, which transformed and re-framed it as "our house," i.e. normal British middle and working class homes. While this performance on the one hand celebrated British working- and middle-class life and can be interpreted as appropriation of the palace, it also, on the other hand, highlighted the differences in status between 'ordinary' audience – and maybe even artists – and the monarchy, who live in the luxurious palace that is big enough to work as a screen for several terraced houses. The role and status of the members of the royal family, who were part of this spectacle's audience, but were also set apart from other members of the spectators, e.g. through such performances or the hosts' comments, will be the focus of the following section.

THE ROLE OF THE ROYAL FAMILY IN THE CONTEXT OF THE CONCERTS: AN EXAMPLE OF ROYAL 'ORDINARINESS'?

The roles Elizabeth II and her family embody during the celebrations vary considerably and oscillate between royal extraordinariness and ordinariness. On the one hand, the queen's Jubilee is the sole (official) cause for the celebrations and the queen is consequently at their center. On the other hand, during many parts of the festivities – especially popular cultural ones – the queen and the royal family become a more or less passive part of the audience, almost like 'ordinary' citizens. Interestingly enough, through the functions they fulfill during the concerts, they are rather associated with their subjects in the audience than with the 'celebrities,' i.e. the performing artists. However, the equilibrium of 'same but different,' which is probably one of today's most potent modes of establishing a successful and appealing public image of the monarchy and the basis for 'royal ordinariness,' is carefully upheld in the context of such occasions. A striking example is the queen's presence during the concerts. While the other members of the royal family were present from the very beginning of both concerts, the queen (and Prince Philip in 2002; he was not present in 2012 due to a bladder infection treated in hospital) joined the concerts significantly later, i.e. about two hours after their respective beginnings. With her separate and special entry, not only her special status is highlighted, but also the exceptionality of her presence during a pop and rock concert is underlined. *The Guardian*'s music blog commented live on the queen's absence: "8.13pm: A few people asking on the Twitter where the bloody 'eck the Queen is. Do you really think the Queen is the kind of gal who turns up early to watch the support acts?" ("The Queen's Diamond Jubilee Concert" 2012: n. pag.) Although she becomes part of the audience – albeit in the royal box – she is still set apart from the rest of the attendees, even of her own family. However, this special treatment and staging of the queen's entry adds a dramaturgy to the events, which creates suspense and is of utmost importance for keeping up the magical aura that render the concerts such special and extraordinary events.

In addition, the queen's (and the royal family's) attendance is of significance for shaping the monarchy's public image and the perception of their cultural work. Chris Rojek explains that "[t]he monarch can no longer be completely above the people, since this would be perceived as haughty, imperious and out of touch. The most favourable option is to be for the people by engaging in deserving causes and acting as a tribune for the public interest." (2002: 112) Although the concerts are not a charitable cause in the classic sense, they add a new layer to the monarchy's service for the public good as they are widely perceived as free entertainment 'for the people.' While typical welfare activities are often dedicated to minorities, socially underprivileged, or handicapped people, this newly invented tradition might thus enhance the scope of traditional royal welfare activities by appealing to a much broader target group.

Moreover, the royal family's public participation in the concerts allows for a rather private approach to the monarchy as people get a glimpse at royal 'pastime activities' (albeit their rather staged nature in this case). David Chaney describes that beginning with the televised coronation, people have developed a "quasi-intimate relationship" (2001: 215) with the royals, who, in this process, have become "secular celebrities" (ibid: 214) and "familiarized" (ibid), which distinguishes them from other celebrities, such as e.g. the artists actively participating in the concerts. However, there are clear similarities between royal and 'normal' celebrity in the 21st century. Widholm and Becker argue that just like other celebrities, monarchs are part of discourses surrounding "an illusion of intimacy" (2015: 10). This illusion is strategically granted not only during royal celebrations, but, as I have argued elsewhere (cf. Jordan 2019), especially in programs that allow a look behind usually closed royal doors and into pastime, private situations. Nevertheless, the equilibrium of familiarity and inequality is also at stake here: Nick Couldry explains that the British monarchy has tried to present itself as an 'ordinary' family since the early 20th century (cf. 2001: 224-225). On the other hand, Michael Billig has found that, whereas differences in status seem to disappear when meeting members of the royal family, "[t]he inequalities must persist, in order to make those desired moments of equality so magical" (1991: 82). This might succeed last but not least due to the royal family's special celebrity status, which is ascribed and inherited by birth, not achieved like that of other celebrities (cf. Rojek 2002: 105; Couldry 2001: 223). Interestingly enough, in his speeches after both concerts, Prince Charles toyed with this idea and opened up a difference in status between the queen and Prince Philip on the one hand and the rest of the royal family on the other hand, whom he put on one level with British citizens. Towards the end of his speech in 2012, he said: "So as a nation, this is our opportunity to thank you and my father for always being there for us, for inspiring us with your selfless duty and service and for making us proud to be British." (*The Diamond Jubilee Concert* 03:11:50-03:12:00) By using the "us" as personal pronoun, Charles fraternized with the public. He staged himself as an ordinary subject, highlighting his status as a citizen of the nation rather than the heir to the throne, thus renegotiating his own position between royalty and ordinariness.

As these examples show, the careful equilibrium between extraordinariness and ordinariness, between being a royal family and an ordinary family, and between aloofness and sociability comes to the fore particularly in the realm of popular cultural celebrations and consequently renders them a highly interesting subject for both cultural and royal studies. Moreover, scrutinizing the cultural work of the younger royal generations, especially with regard to how they position themselves between these different, partly contradictory conceptions of modern royalty remains of interest for future studies dedicated to contemporary monarchies.

CONCLUSION: A NEW GENERATION OF INVENTED ROYAL TRADITIONS

Contemporary monarchies with their rather limited political capacities fulfil first and foremost symbolic and cultural functions in the realms of (state) representation and welfare. The integration of popular cultural elements next to traditional pageantry during royal celebrations shows that the British monarchy has found an additional and new way to remain valuable for society and to update their public image, which needs to correspond to the demands and conditions of a modern, multicultural, and diverse Britain and Commonwealth. Chris Rojek claims that "[i]f the primary function of the monarch today is symbolic, it will be up to Charles, William and their advisers to construct a symbol that can embrace a multicultural Britain" (2002: 110). The symbolic character of integrative events such as the concerts, which incorporated a plethora of artists from Britain and abroad, with different ethnicities, religious attitudes, and personal (partly troubled) backgrounds is telling as it shows new directions in the monarchy's cultural work and attitude towards everyday culture. As an additional synergetic effect, the participation of these artists in the concerts suggests that, however diverse they are, they support Elizabeth II as Britain's sovereign and head of the Commonwealth and thus the monarchy as institution. This 'soft power' that celebrities – both artists and hosts of the concerts – exercise should not be underestimated, as their fans might reflect on the celebrities' alliances. Moreover, my analysis has suggested that popular cultural events such as concerts are an effective way of involving subjects who are usually not in favor of the monarchy since many of them do not regard their dislike as an obstacle for joining the celebrations. Nonetheless, it remains highly unlikely that such mass events convince people to fundamentally change their minds or political convictions.

Conceiving of the concerts as invented traditions, it can be expected that grand and happy royal occasions which are not primarily family rituals like weddings, christenings, or funerals, but rather state occasions (such as the next crown jubilees or the coronation of the next monarch) will be accompanied by popular cultural celebrations as well. Another recent example is the *Concert for Diana* in 2007, which was hosted by her sons William and Harry on what would have been her 46th birthday to commemorate the 10th anniversary of her death. This benefit concert did not only form part of this newly invented tradition, but succeeded to combine the cultural functions of remembering Diana, donating the returns to royal charities, entertaining the masses and associating the (younger) royal family[7] with popular culture and celebrities.

To sum up, this article has shown that popular cultural events such as concerts represent a new generation of invented royal traditions, as they have by now become anticipated elements of large-scale royal celebrations. They are of high interest for royal studies, especially from a cultural studies perspective, as their analyses reveal much about the British monarchy's current position in society, their relation to the public and the Crown's image that is established and perpetuated in

---

7   Both the queen and Prince Charles were not present during the concert.

these widely received media events. Not only are the concerts a new and spectacular way of putting the monarchy and its royal protagonists in the national and international limelight, they also have the potential to successfully update the monarchy's image by demonstrating their association with popular culture and music, giving a new meaning to traditional royal landmarks like Buckingham Palace, and last but not least by renegotiating and reaccentuating the Crown's role in Britain's cultural landscape.

WORKS CITED

"40 Facts about Buckingham Palace", n. d., accessed November 5, 2019 (https://web.archive.org/web/20111104182150/http://www.royal.gov.uk/latestnewsanddiary/factfiles/40factsaboutbuckinghampalace.aspx).

"50 Facts on the Queen's Golden Jubilee Year", 7 August, 2002, accessed October 29, 2019 (https://web.archive.org/web/20090216150003/http://www.royal.gov.uk/LatestNewsandDiary/Pressreleases/2002/50factsonTheQueensGoldenJubileeyear-2002.aspx).

"60 Facts About the Diamond Jubilee Celebrations in the UK", September 15, 2012, accessed July 29, 2019 (https://www.royal.uk/60-facts-about-diamond-jubilee-celebrations-uk).

Adams, Ruth (2016): "The Queen on the Big Screen(s): Outdoor Screens and Public Congregations." In: Mandy Merck (ed.), The British Monarchy on Screen, Manchester: Manchester University Press, pp. 264-287.

Arnold, Matthew (1993 [1869]): Culture and Anarchy and Other Writings, edited by Stefan Collini. Cambridge: Cambridge University Press.

Billig, Michael (1991): Talking of the Royal Family, London: Taylor and Francis.

Brauer, Juliane (2012): "'...das Lied zum Ausdruck der Empfindungen werden kann': Singen und Gefühlserziehung in der frühen DDR." In: Marcelo Caruso/Ute Frevert (eds.), Emotionen in der Bildungsgeschichte (= Jahrbuch für Historische Bildungsforschung 18), Bad Heilbrunn: Klinkhardt, pp. 126-145.

Brunt, Rosalind (1992): "A 'Divine Gift to Inspire'? Popular Cultural Representation, Nationhood and The British Monarchy." In: Dominic Strinati/Stephen Wagg (eds.), Come on Down? Popular Media Culture in Post-War Britain, London and New York: Routledge, pp. 285-301.

Cannadine, David (1983): "The Context, Performance and Meaning of Ritual: The British Monarchy and the 'Invention of Tradition', c. 1820-1977." In: Eric Hobsbawm/Terence Ranger (eds.), The Invention of Tradition, Cambridge and New York: Cambridge University Press, pp. 101-164.

Chaney, David (2001). "The Mediated Monarchy." In: David Morley/Kevin Robins (eds.), British Cultural Studies. Geography, Nationality, and Identity, Oxford: Oxford University Press, pp. 207-219.

Couldry, Nick (2001). "Everyday Royal Celebrity." In: David Morley/Kevin Robins (eds.), British Cultural Studies. Geography, Nationality, and Identity, Oxford: Oxford University Press, pp. 221-233.

Farrell, Terry (2002): "Parks and Palaces. How Monarchy Reigns over Public Spaces." In: Tom Bentley/James Wilsdon (eds.), Monarchies (= Demos Collection Issues 17), London: Demos, pp. 90-96.

"Golden Jubilee Speech at London's Guildhall", June 4, 2002, accessed October 31, 2019 (http://edition.cnn.com/2002/WORLD/europe/06/04/uk.jubilee.text/index.html).

Hobsbawm, Eric/Ranger, Terence (eds.) (1983): The Invention of Tradition, Cambridge and New York: Cambridge University Press.

Huq, Rupa (2010): "Labouring the Point? The Politics of Britpop in 'New Britain'." In: Andy Bennett/Jon Stratton (eds.), Britpop and the English Music Tradition, Farnham and Burlington: Ashgate, pp. 89-102.

Jordan, Christina (2019): "From Private to Public: Royal Family Memory as Prospective Collective Memory in A Jubilee Tribute to The Queen by The Prince of Wales (2012)." In: Journal of Aesthetics and Culture 11/sup1 (https://doi.org/10.1080/20004214.2019.1635426).

"Jubilee Concert: Big Noise and a Big Gasp as Duke Misses Date with Pop Royalty." In: The Guardian June 4, 2012, accessed July 29, 2019 (https://www.theguardian.com/music/2012/jun/04/diamond-jubilee-concert-buckingham-palace).

Kellner, Douglas (2003): Media Spectacle, London and New York: Routledge.

Laing, Jennifer/Frost, Warwick (2018): Royal Events. Rituals, Innovations, Meanings, Abingdon and New York: Routledge.

O'Donnell, Hugh (2006): "Once in TV's Royal City: Television Coverage of Royal Media Events." In: Godela Weiss-Sussex/Franco Binchini (eds.), Urban Mindscapes of Europe (= European Studies 23), Amsterdam and New York: Rodopi, pp. 163-177.

Pimlott, Ben (2002): "After Deference: the Future of the Monarchy in a Value-For-Money Age." In: Tom Bentley/James Wilsdon (eds.), Monarchies (= Demos Collection Issues 17), London: Demos, pp. 27-32.

Rojek, Chris (2002): "Courting Fame. The Monarchy and Celebrity Culture." In: Tom Bentley/James Wilsdon (eds.), Monarchies (= Demos Collection Issues 17), London: Demos, pp. 105-110.

Rowbottom, Anne (2002): "Following the Queen: The Place of the Royal Family in the Context of Royal Visits and Civil Religion." In: Sociological Research Online 7/2 (http://www.socresonline.org.uk/7/2/rowbottom.html).

"Royal Residences: Buckingham Palace", n. d., accessed November 5, 2019 (https://www.royal.uk/royal-residences-buckingham-palace).

Sex Pistols (1977): "God Save the Queen." Track # four on side one on Never Mind the Bollocks, Here's the Sex Pistols. Virgin Records.

"The Queen's Diamond Jubilee Concert – as It Happened", June 4, 2012, accessed November 20, 2019 (https://www.theguardian.com/music/musicblog/2012/jun/04/queen-diamond-jubilee-concert).

"Treasures of London – The Pearl Sword", August 9, 2013, accessed December 7, 2019 (https://exploring-london.com/2013/08/09/treasures-of-london-the-pearl-sword/).

Stevenson, Clifford/Abell, Jackie (2011): "Enacting National Concerns: Anglo-British Accounts of the 2002 Royal Golden Jubilee." In: Journal of Community & Applied Social Psychology 21/2, pp. 124-137.

Widholm, Andreas/Becker, Karin (2015): "Celebrating with the Celebrities: Television in Public Space during Two Royal Weddings." In: Celebrity Studies 6/1, pp. 6-22.

Williams, Raymond (2008 [1958]): "Culture is Ordinary." In: Neil Badmington/ Julia Thomas (eds.), The Routledge Critical and Cultural Theory Reader, London and New York: Routledge, pp.82-94.

Films and Television

The Crown. Created by Peter Morgan. 2016–. Netflix.
The Queen. Directed by Stephen Frears. 2006. Pathé.
Party at the Palace. 2002. BBC.
The Diamond Jubilee Concert. 2012. BBC.

Afterword

Afterword:
The British Monarchy and Brexit

Imke Polland

I am writing the largest part of this in August 2019,[1] in the middle of discussions about a possible no confidence vote against Prime Minister Boris Johnson when no outcome seems certain except for the chaos of the status quo. More than three years after the in/out referendum on Britain's EU membership, with Brexit looming on the horizon (the leave-date now being January 31, 2020), the question of what role one of Britain's major institutions of the establishment, the monarchy, plays in this increasingly opaque process seems to become more pressing. With the Labour Party ostensibly plotting to involve the palace in a coup against Prime Minister Boris Johnson (cf. Yorke/Tominey 2019: n. pag.), and incessant speculations about the queen's personal opinions on the matter of Brexit in the British press, another layer of uncertainty and speculation is added to the already unsettled and seemingly haphazard discussions in the political arena. The British monarchy, allegedly a "post-political" (Higson 2016: 360) institution (even though it is very much political indeed – in the form of its representational politics and soft power influence [cf. Nye 2004; Müller/Mehrkens 2016], for example), is increasingly involved in public speculations about Brexit. The monarchy holds a powerful position in these debates, because of the central values it is conceived to embody: stability and continuity. In the following, I will offer some thoughts on the role of the British royals in current times of uncertainty, particularly in the context of ongoing Brexit negotiations based on a review of recent British media coverage.

---

1 Some additions to this essay were made throughout the publication process to keep it as updated as possible. The final remarks were added in early November 2019, after a new date for the UK's withdrawal from the EU had been set and the British parliament had agreed to hold a general election in December 2019.

TWO REFERENDA AND THE 'POLITICS' OF ROYALTY

Already in 2014, when the Scottish referendum on independence was held, the role of the royal family was debated in the British media, as the vote on independence also unavoidably raised the question of Scotland's state form, i.e. the possibility of the country becoming a republic. More than five years ago, during the referendum campaigns, it was made clear that irrespective of the vote's outcome, Elizabeth II would remain the Queen of Scotland. At the time, 54% of Scots favored retaining the monarchy (see Webber 2014: n. pag.). As recent polls suggest, the renewed debate on a possible Scottish independence after the Brexit vote has not affected this general opinion (yet) (cf. YouGov 2018).

At the time, both the political role of the monarchy and the queen's personal views on Scottish independence were subject of intent speculations. A comment she made to a well-wisher after a church visit near her Balmoral estate in Scotland was understood as a political reference. *The Guardian* wrote:

> "The Queen made a rare intervention on the political stage when she expressed the hope that voters will 'think very carefully about the future' before the Scottish independence referendum on Thursday. [...] The Queen's remarks were interpreted by no campaigners as helpful to their cause. They were seen to tally with a warning the prime minister will deliver in Scotland on Monday, on his final visit north of the border before Thursday's vote, that a vote for independence would lead to an irrevocable break with the UK." (Watt/Carrell/Quinn 2014: n. pag.)

What is particularly interesting with regards to allegedly political statements of the monarch (or members of the royal family) is that they are never direct comments or references to the political decisions and events in question. Rather, they generally are statements made in different contexts, e.g. in speeches or conversations, and interpreted by journalists or even instrumentalized by parties to have a certain political meaning in the respective context.

A similar occurrence concerns the monarch's Christmas broadcast in 2018, which focused on the theme of compromise, respect, and mutual understanding. Not surprisingly, this broadcast was perceived as a "veiled Brexit reference" to the country divided over the referendum outcome (Khan 2018: n. pag.). To this *The Daily Telegraph*'s Hannah Furness adds: "While Buckingham Palace is always quick to deny political motives behind anything the Queen says, she has in the past used subtle comments to influence the public's thinking on political matters (2018: n. pag.). While it is questionable in how far these referenced occurrences really were strategic utterances on the side of the queen and whether the impression does not rather result from the public's interpretations of statements, the influence was effective and clearly noticeable.

Yet another instance soon after that, in January 2019, reinforced this perception as various papers wrote about a speech given by the queen at the Sandringham Women's Institute, which was seen by commentators to give further insight on the monarch's view on Brexit. While she actually spoke about "the virtues of respecting other people's points of view," her remarks were "widely interpreted as a veiled reference to the toxic debate around Brexit" (Topping 2019: n. pag.).

The articles picking up on those illusive statements fashion them as reassuring and give the impression that the queen, as head of state, can mediate in politically difficult situations and thus contribute to preserve stability and order. And indeed, the queen does constitutionally have "the right to warn" (Bagehot 2001 [1867]: 64), a right, like the other two royal prerogatives,[2] which the queen is expected to exercise cautiously in her weekly meetings with the prime minister. According to the official website of the royal family, throughout the 'Audience' "[t]he Queen remains politically neutral on all matters, she is able to 'advise and warn' her ministers – including her Prime Minister – when necessary" ("Audiences" n. d.: n. pag.). The queen's role is thus more than implicitly political.

In the face of such commentary that alludes to the prerogatives, therefore, it almost seems as if there was a public longing to know about the political opinions of members of the royal family in order to gauge the political role of the one governmental institution conceived to be above politics or politically neutral. It is important to note, however, that these representations are all interpretations and never authorized by the palace. And this is what does the trick. By being illusive, the monarchy accumulates more symbolic relevance than by being outspoken; which, in turn, can have the opposite effect. When the supposedly politically neutral royals deviate from their assigned role and comment on the politics of the day they have to expect severe criticism – even if only temporarily. Recall for example Princess Diana's famous campaign in the context of the landmine crisis in Angola. At the time it was criticized as interference in what was perceived as a highly political issue. In hindsight, she is now praised for her activism in this matter, as can be seen, for example, in the 2019 ITV documentary entitled "An African Journey" on Prince Harry and Meghan's royal tour to Africa, where Harry followed in his mother's footsteps. Moreover, royal 'outspokenness' can complicate or destabilize the system and further divide public opinion along the lines of royalist/republican.

---

2   The other two prerogatives as seminally outlined by Bagehot (2001 [1867]) are the right to be consulted and to encourage.

While these examples serve to show not only the symbolic roles the monarchy still holds in contemporary Britain, it also highlights the soft power wielded by the members of the royal family.[3] An interesting case in the context of Brexit negotiations are the travels of the younger royals to European countries in the aftermath of the referendum, which are prime examples of the exertion of royal soft power influence.

THE ROYALS AS AMBASSADORS

For a long time, royal tours have been a key element in Britain's foreign policy and relations (cf. Glencross 2015). During carefully planned, orchestrated, and medialized state visits, royal diplomacy served (and indeed serves) as a powerful political tool. It does not come as a surprise that this was again activated after the Brexit referendum. In spring and summer 2017, Prince William and Catherine toured France, Poland, and Germany (notably some of the largest European countries and strongest partners of the UK).[4] As Kim Willsher wrote in *The Guardian*, their "trip is part of a campaign of 'soft' diplomacy aimed at forging links on the continent as Britain starts delicate and complicated Brexit negotiations" (2017: n. pag.). The royals, in this case, served as ambassadors for their country in that they supported a specific cause, i.e. showing unchanged will to retain close ties to the European partners. While they act as spokespersons of their countrymen, one could critically note that these visits might be interpreted as representing only one 'camp' of the British population after the vote. Especially because the royals do not stand for a particular political program, however, their diplomatic endeavor is valuable and of a different quality to that of the role of the UK's ambassadors stationed in the partner countries.

---

3 According to the seminal definition of soft power by Joseph Nye, it refers to the power of achieving an intended outcome not by coercion but by means of appeal, persuasion and attraction (cf. Nye 2004: 5-7). The British royals exert soft power in manifold ways also pertaining to different generational behaviour (cf. Polland forthcoming), e.g. by setting examples for consumption practices, that is what Otnes and Maclaran have termed "the Kate effect" (2015: 280).

4 Interestingly, the Spanish King and Queen came to the UK on a state visit the same year. Thus, all the major countries of the European Union (except for Italy) in terms of population, publicly staged their ties and their spirit of cooperation with the United Kingdom in the year after the Brexit vote.

William and Catherine's visits were openly discussed as conciliatory gestures and the symbolic reaffirmation of Britain's close ties to Europe both in British media and those of the respective countries. Then, as negotiations were prolonged, Prince Charles and the Duchess of Cornwall visited Germany in May 2019 for what, again, was widely framed as a charm offensive by both the German and the British press (notably by papers largely supportive of both the Leave and the Remain 'camp').[5] The royals' state visits, therefore, took on cultural functions of, for example, re-establishing and emphasizing British relations to EU countries, staging an important element of the 'brand of Britain' that appeals to many people abroad, too, and thus promoting a positive image of Britain. It is in this sense that what Walter Bagehot called "an accepted secret doctrine" 150 years ago, still seems to hold true today; namely "that the Crown does more than it seems" (2001 [1867]: 54-55). The cultural significance of the royals' role performed during these state visits and their (medial) ramifications are not to be underestimated. Consequentially, it is exactly by being above politics that the monarchy (is supposed to) influence(s) the politics of the day.

DEMANDING ROYAL INTERVENTION?

While the role of the monarchy nowadays is officially supposed to be unpolitical and even fervent supporters of the institution know that in order to remain popular the monarchy has to act neutrally, this self-evident fact might have lost some of its obviousness in the face of the insecurities caused by the long Brexit negotiation process.

On 23 March, 2019, at the so-called "March on London," protesters sported the image of the young Queen Elizabeth II as a figurehead for their demand to "stop Brexit."

---

5   It can be noted that papers, which may be said to be supportive of either field, reported quite favorably on these royal 'charm offensives.'

"Stop Brexit" artwork at the People's Vote March in London, 23rd March, 2019

Source: Wikimedia Commons 2019

It is one of the most reproduced portraits as it has also adorned British stamps for more than 50 years and is thus instantly recognizable. Moreover, it can be read in at least two ways. First, it may constitute a demand for the queen to intervene in the political process by literally 'stopping Brexit' through exercising the royal "right to warn" not as is usually the case, on the advice of her government, but rather countering it. Second, it can point towards the significance of the monarchy for the British cultural imaginary. By using the image of the young queen, the protesters indirectly also reference the hopes connected to the advent of a 'new Elizabethan age' that accompanied her accession to the throne more than 65 years ago. In times of political upheaval, insecurities and apprehensions, people tend to seek comfort in the familiar, in a nostalgically glorified past, in traditions and institutions that may provide feelings of security, coherence, and order; as is the case with the monarchy. Public support of the institution has been on a high tide for roughly the last decade. As the monarchy only exists today because people still want it to exist, this – somewhat paradoxically – renders one of the most undemocratic institutions in contemporary European society democratic. The absurd 'democracy of royalty' results from the fact that its mere existence represents the will of the people.

"However pervasive the presence *within* the political machine, the monarchy is only as strong as its hold on the whole nation's imagination. Its authority is based on an illusion that it is what people want; that, as an aggregate of their wishes, it represents an expression of the power of the people." (Douglas-Home 2000: 214)

While this is reminiscent of the argumentation brought forth by supporters of the Leave camp about Brexit – namely that it is the will of the people[6] – the important point rather is the 'illusionary' aspect of the monarchy evoked by this notion. The potency of the monarchy lies in the potential it creates for speculations. Nonetheless, this also reveals the difficulty of the royals' constitutional role, which is vulnerable to utilization. This was said to be the case with the queen's speech on October 14, 2019 denounced as a "farcical […] stunt" that "dragged Her Majesty into politics" in the *Daily Mirror* (Maguire 2019: n. pag.). And it has been for a long time within the negotiation process. On March 8, 2017, for example, "*The Sun* ran a front-page story with the headline 'Queen Backs Brexit' based purely on anonymous sources. After Buckingham Palace lodged a complaint, Britain's press watchdog IPSO judged the headline was 'significantly misleading' and not backed up by the text" (Harding 2017: 12). Such an employment of the monarch's role reveals the monarchy's value for implicit political exploitation.

THE BENEFITS OF AN INSTITUTION 'ABOVE' POLITICS

Next to such occasions of political uses of the monarchy or of the press' influence on public opinion by employing the (symbolic power of) monarchy, there also has been royal intervention in politics in the recent past; most notably Prince Charles' so-called 'black spider memos' of 2004 and 2005. The heir apparent wrote these letters, revealed only in 2010, to members of Parliament outlining his private views on political matters and giving advice on certain issues. The letters were widely seen as instances of lobbying and have spurred heated debates on his role as future monarch (cf. Booth/Taylor 2015: n. pag.). Nonetheless, the monarchy is still widely perceived as adhering to its neutral constitutional role by being 'above' politics. The benefits of such a position are, on the one hand, that it allows for speculations and accusations, but, on the other hand, also for hopes, projections, and demands; hence generally enabling a possible affective engagement with the institution. Walter Bagehot has captured this position in his seminal treatise as follows:

---

6   One is tempted to add that the slight majority of the Leave vote can hardly be called to represent the will of 'the people.'

"The nation is divided into parties, but the Crown is of no party. Its apparent separation from business is that which removes it both from enmities and from desecration, which preserves its mystery, which enables it to combine the affection of conflicting parties, – to be a visible symbol of unity to those still so imperfectly educated as to need a symbol." (Bagehot 2001 [1867]: 45)

While it is not necessarily a symbol of unity, the monarchy still serves symbolic purposes. As Anette Pankratz has pointed out, "[a]s long as the monarchy provides entertainment for its audiences, the institution survives. Royals do not have to be afraid of criticism and scandals, but indifference" (2017: 60). By thus becoming part of a cultural and an illusionary realm, the monarchy becomes almost unassailable. Its position above politics equips it with the symbolic power that has repeatedly been evoked by the British press and the people throughout the Brexit negotiations. This symbolic power refers to its position within notions of national identity. As Michael Billig observed already more than 20 years ago,

"[t]he equation of monarchy with nation implies that an attack upon monarchy is an attack upon the fundamental uniqueness of the nation. If 'our' selves are equated with the nation, then the attack is also a threat to the unique identity of 'our' national selves. To imagine the imagined community without monarchy is to do more than de-imagine the nation: it is to de-imagine 'our' selves." (1992: 34)

As questions of national identity and the meanings of Britishness have been asked anew on occasion of the Brexit referendum debate and the clashes and divisions it revealed in British society, the role of the monarchy for this discourse and within conceptions of national identity are and will be renegotiated, too. As the monarchy apparently remains a space for projections and a possible focal point for hopes it will probably – to venture a reasonable guess – also remain important for British self-understandings in the years to come, once Brexit is implemented. Hope is the main driving force of utopia, and as Jon Day has determined, Brexit "was always a profoundly fictional project" (2017: n. pag.). The 'royal story' is intricately weaved into British national identity, history, and culture and will most probably continue to play a vital role, e.g. by providing coherence and a common frame of reference amidst the insecurities of the 21st century.

WORKS CITED

"Audiences", n. d., accessed November 11, 2019 (https://www.royal.uk/audiences).

Bagehot, Walter (2001 [1867]): The English Constitution, Oxford: Oxford University Press.

Booth, Robert/Matthew Taylor (2015): "Prince Charles's 'black spider memos' show lobbying at highest political level." In: The Guardian May 13, accessed October 31, 2019 (https://www.theguardian.com/uk-news/2015/may/13/prince-charles-black-spider-memos-lobbying-ministers-tony-blair).

Day, Jon (2017): "Brexlit: the new landscape of British fiction." In: Financial Times July 28, 2017, accessed October 31, 2019 (https://www.ft.com/content/30ec47b4-7204-11e7-93ff-99f383b09ff9).

Douglas-Home, Charles (completed by Saul Kelly) (2000): Dignified & Efficient. The British Monarchy in the Twentieth Century, Brinkworth: Claridge Press.

Furness, Hannah (2018): "Queen to urge Britain to put aside its 'deeply held differences' in last Christmas speech before Brexit." In: The Daily Telegraph December 24, accessed August 26, 2019 (https://www.telegraph.co.uk/royal-family/2018/12/24/queen-urge-britain-put-aside-deeply-held-differences-last-christmas/).

Glencross, Matthew (2015): The State Visits of Edward VII. Reinventing Royal Diplomacy for the Twentieth Century, London: Palgrave Macmillan.

Harding, Gareth (2017): "Media Lies and Brexit: A Double Hammer-Blow to Europe and Ethical Journalism." In: Aiden White (ed.), Ethics in the News. EJN Report on Challenges for Journalism in the Post-truth Era. London: Ethical Journalism Network (https://ethicaljournalismnetwork.org/wp-content/uploads/2017/01/ejn-ethics-in-the-news.pdf).

Higson, Andrew (2016): "From Political Power to the Power of the Image: Contemporary 'British' Cinema and the Nation's Monarchs." In: Mandy Merck (ed.), The British Monarchy on Screen, Manchester: Manchester University Press, pp. 339-362.

Khan, Shehab (2018): "The Queen's Christmas message: Monarch calls for those with 'deeply held differences' to treat each other with respect in veiled Brexit reference." In: Independent December 25, accessed August 26, 2019 (https://www.independent.co.uk/news/uk/home-news/queens-christmas-day-speech-christmas-brexit-annual-a8699006.html).

Maguire, Kevin (2019): "Boris Johnson's farcical Queen's Speech stunt dragged Her Majesty into politics." In: The Daily Mirror October 14, 2019, accessed

October 31, 2019 (https://www.mirror.co.uk/news/politics/boris-johnsons-farcical-queens-speech-20577997).

Nye, Joseph (2004): Soft Power. The Means to Success in World Politics, New York: Public Affairs.

Otnes, Cele C./Maclaran, Pauline (2015): Royal Fever. The British Monarchy in Consumer Culture, Oakland: University of California Press.

Pankratz, Anette (2017): "'That's Entertainment': Monarchy as Performance." In: Anette Pankratz/Claus-Ulrich Viol (eds.), (Un)Making the Monarchy, Heidelberg: Winter, pp. 41-64.

Polland, Imke (forthcoming): 'For Better, For Worse'? Royal Heirs between Continuity and Change in Media Representations of British Royal Weddings (2005-2011). Trier: WVT.

Topping, Alexandra (2019): "Tories praise Queen's common ground 'Brexit speech.'" In: The Guardian January, 25, accessed August 26, 2019 (https://www.theguardian.com/uk-news/2019/jan/25/queen-speech-common-ground-conservative-ministers-brexit).

Watt, Nicholas/Carrell, Severin/Quinn, Ben (2014): "Scottish independence: the Queen makes rare comment on referendum." In: The Guardian September 14, accessed August 26, 2019 (https://www.theguardian.com/politics/2014/sep/14/scottish-independence-queen-remark-welcomed-no-vote).

Webber, Esther (2014): "Scottish Independence: What will Happen to the Queen?" In: BBC News September 11, accessed June 26, 2019 (https://www.bbc.com/news/uk-29126569).

"Wikimedia Commons" (2019): Author Philipjohn21, accessed October 31, 2019 (https://upload.wikimedia.org/wikipedia/commons/b/b6/%22Stop_Brexit%22_artwork_at_the_People%27s_Vote_March_in_London%2C_23rd_March_2019.jpg), link to license (https://creativecommons.org/licenses/by-sa/4.0/deed.en).

Willsher, Kim (2017): "Prince William in Paris on first official visit since mother Diana's death." In: The Guardian March 17, 2017, accessed October 31, 2019 (https://www.theguardian.com/uk-news/2017/mar/17/prince-william-visits-paris-for-the-first-time-since-mother-dianas-death).

Yorke, Harry/Tominey, Camilla (2019): "John McDonnell threatens to march on palace and tell Queen: 'We're taking over' if Boris Johnson loses no confidence vote." In: The Daily Telegraph August 7, 2019, accessed August 26, 2019 (https://www.telegraph.co.uk/politics/2019/08/07/john-mcdonnell-threatens-march-palace-tell-queen-taking-boris1/).

"YouGov", May 8-9, 2018, accessed June 26, 2019 (https://d25d2506sfb94s.cloudfront.net/cumulus_uploads/document/m06kzwjbml/InternalResults_180509_RoyalWedding_w.pdf).

Films and Television

Harry and Meghan: An African Journey. Directed by Nathaniel Lippiett. 2019. ITV.

Authors

Aldrich, Robert, Professor of European History at the University of Sydney, teaches and carries out research in modern European and colonial history, including the history of France since the Revolution, the history of the French and British overseas empires, the history of 'sites of memory' and the history of gender and sexuality. He has been engaged in several research projects concerning colonialism and monarchy in the modern world. With Cindy McCreery, Robert Aldrich has edited *Crowns and Colonies: European Monarchies and Overseas Empires* (Manchester University Press 2016) and *Royals on Tour: Politics, Pageantry and Colonialism* (Manchester University Press 2018) and *Monarchies and Decolonisation in Asia* (Manchester University Press forthcoming in 2020). They also edited, in 2018, a special issue of the *Royal Studies Journal* on British royal tours of the Dominions of Australia, Canada, New Zealand and South Africa in the 20th century.

Gilfedder, Deirdre is professor of English at the University of Paris-Dauphine. She specializes in Australian history and cultural studies and has published widely on First World War commemoration, as well as on film, literature, Australian indigenous issues of testimony and representations of monarchy and republicanism. She is the author of the first book on Australians in the First World War in French, *L'Australie et la Grande Guerre* (editions Michel Houdiard Editeur 2015).

Jordan, Christina holds an M.A. in English and German Studies as well as Cultural Anthropology from Goethe University Frankfurt and currently is a PhD candidate at Justus Liebig University Giessen. Her dissertation project analyzes Queen Elizabeth II's Golden and Diamond Jubilee as staged media events. She taught Literature and Culture at the Department of English at Justus Liebig University Giessen, coordinated an international PhD program, and has published on the intersection of monarchy, media and memory as well as on contemporary artistic depictions of the British monarchy.

Kirbach, Eva studied Drama and Theatre Studies as well as British Studies at the universities of Leipzig and Aberystwyth. She currently works at the English Department of Justus Liebig University Giessen. Her Ph.D. project is concerned with the representation of the bodies of political figures in contemporary British plays, focusing on former prime ministers, members of the royal family and MPs. Her main research interests and teaching include historiography and historiographic metafiction as well as the construction of (British) identity, in particular with regard to nation, gender and class.

Maclaran, Pauline is Professor of Marketing and Consumer Research at Royal Holloway University of London, United Kingdom. Her research interests focus on cultural aspects of contemporary consumption, and she adopts a critical perspective to analyze the ideological assumptions that underpin many marketing activities, especially in relation to gender. She co-authored *Royal Fever: The British Monarchy in Consumer Culture* with Professor Cele Otnes (University of California Press 2015) and has also co-edited many books including the *Sage Handbook of Consumer Culture* (2018) and *Motherhoods, Markets and Consumption: The Making of Mothers in Contemporary Western Cultures* (Routledge 2013).

McCreery, Cindy is a Senior Lecturer in the Department of History at the University of Sydney, Australia. Her current major research focus is monarchy and colonialism. With her colleague Robert Aldrich she has edited three volumes in Manchester University Press's *Studies in Imperialism* series: *Crowns and Colonies: European Monarchies and Overseas Empires* (2016), *Royals on Tour: Politics, Pageantry and Colonialism* (2018), and the forthcoming *Monarchies and Decolonisation in Asia* (2020), as well as a special issue of the *Royal Studies Journal* on 20th-century British royal tours of the Dominions (2018). She is now working on 19th-century global royal travel, examining the journeys of King Kalakaua of Hawai'i (1881), Prince Alfred (1867-1871) and Princes Albert Victor and George (1879-1881) of Great Britain. Honors and decorations feature, in different ways, in all three journeys.

Menzel, Marie received her M.A. degree in English, Musicology, and Economics from Goethe University Frankfurt. She is currently a junior lecturer for English Cultural and Literary Studies at Freie Universität Berlin and is conducting a PhD project on contemporary Shakespeare productions and adaptations.

Otnes, Cele is the Anthony J. Petullo Professor and Head of the Department of Business Administration in the Gies College of Business at the University of Illinois at Urbana-Champaign, USA. She is Adjunct Professor at the Norwegian School of Economics, where she co-teaches a doctoral seminar on qualitative research methods. Her focal research interest is in understanding the interplay between rituals and consumption at the meso-, macro- and marketplace levels. She is co-author with Pauline Maclaran of *Royal Fever: The British Monarchy in Consumer Culture* (University of California Press 2015), and with Elizabeth Pleck of *Cinderella Dreams: the Allure of the Lavish Wedding* (University of California Press, 2003). She has published widely in journals in marketing, advertising, popular culture, and related fields.

Polland, Imke is a postdoctoral researcher and the academic coordinator of the European PhD Network "Literary and Cultural Studies" at the International Graduate Centre for the Study of Culture (GCSC), Justus Liebig University Giessen. She has completed her PhD entitled: *'For Better, For Worse?' Royal Heirs between Continuity and Change in Media Representations of British Royal Weddings (2005-2011)* (WVT 2020) and is now working on the project *Fictions of Brexit*. She is co-editor of the volume *Literature and Crises* (WVT 2017) and the forthcoming books *Europe's Crises and Cultural Resources of Resilience* (WVT 2020) and *Forms at Work* (WVT 2020).

Riotte, Torsten is a Reader of history at Goethe University Frankfurt. Educated at Cologne and Cambridge, he graduated with a thesis on the House of Hanover as Britain's German connection. After seven years in the UK he became Senior Lecturer and later Reader at Goethe University. He has published widely on European history including a comparative study of monarchs in exile. He also co-edited the four volume edition *British Envoys to Germany, 1815-1866* (Cambridge University Press 2000-2010) and he has worked on the cultural history of diplomacy. He is currently finishing his history of Europe from 1850-1870.

Scholz, Susanne is Professor of English Literature and Culture at the University of Frankfurt/Main. She has held teaching posts at the Universities of Frankfurt, Siegen and Paderborn. Her main research interests and publications are in the field of early modern, 18th- and 19th-century English literature, gender studies, medical humanities and visual culture studies. She has recently completed a research project on visual practices at the court of Elizabeth I and is now working on a book project about face-fashioning in late 19th- and early 20th-century English literature. Her major book publications are: *Body Narratives: Writing the Nation and Fashioning the Subject in Early Modern England* (Macmillan 2000); *Objekte und Erzählungen. Subjektivität und kultureller Dinggebrauch im England des frühen 18. Jahrhunderts* (Helmer 2004); with Julika Griem (eds.) *Medialisierungen des Unsichtbaren um 1900* (Fink 2010); with Daniel Dornhofer (eds.) Spectatorship at the Elizabethan Court. *Zeitsprünge. Forschungen zur Frühen Neuzeit* 17 (2013); *Phantasmatic Knowledge: Visions of the Human and the Scientific Gaze in English Literature, 1880-1930* (Winter 2013); with Ulrike Vedder (eds.) *Handbuch Literatur und Materielle Kultur* (De Gruyter) 2018.

Stickel, Marie-Theres studied English, French, German, and business studies in Giessen (Germany) and Dijon (France). She graduated in Comparative Literary and Cultural Studies with a master thesis on the changing reading materialities, modes, and media between page and screen in the context of the highly digitalized 21st century. She has done further research dealing with questions of how digitization processes have fundamentally changed the literary system, and published on branding and design strategies publishing houses currently apply with classic books series.

Trajković Filipović, Stefan is a doctoral candidate at the Faculty of History and Cultural Studies at Justus Liebig University Giessen. Having a background in Medieval studies (M.A. in medieval studies from the Central European University), his doctoral research is concerned with modern and contemporary interpretations of medieval and early modern history. He is especially interested in the constructions of relevant figures of memory. From 2016 to 2019 he was a member of the International Graduate Centre for the Study of Culture in Giessen (GCSC). From 2017 to 2019 he held a scholarship for doctoral studies from Gerda Henkel Foundation and in 2019/2020 his research is supported with a stipend from the Collaborative Research Centre 948 "Heroes – Heroizations – Heroisms" at the University of Freiburg.

Veith, Natalie studied English and German literature and culture at the universities of Frankfurt and Cardiff. She has in the past been a research fellow at the University of Frankfurt and currently holds a position at the University of Stuttgart. Her PhD project is dedicated to British neo-Victorian comic books; other fields of interest in research and teaching include visual culture studies and pluricodal media, gender studies, and postclassical narratology.

Cultural Studies

Elisa Ganivet
Border Wall Aesthetics
Artworks in Border Spaces

2019, 250 p., hardcover, ill.
79,99 € (DE), 978-3-8376-4777-8
E-Book: 79,99 € (DE), ISBN 978-3-8394-4777-2

Jocelyne Porcher, Jean Estebanez (eds.)
Animal Labor
A New Perspective on Human-Animal Relations

2019, 182 p., hardcover
99,99 € (DE), 978-3-8376-4364-0
E-Book: 99,99 € (DE), ISBN 978-3-8394-4364-4

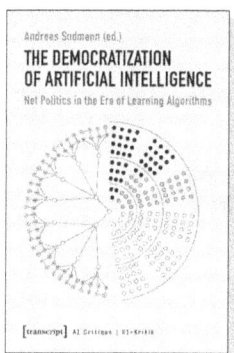

Andreas Sudmann (ed.)
The Democratization of Artificial Intelligence
Net Politics in the Era of Learning Algorithms

2019, 334 p., pb., col. ill.
49,99 € (DE), 978-3-8376-4719-8
E-Book: 49,99 € (DE), ISBN 978-3-8394-4719-2

All print, e-book and open access versions of the titles in our list
are available in our online shop www.transcript-verlag.de/en!

Cultural Studies

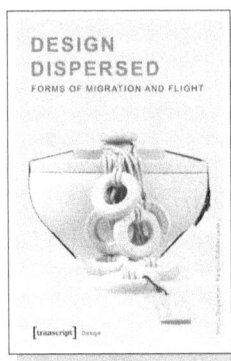

Burcu Dogramaci, Kerstin Pinther (eds.)
Design Dispersed
Forms of Migration and Flight

2019, 274 p., pb., col. ill.
34,99 € (DE), 978-3-8376-4705-1
E-Book: 34,99 € (DE), ISBN 978-3-8394-4705-5

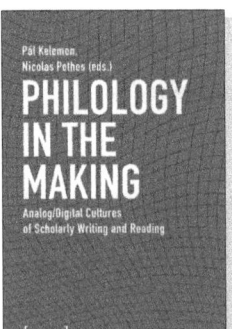

Pál Kelemen, Nicolas Pethes (eds.)
Philology in the Making
Analog/Digital Cultures of Scholarly Writing and Reading

2019, 316 p., pb., ill.
34,99 € (DE), 978-3-8376-4770-9
E-Book: 34,99 € (DE), ISBN 978-3-8394-4770-3

Chris Goldie, Darcy White (eds.)
Northern Light
Landscape, Photography and Evocations of the North

2018, 174 p., hardcover, ill.
79,99 € (DE), 978-3-8376-3975-9
E-Book: 79,99 € (DE), ISBN 978-3-8394-3975-3

**All print, e-book and open access versions of the titles in our list
are available in our online shop www.transcript-verlag.de/en!**

GPSR Authorized Representative: Easy Access System Europe, Mustamäe tee 50, 10621 Tallinn, Estonia, gpsr.requests@easproject.com

www.ingramcontent.com/pod-product-compliance
Lightning Source LLC
Chambersburg PA
CBHW051533020426
42333CB00016B/1900